Immigrant Narratives in Contemporary France

Recent Titles in
Contributions to the Study of World Literature

Immigrant Narratives in Contemporary France

Edited by Susan Ireland
and Patrice J. Proulx

Contributions to the Study of World Literature, Number 106

Greenwood Press
Westport, Connecticut • London

Library of Congress Cataloging-in-Publication Data

Immigrant narratives in contemporary France / edited by Susan Ireland and Patrice J. Proulx.
    p. cm.—(Contributions to the study of world literature, ISSN 0738–9345 ; no. 106)
    Includes bibliographical references and index.
    ISBN 0–313–31593–0 (alk. paper)
    1. French prose literature—20th century—History and criticism. 2. French prose
literature—Minority authors—History and criticism. 3. Immigrants in literature. I.
Ireland, Susan, 1954– II. Proulx, Patrice J. III. Series.
PQ629.I48 2001
848′.9140809920693—dc21   00–052128

British Library Cataloguing in Publication Data is available.

Library of Congress Catalog Card Number: 00–052128
ISBN: 0–313–31593–0
ISSN: 0738–9345

First published in 2001

Greenwood Press, 88 Post Road West, Westport, CT 06881
An imprint of Greenwood Publishing Group, Inc.
www.greenwood.com

Printed in the United States of America

The paper used in this book complies with the
Permanent Paper Standard issued by the National
Information Standards Organization (Z39.48–1984).

10 9 8 7 6 5 4 3 2 1

For Greg and Richard, without whose understanding and support this book would not have been completed.

Contents

Contents   ix

Acknowledgments

The editors are particularly grateful to Gregory Morin, Bev Garcia, and Terri Phipps for their invaluable assistance in the preparation of the manuscript. We also wish to acknowledge Grinnell College and the University of Nebraska at Omaha for providing the editors with one-semester leaves to work on this project.

Introduction

Susan Ireland and Patrice J. Proulx

The presence of ethnic minorities in France has increased dramatically over the last few decades as large numbers of immigrants--mostly from the former French colonies--have taken up residence there for economic or political reasons. As a consequence, the subject of immigration itself has moved to the center of many sensitive social and political debates, and has become the focus of anxieties about national identity. Indeed, recent years have seen a growing emphasis on the topic of immigration in a wide variety of disciplines, from history and economics to sociology and post-colonial studies. This trend derives from the increasing importance of transnational phenomena such as international labor and capital flows and the globalization of economic markets and communications networks. These have led, on the one hand, to a heightened preoccupation with boundaries and border crossings in both the physical and figurative senses, and, on the other, to the valorization of the concepts of hybridity and plurality which problematize monolithic definitions of individual and collective identity. Similarly, in the field of literary theory, the related terms "displacement," "nomadism," and "deterritorialization" are used to characterize key concepts of contemporary textual and cultural analysis. The literary trope of exile, which suggests both geographical displacement and psychological dislocation, has become a recurrent theme in post-colonial texts that seek to give voice to new relationships between place and self which are constructed from the experience of immigration. Many of the texts written by immigrant authors focus attention on the locational concept of territory and the spatially related notions of home and belonging.

Within this general emphasis on immigration, particular attention is being focused in the West on what Stephen Castles calls "new ethnic minorities"[1]--recent immigrants and their descendants who have moved from the Third World to Western industrialized nations. In the case of France, the influx of immigrants since the 1940s is linked to colonialism and its legacy, and the representation of immigrants in the mainstream press remains strongly influenced by the old hierarchical relationship between colonizer and colonized. Unlike the earlier waves of immigration from countries such as Italy and Portugal, the post-World War II non-European immigrants are often perceived as being too culturally different to be successfully integrated into French society. Through them, the colonial relationship is relived and rewritten, this time on France's home territory.

A proliferation of economic, political, historical, and sociological works seek to provide a range of perspectives on the place of immigrants in French society. Like these other analyses of immigration, the literary texts raise the question of the place and voice of the new ethnic minorities in contemporary France. In particular, these texts examine French national and cultural identity, challenging the notion of France as a homogeneous state, while concomitantly suggesting the ways in which immigrants both transform and are transformed by their new country. In this sense, the immigrant perspective voiced in the narratives under consideration in this volume provides a complement to socio-political discourses on issues related to immigration, and proposes an alternative vision of French society that valorizes diversity and that counterbalances the negative one most often presented in the media. Members of the second generation, as well as workers from the French Antilles, for example, are still referred to as immigrants, in what could be considered an implicit attempt to keep them marginalized.

In their compelling discussion of current debates surrounding the negotiation of immigrant identities, Gisela Brinker-Gabler and Sidonie Smith insist on the crucial role played by the literary text, positing that "literary forms are part of the system of cultural representations through which national identities and national subjects come into being. . . . Nations require narratives through which individuals imagine themselves as national subjects and align themselves in the national narrative" (17). They also elaborate on the issue of the "imagined community" (9) which must be reinvented in order to accommodate a large immigrant presence and to take other narratives into account. The authors discussed in this volume all contribute to such a reimagining, redefining what it means to be French and to be a French writer by introducing notions of difference into their narratives. Indeed, the steadily growing corpus of literary texts written by authors of recent immigrant origin reflects the changing composition of French society and could be said to constitute the most vibrant area of French literature today, what Charles Bonn calls "un espace littéraire émergent."[2] These writers, who come from such diverse geographical regions as the Maghreb, sub-Saharan Africa, Asia, the Caribbean, and the Middle East, bring to their work a rich blend of diverse cultural and literary traditions; several of these authors have been the recipients of the Goncourt, France's most prestigious literary prize--Tahar Ben Jelloun (Morocco), Patrick Chamoiseau (Martinique), and Amin Maalouf (Lebanon), for example.

One of the primary aims of *Immigrant Narratives in Contemporary France*, which contains both more general, socio-historical chapters, and chapters that provide detailed analysis of specific texts and authors, is to address the question of the post-war literature of immigration in France in a comprehensive fashion. Most books published in English in the area generally referred to as Francophone literature are devoted primarily to the literature produced in and dealing with the former colonies. Indeed, this study was inspired by Alec Hargreaves's observation that "There has as yet been no systematic study of French fiction dealing with the immigrant community" (4). Given that these texts now constitute a significant corpus, this book will help fill the gap identified by Hargreaves.

Another key objective of this volume is to examine a number of issues dealing with the specificities of the literary production of the different ethnic groups, while taking into account both generational differences and the effect of factors such as class and gender. Although contributors to the collection approach their topics from a variety of critical and theoretical perspectives, they all speak to a series of central questions related to the textualization and theorization of the immigrant experience. The principal questions explored in the volume include the following: How do immigrant writers express the confrontation between different cultural and political economies? Given the fact that most immigrant writers are dealing with multiple or conflicting sites of home, is a reconciliation with their origins possible or even desirable? Do they subscribe to the myth of return? In what ways do the texts deal with the literal and figurative themes of place and displacement--issues of center, periphery, and dislocation? How do these works portray the concept of Frenchness and how do they shape debates about French national and cultural identity? How do they position themselves in relation to notions such as assimilation, integration, and the right to difference? Finally, to what extent do these texts see themselves as undermining ethnic stereotypes or as subverting the traditional canon of French literature?

While recognizing that many issues recur across ethnic groups, we have chosen to organize the chapters into four sections based on geographical origins in order to highlight the multi-cultural nature of French literature and society today. Many of the chapters present the works they discuss as a form of counter-narrative and discuss such themes as the rewriting of immigrant history (see Donadey, Ireland, and Laronde) and the particular difficulties encountered by women immigrants at school, at home, and in the workplace (see Geesey, Hitchcott, and Proulx). At the same time, the chapters in this volume attest to the wide range of styles and genres used by writers of immigrant descent--autobiographical fiction, life stories, realist fiction, epistolary narratives, and experimental texts. The presence of emerging forms raises questions about classification and naming which are addressed in several of the chapters (see Cazenave, McKinney, and Thomas). Contributors also trace out complex interactions between immigrants and majority French society in terms of linguistic identity (see Abu-Haidar), historical relations between the overseas departments and the *métropole* (see Murdoch), changing forms of immigration and their representation (see Rosello), textual inscriptions of immigrant neighborhoods (see Durmelat), and, finally, the experience of alienation and exile for those who have either chosen or been forced to leave their homelands (see Delvaux and Selao). It is our hope that *Immigrant Narratives in Contemporary France* will make a significant contribution to current debates surrounding the relationship of immigration to problematic issues such as cultural hybridity, identity politics, border writing, and the status of "minority" literature within the traditional literary canon, and that it will encourage further explorations of literary and cultural spaces born of the immigrant experience.

NOTES

1. The term "new ethnic minorities" is from the subtitle of Stephen Castles's *Here for Good: Western Europe's New Ethnic Minorities.*

2. "Un espace littéraire émergent" is the title of the first volume of Charles Bonn's *Littératures des immigrations.*

WORKS CITED

Bonn, Charles. "Un espace littéraire émergent." *Littératures des immigrations.* Vol. 1. Paris: L'Harmattan, 1995, 11-14.

Brinker-Gabler, Gisela, and Sidonie Smith. Introduction. *Writing New Identities: Gender, Nation, and Immigration in Contemporary Europe.* Minneapolis: University of Minnesota Press, 1997, 1-27.

Castles, Stephen. *Here for Good: Western Europe's New Ethnic Minorities.* London: Pluto Press, 1984.

Hargreaves, Alec G. *Immigration and Identity in Beur Fiction: Voices from the North African Immigrant Community in France.* Oxford: Berg Publishers, 1997.

OVERVIEW

Perceptions of Ethnic Difference in Post-War France

Alec G. Hargreaves

INTRODUCTION

The writers discussed in this book all have their origins in the broad field of international migration and the minority ethnic groups associated with it. While some were born in France and are not therefore immigrants in the true sense, others migrated to France as adults. Yet few, if any, would customarily be described in French as *écrivains immigrés* (immigrant writers). If this expression sounds almost oxymoronic, it is because its component terms carry semantic accretions acquired in very different fields of usage. Where an *écrivain* operates in the field of culture, often of an élite kind, *immigrés* are generally regarded as economic actors concentrated at the lower end of the social scale.

Strictly speaking, any person living in a country other than that in which he or she was born is an immigrant. If, in everyday discourse, the term is applied only to certain types of immigrants--and at the same time to some non-immigrants--this is because of the historical context in which its usage has been forged. The aims of this chapter are to provide an outline of that context and to explore some of the main terms in which the processes of international migration and minority ethnic settlement have been conceptualized by the majority ethnic population in post-war France. Even when they are not themselves perceived as "immigrants," minority ethnic authors are in varying degrees conscious of this context. Moreover, as they are sometimes taken for "immigrants" (as commonly understood in France), those among them who are not in any real sense immigrants are nevertheless deeply affected by the perceptions of ethnic difference traversing French society. We therefore need to be aware of this context if we are to fully understand their works.

This chapter is divided into three main parts. The first of these provides a historical overview. The second focuses on key words used (as well as some not used) in referring to immigrants and their descendants, while the final section looks at the conceptualization of the processes of social and cultural change associated with minority ethnic settlement.

HISTORY

Historically, two main phases may be distinguished within the postwar period. The first of these stretches from the liberation in 1944 to the first oil crisis of 1973, which marked the end of what subsequently became known as *les trente glorieuses*, a thirty-year period marked (particularly in the second half) by exceptionally high and sustained economic growth. During this first phase, immigration was seldom discussed outside specialist administrative circles. It was a period of loose immigration controls, and brought a steady shift in the ethnic balance of the immigrant population, with post-colonial minorities becoming more visible than Europeans. The second phase, running from 1974 to the present, has been characterized by lower and more fitful economic growth and painful changes in the labor market, with record levels of unemployment and a generalized climate of economic insecurity. It has brought draconian immigration controls and seen "immigration"--understood in France as a label encompassing not only population movements but also the processes of social interaction resulting from minority ethnic settlement--explode into the forefront of political debate and across a growing range of social and cultural spheres.

As France emerged from Nazi occupation, the main problem posed by immigration was that there was not enough of it. The war had left a trail of destruction and depleted the ranks of able-bodied workers. Reconstruction would therefore require assistance from workers brought in from abroad. While this basic premise was accepted on virtually all sides, a vigorous debate took place among specialist government advisers concerning the relative merits of temporary labor migration compared with permanent family settlement. Some argued that family migration was needed because France faced not only a short-term reconstruction problem but also a more structural demographic deficit. In contrast with her faster growing neighbors--most obviously, her arch-rival Germany--France had experienced a long period of population stagnation. Family settlement by immigrants would help to swell not only the labor force but also the long-term demographic profile of the country.

While there was by no means unanimity on the need for permanent settlement of this kind, practically all those involved in the debate agreed that, as in the past, it would be preferable to recruit immigrants in Europe rather than overseas. There was a general consensus in favor firstly of west Europeans such as Italians and Belgians, followed by central and eastern Europeans, with Africans and Asians the least favored groups. At the same time, the horrors associated with the racist policies recently pursued by Nazi Germany made some (though not all) in government circles hesitate to adopt an immigration policy based on openly ethnic criteria.

A rather blurred compromise eventually emerged in which a legal framework facilitating family settlement was put in place without any explicitly codified ethnic hierarchy. At the same time, the authorities responsible for recruiting immigrants effectively worked to a de facto ethnic agenda by prioritizing neighboring countries such as Italy.[1] The practicalities of public policy were also at odds with its legalities in another important respect. Although family immigration was officially welcomed, very little was done to assist incoming families in vital matters such as the provision of adequate housing. The state was mainly concerned with ensuring that France had an adequate labor supply. Beyond that narrow economic focus, immigrants were left to fend largely for themselves.

During the 1950s and 1960s, one of the effects of this was to be the proliferation of *bidonvilles* (shantytowns), groups of improvised shacks thrown up by immigrants on vacant land with little or no access to basic utilities such as running water and electricity. It was not until the 1970s that the authorities decided to eradicate these dwellings, moving their inhabitants initially to *cités de transit*, slightly better quality but still "temporary" accommodations in which some families found themselves trapped for ten years or more. Eventually, most moved on to high-rise, low-quality housing projects generally located in outlying urban areas, where they remain concentrated today.[2]

One further development in the early post-war period needs to be mentioned. In 1947, France granted a new status to her largest North African colony, Algeria, which gave the Muslim majority of the population equal freedom of movement alongside the settler minority. Designed as a symbolic measure aimed at helping stem the growing move towards decolonization, this provision was not intended to encourage migration, but it had the effect of exempting Algerians from immigration controls in metropolitan France, and growing numbers of them took advantage of this to seek work there. As Italians and other Europeans proved less attracted to France than in the pre-war period, a de facto shift in the ethnic balance of migratory flows began to take place, a shift that went against the grain of French expectations. Instead of family settlement from neighboring European countries, there was a growing pattern of labor migration from Algeria and other colonial territories.

This trend accelerated after France divested herself of her overseas empire, a process which culminated with Algerian independence in 1962. Far from bringing an end to population flows between ex-colonies and metropolitan France, decolonization was followed during the 1960s and early 1970s by a sharp rise in immigration from former colonial territories. This was due partly to legal provisions favoring freedom of movement from certain former colonies, notably Algeria; partly to the high levels of unemployment and low standard of living prevailing in those countries; and partly to growing labor shortages in France, where the authorities effectively waived immigration controls, thus permitting employers to hire foreign workers without first applying for the necessary permits. Formal agreements on immigration flows were signed with many Third World countries, as formerly colonized territories in Africa, Asia, and Oceania now became known. Recruitment campaigns were also conducted in remnants of the old empire still under French administration, now known as *Départements d'Outre-Mer* and *Territoires d'Outre-Mer* (Overseas Departments and Overseas Territories) (DOM-TOM). Most migrants from the DOM-TOM came from the Caribbean islands of Guadeloupe and Martinique, where the population was mainly of non-European descent.

Although Portuguese immigrants had also begun arriving in large numbers during the early 1970s, joining other Europeans who had settled permanently in France during earlier periods of mass migration, the census of 1982 would show that for the first time Europeans accounted for less than half of France's foreign population. Among the remainder, Maghrebis (North Africans) were by far the largest group, with smaller numbers of sub-Saharan Africans and Asians also present. The decline in the relative importance of Europeans--who until this period had been overwhelmingly dominant among the immigrant population--was also accompanied by a rise in family settlement by immigrants of Third World origin, which gathered speed during the 1970s.

By a deep historical irony, this shift towards permanent settlement by non-Europeans became increasingly visible at precisely the moment when the economic boom which had fueled the recruitment of immigrant labor collapsed. The oil crisis of 1973 and subsequent changes in the economic climate prompted a raft of policy measures, beginning in 1974, designed to halt and if possible reverse migratory flows from Third World countries. The period since then has been marked by a complex web of contradictory trends: the demographic consolidation of post-colonial minorities has been accompanied by their political and economic destabilization and, more recently, by their emergence as significant actors in the transformation of French popular culture.

The formal termination of labor migration from Third World countries did not bring an end to population inflows from Africa and Asia. Families continued to join breadwinners already in France, and the ranks of post-colonial minorities were further augmented by political refugees. The largest influx of this kind came from Southeast Asia following the Communist victory which ended the Vietnam War in 1975. Many opponents of the new regime fled, often as "boat people," and a significant proportion of them found refuge in France, which until 1954 had been the colonial power in Indochina. Compared with the mainly unskilled labor migrants who came to France from the Maghreb and sub-Saharan Africa, those who fled Southeast Asia tended to be more middle-class, carrying with them significant business skills. They were seen less as former colonial "natives" and more as victims of the Cold War suffering at the hands of the West's ideological adversaries. For this reason, they tended to be accepted more readily than other post-colonial minorities.

At the same time, this influx of Southeast Asians helped to erode the distinction between economic migrants and political refugees, for it was not always clear whether they were genuinely fleeing persecution or simply seeking better economic opportunities. During the 1980s and early 1990s, the number of asylum-seekers from Africa, the Middle East, and Asia rose rapidly. Suspecting that they were attempting to circumvent the ban on labor migration, the authorities refused residence permits to the vast majority of them. Many unsuccessful asylum-seekers nevertheless remained in France, swelling the ranks of what became generally known during the 1990s as *sans-papiers*, undocumented or illegal immigrants. Other *sans-papiers* were victims of the Pasqua laws of 1993 which, in attempting to curb family reunification and other modes of access to French residence permits, threw tens of thousands into a legal no man's land.[3]

Residence permits and even French citizenship--which a growing proportion of these new immigrant minorities possess--have been no guarantee of security. The seemingly unstoppable rise in unemployment witnessed between the mid-1970s and the mid-1990s hit minority groups particularly hard. Unemployment rates have run far higher among post-colonial minorities than among the majority ethnic population and European immigrants. If this discrepancy is partly attributable to the lower levels of certified skills generally found among Third World minorities, there can be no doubt that it is also due in part to racial discrimination on the part of employers. There is now a growing body of evidence to show that young people of Maghrebi, sub-Saharan, and Caribbean descent encounter widespread discrimination in the search for jobs and housing as well as in gaining access to leisure facilities such as nightclubs. The color of their skin, the spelling of their names, or simply a reference to their address is often sufficient to disqualify them in the eyes of an employer.[4]

The addresses which resonate in this way are located in neighborhoods which have come to be known as the *banlieues*. Until the 1980s, the *banlieue* was a generic term encompassing all suburban areas of French cities, but as post-colonial minorities became increasingly concentrated in suburban neighborhoods characterized by low-quality social housing and high levels of unemployment, these districts in particular were singled out in media usage of the *banlieue* label. In everyday discourse, the *banlieue* now functions as a synonym for ethnic alterity, social disadvantage, drugs, and crime.[5]

The main cultural marker of that ethnic alterity is Islam, the religion of almost all Maghrebi immigrants and of a significant proportion of sub-Saharan Africans. Little known in France before the 1970s, Islam is now the country's second largest religious faith, behind Catholicism but well ahead of Protestantism and Judaism. Associated with anti-French nationalism during the Algerian war of independence and with other anti-Western movements such as pro-Palestinian terrorism and the Iranian revolution of 1979, Islam has frequently been seen as a threat to the cultural integrity of France. There is a sharp contrast here with Buddhism, now the country's fifth largest religion. Introduced into France by migrants and refugees from Southeast Asia, Buddhism has a much more peace-loving image than Islam. Majority ethnic converts account for over half the estimated 400,000 Buddhists in France but only about 1 percent of the country's estimated 4 million Muslims.

The media hysteria which surrounded the Islamic headscarf affairs of 1989 and 1994 typified the vilification to which Muslims are often subjected.[6] In reality, contrary to popular prejudices, the vast majority of Muslims are entirely respectful of the prevailing social order in France. Moreover, the tiny number of Muslim girls choosing to wear headscarves at school--which they are by law entitled to do--testifies amply to the much weaker hold of Islam on second- and third-generation members of Maghrebi and other post-colonial minorities, compared with their immigrant parents or grandparents. It is abundantly clear that these new generations have been putting the main weight of their cultural energies not into Islam but into popular cultural forms forged primarily in the secular West. One of the most striking features of the second half of the 1990s has been the way in which multi-ethnic rap bands and other musical groups have emerged from the *banlieues* and entered the mainstream of French popular culture. Performers such as IAM, NTM, and Zebda are now among the top-selling artists in France.[7]

These developments are linked with the wider phenomenon of globalization now traversing France. While political elites have been struggling to resist this process, proclaiming their dedication to the protection of the nation-state, young people in France appear more willing to embrace the horizons opened up by globalization. Minority ethnic youths were particularly well placed to lead the way. Their immigrant origins made cultural hybridity part of everyday life, and their first-hand knowledge of social disadvantage and discrimination made it easy for them to identify with the experiences in which the hip hop culture of African Americans was forged. The prestige enjoyed by American popular culture, in contrast with the sensitivity about France's colonial past, also provided a terrain on which minority and majority ethnic youths could meet without either side feeling that it was yielding territory to the other. From these disparate elements, a space has been opened up inside French popular culture that is multi-ethnic with respect to its origins, practitioners, and audiences. In this way, despite the barriers often placed in their way, there are signs that minority ethnic groups are at last helping to reshape the contours of majority ethnic identities, rather than simply standing in their shadow.

PEOPLE

It is often said that there is no public recognition of ethnicity in France. This is at best a half truth. Although public officials never use terms such as "ethnic minorities"--the notion of a minority is officially as taboo as that of ethnicity--the semantic field covered by such terms is frequently evoked under different lexical markers in political as well as everyday discourse. Much of the talk about ethnicity is subterranean, in the sense that it circulates through words that have no explicit connection with ethnic differences. The *banlieues*--urban spaces that have become a byword for concentrations of minority ethnic groups--are an obvious example of this. In official discourse, exemplified in legal and administrative documents, even the word *immigré* (immigrant) features less frequently than might be expected. The primary distinction in official thinking is between French nationals and foreigners. Although this clearly overlaps with the distinction between immigrants and non-immigrants and between majority and minority ethnic groups, these different lines of demarcation are by no means identical.

It is only in the last ten years or so that public bodies responsible for studying the population of France have begun to acknowledge that the concept of an *immigré*--as distinct from that of an *étranger* (foreigner)--may be legitimately and even usefully employed. Led principally by Michèle Tribalat, a number of studies sponsored by the Institut National de la Statistique et des Etudes Economiques (INSEE) and the Institut National d'Etudes Démographiques (INED) have begun to examine the size and significance of the immigrant population within French society.[8] As defined in these studies, an immigrant is a person born abroad without French nationality and who is now resident in France. This definition officially excludes almost a third of the people now living in France who were born elsewhere. Most of those left out in this way are classed as *rapatriés* (repatriates), a term applied primarily to colonial settlers of European descent who moved to France with the advent of decolonization; the remainder come mainly from the DOM-TOM. As they were all born with French nationality, they fall outside the parameters by which immigrants are formally defined, despite the fact that they have physically migrated from one territory to another.

These distinctions show clearly that geographical mobility does not on its own define the condition of an immigrant. At least as important as spatial movements are the socially constructed boundaries by which collective identities are defined. An immigrant is someone born outside the political and cultural--not simply territorial--boundaries of the French nation-state. Such a person may be allowed to enter the territory of France, but will not be formally recognized as fully belonging there unless and until he or she becomes a French citizen. If and when the immigrant crosses over that juridical boundary, his or her immigrant origins cease to have any official significance, for all members of the French nation-state are formally regarded as individuals equal in the eyes of the law, which gives no recognition to minority ethnic groups.

That at least is the theory. The day-to-day experiences of migrants are often very different. For instance, although migrants from the DOM-TOM are not formally classed as *immigrés*, that is nevertheless how they are seen by many members of the majority ethnic population. Their juridical status as French citizens is invisible to the man or woman in the street, in whose eyes their dark skins are frequently taken to signify immigrant status and, by the same token, a lesser degree of belonging or legitimacy within French society. Similar problems afflict the *harkis*, *rapatriés* of Algerian (rather than European) descent.

Officially classified today as *rapatriés d'origine nord-africaine* (repatriates of North African origin; RONA)--and as such, living proof that the French state is in practice not immune to the recognition of ethnic differences--the *harkis* were Muslim troops who fought on the side of the French during the Algerian war of independence. Until the creation of an independent Algerian state in 1962, all inhabitants of Algeria were officially French nationals. With the end of French rule, virtually all those of non-European origin, including migrants in France, lost French citizenship and became Algerian nationals. But those *harkis* who managed to flee to France--many others died in bloody reprisals during the transition to independence--remained French. Their formal identity papers and past efforts on behalf of French sovereignty overseas were, however, to prove no protection from the hostility shown by a large part of the majority ethnic population within France towards anyone seen as an *Algérien*, an *Arabe* or simply as an *immigré*.[9]

By the 1970s, these three terms--along with *Maghrébin*, which since decolonization had been gaining currency as a substitute for *Nord-Africain*--had become virtually interchangeable in popular discourse. This reflected both the rising numbers of post-colonial migrants in France and the sweeping ways in which ethnic boundaries were drawn in the minds of ordinary people on the basis of skin color and other somatic features which were taken to signify unbridgeable cultural differences associated primarily with Islam. Anyone with a southern Mediterranean appearance was likely to be taken for an Arab or a Maghrebi, terms which in turn were treated as synonyms for Algerians. Few people realized that many North Africans were Berbers, not Arabs, or that the number of immigrants originating in Morocco and Tunisia was rapidly catching up with those from Algeria. In everyday language, immigrants were equated with people of color: most were assumed to be Algerians and by the same token Muslims, and all were exposed to prejudice and discrimination rooted in the long-standing distrust of immigrant "outsiders" that was now compounded by the bitter legacy of the colonial system and its bloody end in Algeria.[10]

These popular images of immigrants, which have remained largely in place since the 1970s, differ greatly from the scholarly demographic definitions and the juridical contours of formal citizenship. As popularly understood, immigrants are both a narrower and a wider category than in academic or legal discourse. Very large numbers of immigrants in the true sense are not perceived as immigrants at all. Although post-colonial groups have dominated recent migratory inflows, Europeans still account for half of the immigrants living in France, defined as people born abroad without French nationality.[11] Yet Europeans are today almost never referred to as immigrants. If this is partly due to skin color and racially tainted notions of cultural alterity inherited from the colonial period, it is also connected with patterns of social stratification.

Mass migration to France has always been dominated by manual workers, who are often unskilled. Earlier in the twentieth century, when Europeans accounted for the vast majority of foreign workers, they were commonly referred to as *travailleurs immigrés* (immigrant workers) or simply as *immigrés*. After World War II, unskilled workers came increasingly from Third World countries, while European migrants tended to fill more skilled positions. Consequently, since the stereotypical image of an immigrant connoted manual labor, it came to be associated more readily with people of color than with Europeans, who were assumed to be white. Class and color--together with hierarchical notions of cultural difference associated with the latter--thus reinforced each other in this new demarcation of immigrants.

In a relatively small number of cases, class can sometimes work to free individuals from the stigmatizing gaze of the majority ethnic "Other." Professional people of Third World origin are often exempted from the "immigrant worker" label despite the fact that they are migrants and--in the generic sense of the word--workers. When recognized as businesspeople, academics, or writers, migrants from Africa, the Middle East, or Asia are more likely to be seen as "foreigners" than as "immigrants," even when they match all the formal criteria by which immigrants are defined.[12] The ambiguous position of post-colonial élites living in France is exemplified in the following remarks made by the Moroccan-born author Tahar Ben Jelloun, writing during an upsurge of racist violence in the early 1980s:

It's a privilege for a Maghrebi living in France not to be directly subjected at a physical level to everyday racism. But it's a bitter privilege. A sickening shroud of contempt is thrown across untold numbers of men and women, refusing to look at or acknowledge them while at the same time stigmatizing them. Perversely, this contempt often spares a few people--writers, intellectuals, exponents of the French language: beings who appear less strange, more easily assimilable, in the final analysis not all that different from France's half-open heart. . . .

Yet there are times when I do feel like a stranger, every time racism rears its ugly or covert head, every time lines are drawn that can't be crossed. . . . The almost neurotic rejection of everything associated with Islam and the Third World weighs upon the whole community together, working men and intellectuals alike.[13] (157-158)

Ben Jelloun's remarks illustrate both the distance that often separates writers from the mass of immigrant workers and the underlying importance of ethnic affiliations, especially in the face of majority ethnic racism.

While working at one level of the popular imagination to narrow the category of immigrants by removing Europeans from the frame, color also works in the opposite direction by adding large numbers of non-immigrants to those who are perceived as immigrants. Born in the country where their parents or grandparents settled, the descendants of post-colonial migrants are not themselves immigrants, but they are often perceived as such by the majority ethnic population. Even when majority ethnic observers know that they are looking at people born in France, they sometimes remain trapped within mindsets that equate colored skins with immigrant status and less than full legitimacy within French society.

These perceptual problems may be illustrated by quoting from a bibliography of early publications dealing with second-generation members of the new immigrant minorities which were beginning to emerge in France during the late 1970s. Writing in 1980, Marie-Claude Munoz listed the following terms as those most commonly employed to designate this new generation: "Young migrants, young migrant workers, young immigrants, foreign youths, young emigrants, foreign immigrant youths, immigrant youths, youths of Maghrebi origin, young Algerians in France, sons of migrants, second-generation migrants, second-generation immigrants, second-generation newcomers, 'illegitimate children' " (7).[14] Practically all the terms quoted here were quite inappropriate, for most of the young people they were meant to describe were neither migrants nor workers, but the children of immigrant workers. Although some had been brought to France by their parents during childhood or adolescence, most were born there. By no means all of them were foreigners, and a large proportion would automatically receive French citizenship on reaching the age of majority if they had not already received it at birth. The final expression listed by Munoz reveals some of the unspoken assumptions behind many of the others: this new generation was seen as "illegitimate" because it cut across the expectations customarily associated with migrants, especially those of Third World origin. Instead of a temporary labor force free of family attachments in France, here was a new generation betokening the permanent settlement of post-colonial minorities. The gendered stereotyping implicit in Munoz's list and in the title of her bibliography should also be noted. The stereotypical image of migrants as male workers is reflected in the references to "sons" of migrants. There is no reference to female members of the new generation, nor for that matter to female migrants, as if the children of immigrants could only be conceived of as an extension of the male labor force.

During the early 1980s, a new designation for second-generation Maghrebis entered circulation: *Beurs*. This term had originally been adopted by young Maghrebis in the *banlieues* of Paris who were tired of the pejorative connotations attached to majority ethnic usage of the word *Arabe*. A *verlan* (back-slang) expression formed by inverting and partially truncating the syllables of the word *Arabe*, *Beur* initially functioned as a valorizing self-designation not understood by the rest of the population. By the late 1980s, however, it had become widely used by the mass media, principally in contexts highlighting problems associated with stereotypical ideas of "immigration" and the *banlieues*. The negative stereotypes attached in this way to the *Beur* label led to its rejection by most of those to whom it was applied. In a 1991 interview, Ben Jelloun indicated that he would never call his daughter a *Beur* despite the fact that she was born in France of Maghrebi parentage, for *Beur* was synonymous with proletarian origins (in contrast with the middle-class status of Ben Jelloun) and signified continuing social disadvantage: " 'Beur' automatically means the *banlieue*, a dead-end world, problems of social adjustment, etc." (Spear 33).[15] Many second-generation Maghrebi authors raised in this milieu have experienced and written about the stigmatization of the *banlieue*, a stigmatization that has led to their being subsumed within the negatively connoted field of "immigration."[16] For similar reasons, most of them too now reject the *Beur* label.[17]

PROCESSES

France is often said to have an assimilationist tradition in relation to immigrant minorities. Like the idea of France as a country where ethnicity has no public role, this too is a half truth. Compared with other countries such as Germany, France has certainly been more open to the permanent settlement of immigrants and has made access to citizenship relatively easy. But there has never been unanimous support for these policies, and at times contrary positions have gained considerable momentum. At a popular level, the stigmatization of the *banlieues* is symptomatic of these exclusionary tendencies. Moreover, even when a basically assimilationist approach has been pursued--as has generally been the case in educational and cultural policies--it has not always had the steamroller effect frequently attributed to it.

For instance, it is now almost a century since a significant part of the Armenian diaspora settled in France following the massacres carried out in their homeland during World War I. Three or four generations later, a strong sense of ethnic specificity remains present among the descendants of Armenian refugees. Their lobbying power was sufficiently strong to persuade the French National Assembly to pass a resolution in 1998 officially recognizing the massacres of 1915 as genocidal in nature.[18] Youri Djorkaeff, one of two players of Armenian descent in the soccer squad that brought France her World Cup victory a few weeks later, said he had been inspired by the National Assembly vote to score during the tournament. In a report on Djorkaeff's close links with the Armenian minority in the Lyons suburb of Décines, a journalist in *Le Monde* described it as "a community constantly referred to in the *banlieues* of Lyons as a model of integration, faithful both to its cultural roots and to France, venerated as a second homeland" (Tincq).[19]

The same report noted it had not always been thus: "Sitting down to a dish of *tchi keufte* [raw meat], the older ones [Armenians] recall the time when their classmates treated them as 'animals' because they ate raw meat and vine leaves" (Tincq).[20] Many other Europeans in that age group had been treated with similar disdain and labelled as "unassimilable" while working or growing up in France, especially during periods of heightened economic insecurity. François Cavanna, for example, has written eloquently of the jibes and discrimination suffered by the Italian minority during the 1930s slump.[21] During the same period, Poles who had been hired ten or fifteen years earlier to plug gaps in the labor force left by the carnage of World War I were branded as unassimilable (sometimes on the grounds that they brought their own Catholic priests with them!) and were repatriated by the trainload.[22]

While generally pursuing an assimilationist policy, the authorities in France have always retained and have sometimes been tempted to use reserve powers permitting them to remove immigrants at will. Those who have been allowed to stay have certainly been expected to assimilate, and the full weight of the educational system has been used in support of this, but the Armenian example shows that the myth of France as wholly assimilationist is overly simple. Immigrant minorities have always retained the right to a private sphere of their own making, even if this has been hemmed in by various restrictions, and the Armenians of Lyons, like the Poles of northern France,[23] bear witness to the fact that recognizable minority identities have often been sustained through succeeding generations. So, far from being a consistent and even-handed policy, the notion of "assimilation" has not uncommonly served as a justification for selecting and/or rejecting immigrants, depending on changing circumstances, and where applied, its impact has been less than total.

The concept of assimilation was partly forged in the colonial arena, where it was intended to be the process through which France's self-appointed "civilizing mission" would come to fruition.[24] The monopoly of power enjoyed by the French was justified on the grounds that it would enable them to organize structures within which the "native" masses would eventually be taught to replicate and share equally in French civilization. The theory of assimilation had two main weaknesses: it was never matched by the material resources that would have been required to make a reality of it, and it was founded on a crude hierarchical model which assumed that indigenous cultures contained nothing worthy of preservation.

With the collapse of the overseas empire, the concept of assimilation lost much of its credibility. It was further weakened by the radical critique of internal centralization voiced during the student demonstrations of 1968, which sharply challenged the idea that a single cultural model could be valid for the whole of French society. Yet even when not explicitly enunciated (words such as *adaptation* and *intégration* were used instead), the idea of assimilation continued in many ways to inform both popular and public thinking in relation to immigrant minorities.

When the economy turned sour in the second half of the 1970s and the French authorities wanted to improve labor market conditions for the majority ethnic population, Third World immigrants--especially those of Maghrebi origin--were targeted for repatriation on the grounds that they were the least assimilable. Europeans, who during earlier economic downturns had also been treated as unassimilable, were now described as models of successful "integration," a term that was to become the centerpiece of public policy towards immigrant minorities from the late 1980s onwards.

The current consensus of all the main parties--except for the extreme right-wing National Front (FN)--around the slogan of *intégration* emerged after more than a decade of political turmoil during which assimilation seemed in many ways to disappear from the political agenda. The center-right governments in office during the late 1970s not only sought to repatriate immigrants, but they also put in place educational programs conceived with the specific objective of avoiding assimilation. By permitting "home country" governments to fund mother-tongue teaching in French schools, it was hoped that this would help prepare immigrant families for repatriation to their countries of origin. These and other measures, including financial incentives designed to encourage repatriation, proved largely unsuccessful. When the left came to power in 1981, it scrapped the repatriation program but retained mother-tongue classes and brought in other measures to support minority cultures, but with a different objective from the previous administration. Influenced by the legacy of 1968, the Socialist Party was committed both to political decentralization and to greater cultural pluralism. Instead of the old idea of assimilation or the later watchword of integration, the new administration advocated what it called the "insertion" of immigrant minorities. This meant facilitating their social, economic, and political incorporation while respecting their right to retain cultural differences, a right embodied in the slogan of *le droit à la différence* (the right to difference).[25]

With the emergence of the Front National (FN) as a major political actor in the mid-1980s, the left abandoned these slogans and sought to construct a new consensus, which the center-right parties eventually joined, around the concept of integration. This was closely connected with a renewed emphasis on the "universal" values of French republicanism, said to be exemplified in the integration of individuals--but not of communities--of immigrant origin.[26]

While integration has remained unquestionably the dominant concept in political discourse relating to immigrant minorities in France, it is drenched in ambiguities. Seen by some as a half-way house or as a third way between the centripetal steamroller of assimilation and the centrifugal dangers of insertion, integration was interpreted by a few on the left as simply a new word for insertion while many on the right as well as in the center and in some cases on the left of the political spectrum have used it as a camouflage for the concept of assimilation.[27]

To find our way through these ambiguities, it is useful to distinguish between assimilation and acculturation. Where acculturation signifies the internalization of a given cultural system, assimilation implies in addition the abandoning or obliteration of all other cultural affiliations. Just as it would be absurd to suggest that the acquisition of a second language necessarily implies forgetting or abandoning one's first language, so it is unreasonable to assume that the internalization of French culture necessarily implies the abandoning of all others. Second- and third-generation members of minority ethnic groups have readily acculturated to the norms dominant in France while often complementing and widening them with additional elements drawn from their migratory heritage. This does not--or should not--make them any less "integrated."

The supposed antithesis of integration is commonly demonized as *communautarisme*, a kind of ethnic separatism exemplified in lurid references to the Lebanese civil war, the break-up of Yugoslavia, or, more commonly, the dangers of the so-called Anglo-Saxon model, said to be synonymous with the formation of ethnic ghettoes.[28] These grotesque caricatures are designed to reassure French public opinion that national cohesion is safe thanks to the unique virtues of the republican model of integration. One effect of this has been to make it virtually impossible for words such as "multi-culturalism"--routinely condemned as an Anglo-Saxon invention--to receive a fair hearing in France.[29]

But we should not allow this intimidating discourse to blind us to what is actually happening on the ground. Although almost no one speaks explicitly in favor of multi-culturalism, cultural pluralism is often defended in more indirect ways, and it is clear that cultural hybridity is increasingly evident in France. As noted above, French rap, ragga, and raï bands combining cultural influences from Europe, Africa, and North America now routinely top the charts.

The multi-ethnic soccer team that won the World Cup in 1998 has also helped widen popular appreciation of the contribution of immigrants to the achievements of France as a nation. Half of the French squad was born outside metropolitan France or of immigrant parents. The crucial role played by Zinedine Zidane, a second-generation Algerian whose goal-scoring talents made him a national hero overnight, dealt a severe blow to the myth that post-colonial minorities--especially those of Muslim heritage--could not, would not, or should not be "integrated" into French society. While Muslims do not yet enjoy the degree of respect accorded to Christian minorities such as the Armenians, a model of integration may be emerging--exemplified in the *Le Monde* article on Djorkaeff--within which ethnic specificities are acknowledged as legitimate provided they are seen to function in tandem with a fundamental sense of belonging in France.

CONCLUSION

It would be unwise to imagine that the feel-good factor generated by a soccer tournament will suffice on its own to turn the tide of racial discrimination frequently encountered by France's post-colonial minorities. But the late 1990s brought two other encouraging developments. One is the first sustained fall in unemployment seen in France in over twenty years. Opinion surveys show that the greater sense of economic security associated with this has been reflected in reduced levels of antipathy towards immigrants and minority ethnic groups.[30] At the same time, the Socialist-led government in office since 1997 has had the courage to tackle the problem of the *sans-papiers*, granting residence permits to most of them, and has been moving towards tougher anti-discriminatory measures which may in the future provide more effective protection for minority groups. While prejudice and bigotry are unlikely to disappear overnight, it is clear that perceptions of ethnic differences are by no means immutably fixed. Writing from the other side of the ethnic divide, the authors examined in the rest of this volume testify in their own terms to the complex and shifting ways in which those differences resonate and evolve.

NOTES

1. For detailed and highly informative accounts of this period, see Patrick Weil's *La France et ses étrangers* and Vincent Viet's *La France immigrée.*
2. See Mehdi Lallaoui's *Du bidonville aux HLM.*
3. The *sans-papiers* crisis of the 1990s was by no means the first. On earlier crises of this kind (when undocumented migrants were more commonly referred to as *clandestins* [illegal immigrants]), see Johanna Simeant's *La cause des sans-papiers.*
4. See, for example, Inspection Générale des Affaires Sociales, *Enquête sur l'insertion des jeunes immigrés dans l'entreprise* and Philippe Bataille's *Le racisme au travail.*
5. See Alec G. Hargreaves, "A Deviant Construction: The French Media and the 'Banlieues.' "
6. See Françoise Gaspard and Farhad Khosrokhavar, *Le foulard et la République.*

7. See Steve Cannon's "*Paname City Rapping*: B-Boys in the *Banlieues* and Beyond."

8. The most important of these studies are Michèle Tribalat's *Cent ans d'immigration* and her *De l'immigration à l'assimilation*, and INSEE, *Les immigrés en France.*

9. Through its census data collection agency INSEE, the French state also separated *harkis* from other French nationals, classifying them as *français musulmans* (French Muslims) in the 1968 census. This had the effect of perpetuating distinctions drawn during the colonial period between "ordinary" French nationals and those of Algerian origin, who were classified separately. Although *français musulmans* disappeared as a separate category in the 1975 census, the distinctions on which it was based are still used by government departments in relation to those now labeled as RONA. Clearly visible here, ethnic criteria are also evident in the fact that, unlike *harkis*, Algerian economic migrants are today formally classified by INSEE as *immigrés* despite the fact that, as most were born prior to Algerian independence, they were French nationals at birth. Strictly speaking, they are in this respect on a par with those classified as *rapatriés* who, because they were born abroad as French nationals, are not regarded as *immigrés*; see *Les immigrés en France* (17). Through distinctions of this kind, it can be seen that ethnic and political considerations play a more significant role than is commonly thought in official French thinking.

10. These and related issues are examined in greater detail in Abdelmalek Sayad's "Qu'est-ce qu'un immigré?" and in Benjamin Stora's *Le transfert d'une mémoire. De l'Algérie française au racisme anti-arabe.*

11. Because they have relatively high rates of naturalization, by which French citizenship is acquired after a period of residence in France, Europeans accounted for 50 percent of immigrants (as defined by INSEE) but only 40 percent of the foreign population in the 1990 census.

12. On these more élite migrant groups, see Anne-Catherine Wagner's *Les nouvelles élites de la mondialisation: une immigration dorée en France.*

13. "C'est un privilège pour un Maghrébin vivant en France de ne pas subir directement, sur son propre corps, le racisme ordinaire. Un privilège amer. Le mépris est ce drap nauséabond jeté sur une quantité indiscernable d'hommes et de femmes pour ne pas les voir, pour ne pas les nommer et aussi pour les désigner au refus. Ce mépris a cependant sa perversité: il est fréquent qu'il épargne quelques-uns. Ecrivains, intellectuels, promoteurs de la langue française: êtres moins étranges, plus assimilables et, tout compte fait, assez proches d'une France à l'âme entrouverte. . . .

Et pourtant, il m'arrive de me sentir étranger, chaque fois que le racisme virulent ou larvé se manifeste, chaque fois qu'on dessine des limites à ne pas dépasser. . . . Le refus quasi névrotique depuis quelque temps de ce qui porte l'empreinte de l'islam et du Tiers-Monde englobe dans le même fardeau toute une communauté, manoeuvres et intellectuels."

14. "jeunes migrants, jeunes travailleurs migrants, jeunes immigrés, jeunes étrangers, jeunes émigrés, jeunes immigrés étrangers, adolescents immigrés, adolescents d'origine maghrébine, jeunesse algérienne en France, fils de migrants, migrants de la seconde génération, seconde génération d'immigrés, deuxième génération d'immigrants, 'enfants illégitimes.' "

15. See Thomas Spear's "Politics and Literature: An Interview with Tahar Ben Jelloun." I am grateful to Thomas Spear for permitting me to consult the French transcript of his interview with Ben Jelloun, whose original words were: " 'Beur' désigne automatiquement la banlieue, la galère, les problèmes d'insertion, etc."

16. See Alec G. Hargreaves's *Immigration and Identity in Beur Fiction: Voices from the North African Immigrant Community in France.*

17. See Sylvie Durmelat's "Petite histoire du mot *beur*."
18. See Clarisse Fabre's "L'Assemblée Nationale proclame: 'La France reconnaît le génocide arménien de 1915.' "
19. "une communauté toujours citée dans les banlieues de Lyon comme un modèle d'intégration, fidèle à sa culture d'origine et à une France vénérée comme une deuxième patrie."
20. "Au restaurant arménien, attablés autour d'un tchi keufte (viande crue), les plus anciens se souviennent de l'époque où leurs camarades de classe les traitaient d''animaux' parce qu'ils mangeaient de la viande crue et des feuilles de vigne."
21. See Cavanna's *Les ritals*.
22. See Janine Ponty's *Polonais méconnus: histoire des travailleurs immigrés en France dans l'entre-deux-guerres*.
23. See Ponty's "L'apport des Polonais dans la région du Nord."
24. See Raymond F. Betts, *Assimilation and Association in French Colonial Theory and Practice*.
25. For a provocative critique of this slogan from a minority ethnic perspective, see Farida Belghoul, "Le droit à la différence: une forme voilée de l'exclusion."
26. See Françoise Lorcerie's "Les sciences sociales au service de l'identité nationale: le débat sur l'intégration en France au début des années 1990" and Jean-Philippe Mathy's "Repli sur la République: la nouvelle donne des intellectuels français."
27. See Françoise Gaspard's "Assimilation, insertion, intégration: les mots pour 'devenir français.' "
28. See Loïc Wacquant's "Banlieues françaises et ghetto noir américain: de l'amalgame à la comparaison."
29. See Alec G. Hargreaves's "Multiculturalism."
30. See the CSA opinion polls in *Le Monde*, November 21, 1998 and March 25, 1999.

WORKS CITED
Bataille, Philippe. *Le racisme au travail*. Paris: La Découverte, 1997.
Belghoul, Farida. "Le droit à la différence: une forme voilée de l'exclusion." *Vivre ensemble avec nos différences*. Paris: Editions Différences, 1984, 18-19, 74.
Ben Jelloun, Tahar. *Hospitalité française: racisme et immigration maghrébine*. Paris: Seuil, 1984.
Betts, Raymond F. *Assimilation and Association in French Colonial Theory and Practice*. New York: Columbia University Press, 1961.
Cannon, Steve. *"Paname City Rapping*: B-Boys in the *Banlieues* and Beyond." *Post-Colonial Cultures in France*. Ed. Alec G. Hargreaves and Mark McKinney. London/New York: Routledge, 1997, 150-166.
Cavanna, François. *Les ritals*. Paris: Belfond, 1978.
CSA opinion poll. *Le Monde*, November 21, 1998.
CSA opinion poll. *Le Monde*, March 25, 1999.
Durmelat, Sylvie. "Petite histoire du mot *beur*: ou comment prendre la parole quand on vous la prête." *French Cultural Studies* 9 (1998): 191-207.
Fabre, Clarisse. "L'Assemblée Nationale proclame: 'La France reconnaît le génocide arménien de 1915.' " *Le Monde*, May 30, 1998.
Gaspard, Françoise. "Assimilation, insertion, intégration: les mots pour 'devenir français.' " *Hommes et Migrations* 1154 (May 1992): 14-23.

Gaspard, Françoise, and Farhad Khosrokhavar. *Le foulard et la République*. Paris: La Découverte, 1995.

Hargreaves, Alec G. "A Deviant Construction: The French Media and the 'Banlieues.' " *New Community* 22.4 (October 1996): 607-618.

---. *Immigration and Identity in Beur Fiction: Voices from the North African Immigrant Community in France*. 2nd ed. Oxford/New York: Berg, 1997.

---. "Multiculturalism." *Political Ideologies in Contemporary France*. Ed. Christopher Flood and Laurence Bell. London and Washington: Pinter, 1997, 180-199.

INSEE. *Les immigrés en France*. Paris: INSEE, 1997.

Inspection Générale des Affaires Sociales. *Enquête sur l'insertion des jeunes immigrés dans l'entreprise*. Paris: IGAS, 1992.

Lallaoui, Mehdi. *Du bidonville aux HLM*. Paris: Syros, 1993.

Lorcerie, Françoise. "Les sciences sociales au service de l'identité nationale: le débat sur l'intégration en France au début des années 1990." *Cartes d'identité: comment dit-on "nous" en politique?* Ed. Denis-Constant Martin. Paris: Presses de la Fondation Nationale des Sciences Politiques, 1994, 244-281.

Mathy, Jean-Philippe. "Repli sur la République: la nouvelle donne des intellectuels français." *L'Esprit Créateur* 37.2 (Summer 1997): 41-55.

Munoz, Marie-Claude. *Bibliographie analytique sur les jeunes étrangers (immigrés ou fils d'immigrés)*. Paris: CIEMM, 1980.

Ponty, Janine. *Polonais méconnus: histoire des travailleurs immigrés en France dans l'entre-deux-guerres*. Paris: Publications de la Sorbonne, 1988.

---. "L'apport des Polonais dans la région du Nord." *Hommes et Migrations* 1221 (September-October 1999): 73-83.

Sayad, Abdelmalek. "Qu'est-ce qu'un immigré?" *Peuples Méditerranéens* 7 (April-June 1979): 3-23.

Simeant, Johanna. *La cause des sans-papiers*. Paris: Presses de la Fondation Nationale des Sciences Politiques, 1998.

Spear, Thomas. "Politics and Literature: An Interview with Tahar Ben Jelloun." *Yale French Studies* 82 (1993): 30-43.

Stora, Benjamin. *Le transfert d'une mémoire. De l'Algérie française au racisme anti-arabe*. Paris: La Découverte, 1999.

Tincq, Henri. "Youri Djorkaeff retrouve la 'petite Arménie'." *Le Monde*, June 24, 1998.

Tribalat, Michèle. *Cent ans d'immigration. Etrangers d'hier, Français d'aujourd'hui. Apport démographique, dynamique familiale et économique de l'immigration étrangère*. Paris: INED/PUF, 1991.

---. *De l'immigration à l'assimilation: enquête sur les populations d'origine étrangère en France*. Paris: La Découverte/INED, 1996.

Viet, Vincent. *La France immigrée: construction d'une politique, 1914-1997*. Paris: Fayard, 1998.

Wacquant, Loïc. "Banlieues françaises et ghetto noir américain: de l'amalgame à la comparaison." *French Politics and Society* 10.4 (Autumn 1992): 81–103.

Wagner, Anne-Catherine. *Les nouvelles élites de la mondialisation: une immigration dorée en France*. Paris: PUF, 1999.

Weil, Patrick. *La France et ses étrangers: l'aventure d'une politique de l'immigration de 1938 à nos jours*. 2nd ed. Paris: Seuil, 1995.

First-Generation Immigrant Narratives

Susan Ireland

> I'm going to sketch out for you the itinerary of an immigrant: poverty
> at home--passport--corruption--humiliation--medical examination--
> emigration office--journey--long crossing--makeshift accommoda-
> tions--work--metro--the trunk--masturbation--lightening--the acci-
> dent--hospital or the cemetery--the money order--vacation--
> illusions--the return--customs--the hospital--death--the accident--
> masturbation--the prostitute--the clap--the metro--images--images--
> images...[1] (Ben Jelloun, *Réclusion solitaire* 136)

> You are the one who rapes and who has a hidden knife, never the one
> who is hiding a wonderful dream in his pocket and who built the
> tower blocks.[2] (Mengouchi and Ramdane 78)

It has frequently been observed that first-generation immigrants to France were
a silent generation.[3] Often illiterate and speaking little or no French, they generally had no desire to stand out and attempted to "se faire petits pour passer in-
aperçus" (to make themselves small in order to go unnoticed) (Ben Jelloun,
Hospitalité 23), thus becoming largely invisible in French society. Without a
language in which to express themselves in France, they were at first described
and defined by others. At the same time, their silence was reinforced by the fact
that majority society showed little interest in hearing what they had to say.[4]
However, this first generation represents an important stage of the immigrant
past. As Tahar Ben Jelloun observes, "this generation of fathers who have grown
old before their time carry on their faces the history of immigration, its mean-

ders, its wounds, its disappointments" (*Hospitalité* 26).[5] While in recent years much has been written by and about the more visible and more vocal second generation, in comparison, relatively little attention has been paid to the experiences of their parents. Although there have been many waves of first-generation immigrants to France, this chapter will focus on the migrant workers who came to France as adults in the post-war period (1950s and 1960s) and will examine the ways in which their experiences have been textualized in fictional and autobiographical works.

These narratives fall roughly into three main categories. The earliest works, published for the most part in the 1970s, include oral testimonies and written life stories which are framed, and often transcribed, by a French person-- usually a journalist or anthropologist--and occasionally by a North African of a similar profession. In each case, the voice of the immigrant is mediated by that of a more educated collaborator who validates the narrative. During the same period, a small number of novels written by educated Africans of the same generation as the migrant workers take up their cause and testify to the suffering and hardship that characterize their lives. Finally, in the 1980s and 1990s, the children of first-generation immigrants, who have been raised and educated in France, have claimed a voice for themselves and, while their texts deal primarily with the question of their own place in France, they also evoke the life of their parents, often with the explicit intention of valorizing their experiences and giving them a place in history.[6] Certain topics recur across the three categories of texts, and in all of them, individual stories are generally presented as representative of collective experience. The most common themes evoke various aspects of the typical immigrant trajectory, from recruitment in the home country to raising children in France: nostalgia and the desire to return "home," working conditions, the unpleasant accommodations available to workers and their families, racism and exclusion, and, for North Africans, the experience of living in France during the Algerian War. Although most of the narratives deal primarily with the lives of male workers, those that focus more on women also portray their difficulties adjusting when they join their husbands in France. Furthermore, in most of the texts, the immigrant body--rejected and wounded--stands as a powerful image of immigrant experience, a form of corporeal inscription that speaks eloquently of the hard lives of the first generation.

The literary narratives of first-generation immigration take their place alongside historical, economic, and political accounts of the same events. The standard historical narrative places migrant workers in the first of three phases of immigration which have led to the presence of new ethnic minorities in France.[7] The first phase, which began in 1945 and ended with the oil crisis in the early 1970s, was that of mass labor migration necessitated by the economic boom and low birth-rate that followed World War II (Castles 11). During this period, large numbers of workers came to France from the colonies and former colonies as part of what was then viewed as a temporary solution to post-war problems. Although the biggest percentage of workers came from North Africa, large numbers also emigrated from the former colonies of Senegal, Mali, and Mauritania and from the Overseas Departments of Martinique, Guadeloupe, and Réunion Island (Castles 51). During the following two phases, those of family reunification and of permanent settlement, as the workers' children were raised in France (Castles 13, 15), the first generation who had arrived as temporary migrant workers became fully fledged immigrants who were likely to remain in France on a long-term basis.

The historical narrative is largely dependent on economic factors. The migrant workers who came to rebuild France after the war constituted a convenient source of labor for French industry; since they were recruited from abroad and were required to travel alone even if married, they could easily be sent home or be replaced when no longer needed. Indeed, the economic demand for workers was so great that recruitment not only continued, but even doubled between 1954 and 1962, the period of the Algerian War (Assouline and Lallaoui 16). In this economic account, the migrant workers figure primarily as units of production in industrial centers such as Paris, Marseille, Lyon, and Lille. Selected for their good health and recruited mainly from rural areas, they quickly became an urban labor force, working in unskilled and semi-skilled jobs, very often on an assembly line or in the service sector. Both the economic and historical accounts of immigration are inextricably intertwined with the broader history of French colonialism. The fact that the colonies provided an easy supply of labor encouraged the transposition of hierarchical colonial relationships into the metropolitan context and their perpetuation after decolonization. As Ben Jelloun observes, many supervisors and managers in corporations such as Renault had fought in the Algerian War (*Hospitalité* 95), while thousands of North Africans now work under them in factories and on construction sites. In this sense, the violence that characterized colonialism is relived through the exploitation of immigrant workers who are reduced to faceless, anonymous units of production while little concern is shown for their well-being--"A la blessure coloniale succèdent la haine, l'exclusion et l'exploitation à domicile" (The wound inflicted by colonialism is followed by hatred, exclusion, and exploitation on France's home territory) (Ben Jelloun, *La plus haute* 12).[8]

Towards the end of the Algerian War, and during the economic crisis of the mid-seventies in particular, first-generation immigrants also became part of political discourse. Before then, they did not figure prominently in political debates since France was actively encouraging immigration, and the workers themselves tended to live quiet, invisible lives. Once the policy of family reunification was introduced in 1974, however, the image of immigration changed radically and moved to the center of the political arena. Most importantly, right-wing political parties began to present immigrants as the cause of a range of economic and social ills, from unemployment to crime and other forms of social disorder. This scapegoating was later reinforced in the polemical discourse of the Front National, which declared many immigrants unassimilable and demanded that they return home. In this political narrative, then, immigration moved quite suddenly from being associated with economic growth and prosperity to being portrayed as a threat to national cohesion, a shift expressed in the increasing number of racist attacks on workers and reflected in apocalyptic images of invasion, terrorism, and enemy hordes at the city gates.[9]

From the intersections of these mainstream accounts of first-generation immigration emerged the composite, stereotypical image of the migrant worker, which remained largely unchanged until the second generation moved to the forefront of political debates and media coverage in the 1980s. According to this cliché, the typical worker was a single, illiterate Arab man who lived in squalid conditions and worked on a construction site or an assembly line.[10] It is against the backdrop of these "official" versions of immigrant history that the narratives written by immigrants themselves assume their full significance. Their counter-narratives provide an alternative version of the workers' lives, and this new per-spective serves to give the first generation the place and voice they have tradi-tionally been denied.

LIFE STORIES

The first-generation life stories presented by a collaborator or co-author include Mohamed Belkacemi's and Alain Gheerbrant's *Belka*, Ahmed's *Une vie d'Algérien, est-ce que ça fait un livre que les gens vont lire?*, Mohamed's *Journal de Mohamed*, Christian's *Zistoir Kristian*, Nedjma Plantade's *L'honneur et l'amertume*, Dalila Kerouani's *Une fille d'Algérie éprise de liberté*, and Ben Jelloun's *La plus haute des solitudes*. With the possible exception of Kerouani's narrative, these autobiographical texts all constitute examples of what Philippe Lejeune calls "The Autobiography of Those Who Do Not Write."[11] Indeed, the texts to be discussed here are presented as a form of testimony, as the authentic life story of a kind of "native informant" who recounts the events of his or her life to an interviewer. This emphasis on the authenticity of lived experience con-firms Charles Bonn's observation that "all new literatures will tend to privilege, if not autobiography in the full sense of the term, then at least testimony pre-sented as 'authentic' " (204).[12] When introducing the "slice of life" they are about to present, many of the collaborators explicitly point to their subjects' inability to read and write, thereby creating "un analphabétisme affiché" (insis-tence on illiteracy) (Bonn 205) which suggests that the voice of first-generation immigrants can be heard only through an intermediary.[13] The nature of the rela-tionship between immigrant and interviewer is generally described in a short preface indicating how the narrative was obtained and transcribed, but this in-troductory material ranges in length from a brief reference to the interviewer on the cover page to very extensive editorial commentary including notes and analyses of various kinds. Consequently, the framing of many of the life stories raises important questions about the collaboration between the transcriber and the autobiographical subject, in particular about whose voice is being heard and how the narrative will be read. Even if well-intentioned, the presentation of the narratives often suggests a contemporary version of the anthropologist/native informant paradigm of the colonial period, which turns the immigrant life story into an ethnographic document complete with much of the "exoticism" inherent in the earlier form.

Mohamed's *Journal de Mohamed*, written in collaboration with Maurice Catani, illustrates the problematic nature of the autobiographical sub-ject-transcriber relationship. The narrative is part of Stock's "témoigner" (testi-monial) series, and the short introduction on the inside cover immediately draws attention to the fact that Mohamed is illiterate while at the same time emphasizing his skills as a storyteller. In addition, the importance of testimony as a genre is underscored in the observation that Mohamed's account is more useful as a tool for understanding the problem of immigrant workers (le problème des travailleurs étrangers) than is a theoretical treatise (traité abstrait). The narrative itself recounts Mohamed's twenty-one years in France, focusing in particular on his work on construction sites and the serious health problems he suffers as a result. His lively, informative account provides a wealth of information on the life of a crane operator--the dangers of the job, the long hours often without overtime pay, accidents, and his fear of losing his job during the general strike organized by the Front de Libération Nationale (FLN). At the same time, it portrays Mohamed as a typical "single" worker sending money home to his wife and six children and sometimes experiencing difficult relations with his family during his vacations in Algeria, especially when his wife becomes an FLN militant. The editorial commentary, however, which takes up almost half the book, underscores Catani's role in shaping Mohamed's story and reveals the extent to which the transcriber's voice intrudes into the narrative; it is composed of a foreword describing when the two men met and how the interviews took place, a short summary of Mohamed's story before he tells it himself, statistics on immigration, chapter headings, and a table of contents as well as a series of notes and analyses on topics such as Kabyle culture. This editorial apparatus sets Catani up as a kind of guide and interpreter whose role is to "faciliter la lecture" (to help the reader) (15), as if Mohamed's story would not be intelligible without his aid. This mediation goes beyond simple guidance and is designed to point the reader in specific directions: "on the one hand I make reading the text easier, and on the other I orient the reader in the way that interests me" (159).[14] Indeed, the ethnographic nature of Catani's project becomes increasingly apparent in the analyses following Mohamed's story. Here, he refers explicitly to "incursions dans le domaine de l'ethnographie" (incursions into the domain of ethnography) as being essential for his own research in which Mohamed's life story, along with those of others, will constitute "le matériau de base" (raw material) for a study of migration and acculturation (157).[15] Although Catani has, as he points out, taken care to separate his analyses from Mohamed's narrative by placing them at the end of the book, they nonetheless predominate to the point that Mohamed does not really appear to be speaking for himself. Catani's discussion of the transcription of Mohamed's account reinforces the impression of his role as shaper and interpreter. Not wanting to change the flavor of Mohamed's French, which is described as a "création originale" (original creation) (165), Catani has at times indicated the correct French version of his words in parentheses. Mohamed's "immigrant" French is thus designated as a deviant form, and in this fashion, "creative" becomes synonymous with "exotic"--a variant which must be "translated" in order for it to be comprehensible. The epigraph in particular, with its emphasis on voice and its use of non-standard French, both announces the immigrant's status as outsider and suggests the role his collaborator will play in giving him a voice: "Depuis tant de temps à la France c'est le premier que je parle comme ça avec vous. Jamais je parle avec personne, avec personne" (Since so much time at France it's the first I speak like that with you. Never I speak with nobody, with nobody).

The question of the immigrant voice and its intelligibility is explicitly raised in the title of Ahmed's narrative, *Une vie d'Algérien, est-ce que ça fait un livre que les gens vont lire?* In this text, the short introduction, whose author is not named, presents the goals of the book as educational in nature: to remedy people's ignorance about immigrants[16] and to provide an antidote to the dangerous "exoticism" of certain well-intentioned media reports that seek to inform the public about North Africans (6). Ahmed's story provides these readers with an account which resembles Mohamed's in many respects. The fact that Ahmed is a *harki* adds a further dimension to some of the episodes involving his relations with his fellow Algerians, but the parts of the narrative dealing with his experience of immigration describe problems similar to those evoked by Mohamed: the difficulty of living on low wages and still having enough money to send home, poor accommodations, and general disappointment with life in France, which derives largely from the racism he has encountered. Because of the didactic goals involved in publishing his story, Ahmed appears as more of a type than as an individual. Indeed, the use of his first name only on the title page and cover of the book reinforces the impression of an exemplary, almost anonymous subject. Furthermore, although the transcriber of Ahmed's story insists on the personal nature of the account, describing it as a "cas isolé" (isolated case) (11) which should not be viewed as a "document" (11), he nonetheless observes in the following sentence that "bien des frères du narrateur auraient sans doute pu tenir l'essentiel de ces propos" (many of the narrator's compatriots could undoubtedly have made more or less the same comments) (11). Similarly, although Mohamed, like Ahmed, indicates in his narrative that he does not wish to be identified, the subtitle of *Journal de Mohamed* emphasizes his role as a type, *Un Algérien en France parmi huit cent mille autres*. Catani further highlights Mohamed's role as example in his remark that "Mohamed est certes *un* migrant algérien, mais . . . il est aussi *les* migrants algériens" (Mohamed is indeed *an* immigrant, but . . . he also represents Algerian immigrants) (158), an observation that underscores the tensions inherent in this type of account between the life story of an individual and the accompanying presentation of it as illustrating the characteristics of a particular ethnic and social group. Although the editorial commentary is less extensive in *Une vie d'Algerien* than in *Journal de Mohamed*, it assumes the same form: footnotes, numbered section headings, a short introduction that presents the text as a "scrupulous transcription" of a series of monologues recorded in 1972-1973 and that discusses the oral nature of the testimony, and a conclusion entitled "Une génération sacrifiée?" (A Sacrificed Generation?) (183) which, while it affirms the need to combat prejudice, ends with several paragraphs containing stereotypical observations on Islam.

Belka, the life story of an Algerian immigrant worker who now organizes literacy classes for adults, is the longest narrative to be discussed in this section (365 pages) and has the least amount of editorial framing (barely three pages). Alain Gheerbrant's introduction, which describes his collaboration with Belka as a form of "osmosis" (8), is more impressionistic in nature than the forewords to *Journal de Mohamed* and *Une vie d'Algérien*, but does nonetheless provide information on his role in shaping the text, describing it as the result of two years of piecing together Belka's memories, some of which had been jotted down on paper while others were related to him orally. During this time, he gave structure to the chaotic memories--"je les triais en essayant surtout de ne pas les tuer" (I sorted them, trying more than anything else not to destroy them) (7)--presenting himself as the representative of order, yet trying to minimize his role through the notion of total immersion, as if he had somehow become Belka's mouthpiece: "je parlais Belka, je pensais Belka" (I spoke Belka, I thought Belka) (8).

The fascinating story of Belka's life reads more like a novel than the two narratives already examined. The first part of the text, the story in microcosm of the colonial relationship between France and Algeria, describes the narrator's childhood and adolescence, focusing on his relationship with a French woman, a teacher who makes sure he becomes literate as part of her efforts to "civilize" him--"Rose is the trainer and I the wild animal in the process of being tamed" (103)[17]--and who attempts to poison him when he wants to end the affair. The second half of the book, which deals with Belka's experiences in France, is particularly interesting for its account of immigration during World War II. Belka first leaves for France when he hears that the Vichy government is recruiting factory workers; he initially works in an aluminum factory, but his experience there is short-lived since, when he tries to cross into the Occupied Zone in order to make more money, he is arrested, taken for a member of a smuggling ring, and deported as an "Individu nuisible pour le moral des travailleurs algériens dans la métropole" (Individual harmful for the morale of Algerian workers in France) (188). His account of his second departure for France portrays a different kind of immigration from that of the typical first-generation worker. As an illegal immigrant in Paris in the spring of 1946, he feels completely at home in the North African neighborhood of Pigalle and the Goutte d'Or, making a living on the black market and frequenting nightclubs and colorful characters from the multi-ethnic Parisian underworld at night. At the end of the war, however, and especially after he marries a French nurse, he begins the exhausting, monotonous life of a typical migrant worker by going to work for Simca--"J'avais rejoint le camp des automates" (I had gone over to the side of the robots) (273). The central focus of this part of the narrative--Belka's experiences at Simca during the Algerian War--provides a detailed account of the organization and activities of the FLN in France and its bitter and bloody conflicts with the Mouvement National Algérien (MNA), which was suspected of complicity with the French. Besides highlighting the difficulty of combining the roles of worker and militant, Belka documents the diverse aspects of his eight years of clandestine combat and the final year he spent in the Larzac detention center, an experience which motivated him to tell his life story. In the resulting narrative, he describes the pyramid structure of the FLN, the different activities carried out by its members, the intimidation tactics used by both sides, and both workers' and managers' reactions to the order to strike in solidarity with workers in Algeria. The narrative of Belka's life as an immigrant in France and as a full participant in Algeria's struggle for independence is presented in the final sentence of the text as the story of how he learned to resist marginalization, and the notion of liberation is clearly related to that of voice, hence his decision to organize literacy programs for workers: "Liberation is spelled with an L, an I, a B, an E, an R, an A, a T, an I, an O, an N! LIBERATION is spelled with all the letters of the ALPHABET" (366).[18]

The bilingual autobiographical narrative *Zistoir Kristian*, the story of an immigrant worker from La Réunion who came to France in the 1960s, is, like the others, presented as a "true story,"[19] and the use of the term "Mes-aventures" (My/Misadventures) in the subtitle plays on the notions of authorship and of immigration as disillusionment. In this text, the prefatory material revolves around the question of translation since the original narrative was supposedly written in Creole in the form of a journal, and the foreword is signed by "the translators" (13), who are in fact a group of anti-colonialist Réunionnais students living in Paris (Marimoutou, "Trois regards" 110). Christian's story is thus presented both as an exemplary testimonial narrative and as an experiment in translation designed to demonstrate that Creole can function as a written language rather than being relegated to the status of "vulgaire patois" (vulgar dialect) (5). For this reason, Jean-Claude Marimoutou characterizes the text as a "manifeste linguistique en acte" (a linguistic manifesto in action) ("La faille" 94), questioning the authenticity of the narrative and viewing it rather as an "autobiographie fictive" (fictional autobiography) ("La faille" 94) or an "espèce d'autofiction à thèse" (kind of didactic autofiction) ("Trois regards" 110). Besides discussing the status of Creole, the translators foreground the political dimensions of the narrative, presenting it as a denunciation of colonial exploitation in La Réunion and of French immigration policies, as well as providing some historical background on colonial agricultural practices and on the Bumidom (Bureau pour le Développement des Migrations des Départements d'Outre-Mer), which was created in 1963 to supply French industry with workers from the overseas departments.[20] Christian's account is thus preceded by highly politicized commentary which, like several of the other narratives discussed, presents the narrator's experience as "singulière" (uncommon) while at the same time defining it as emblematic of the trajectory of Réunionnais immigrant workers in general.[21] In many respects Christian's life story is a classic tale of disillusionment and political awakening. The first half of the text, which takes place in La Réunion, depicts the life of poor agricultural workers, while the second focuses on Christian's rapid disenchantment upon his arrival in France--his sense of exclusion underscored by comparisons related to slavery. Christian first comes to France as part of his military service, but stays on in order to take advantage of a training course in masonry, then remains in France as a worker since he is unable to afford a ticket home. At this point, he deals with experiences similar to those of North African workers--racism, exploitation, and low-quality accommodations--but his account also singles out the Bumidom for harsh criticism. A series of short-term jobs constantly brings Christian back to the Bumidom which, along with the Bourse du Travail, is portrayed as the "bourreau" (executioner) (187) of Réunionnais immigrants because, according to Christian, it always sends them to the worst jobs and makes them dependent. The indictment of the Bumidom and of racism serves as the conclusion to the narrative, as Christian compares the situation of immigrants in France with that of French people who work in La Réunion, and his experience of life as a second-class citizen in France can be summarized in his bitter comment that "ça me dégoûte d'être de nationalité française" (it disgusts me to be a French national) (152).

The extent of the collaboration in Dalila Kerouani's *Une fille d'Algérie éprise de liberté*, one of the few accounts by a woman who becomes an immigrant worker,[22] is difficult to determine. The book contains no editorial commentary, and the only reference to the collaborator (Jeanne-Françoise Bayen) appears on the title page inside the novel, not on the cover. Furthermore, since Kerouani indicates that she spoke French well when she emigrated,[23] it is possible that she is the primary author of the text, and it is in any case impossible to determine what kind of editing or shaping Bayen is responsible for. Kerouani's account of immigration is also atypical in several other respects. First, her move to France with her six children in 1973 was not the result of a traditional type of family reunification since the decision to emigrate was Kerouani's alone, and her husband was not informed of her imminent arrival until she was in the departure lounge at the airport. Second, the titles of the two parts of the text devoted to Algeria and France present her trajectory as an immigrant as a move from "La vie soumise" (A Life of Subjugation) to "Le quotidien de la liberté" (Daily Life as a Free Person) (7, 115). While this is not the case in most of the men's narratives, her decision to emigrate constitutes an act of rebellion and is experienced as liberating, even though it entailed a change in economic status. While the narrators of the autobiographies discussed so far were all from poor backgrounds, Kerouani was from a relatively well-off family, but experienced the exhausting life of the typical immigrant worker when her husband became seriously ill and died soon after her arrival in France. In order to support her children, she at first cared for the elderly during the day (cleaning, shopping, and cooking) and worked for a cleaning company at night, then later took a job in a factory where she had been working for ten years when the book was completed. Despite the hard work, hers is presented as the success story of a woman determined to prevail as she raises her six children alone, and the emphasis on gender is underscored in her satisfaction that the sacrifices she has made in order to educate her children will "save" her daughters from the type of life she has had (235).

Nedjma's Plantade's *L'honneur et l'amertume*, a translation into French of Louisa Azzizen's life story recounted in a Kabyle Berber dialect, provides an interesting contrast with *Une fille d'Algérie éprise de liberté*.[24] Like most of the other collaborators, Plantade explains briefly how she has tried to convey the oral tone of the narrative and indicates the significance of the story. Unlike most of the others, however, Plantade is of the same origin as Louisa and goes to great lengths to point out the similarities between them--although they are from different generations, they both emigrated to France during the Algerian War, Plantade at age seven and Louisa at thirty-three. By emphasizing their shared experience as immigrants, she glosses over the differences in their education--Plantade has a doctorate in anthropology--and focuses rather on the fact that she is not affiliated primarily with France. Furthermore, although Plantade, like several of the other collaborators, has an educational role in mind for the narrative, her ideal readers are no longer French, but second-generation immigrants who wish to learn about their North African heritage.[25] For such readers,

Louisa's story provides an example of a traditional family reunification narrative. Indeed, Louisa could well have been featured in the section of Benguigui's documentary devoted to mothers: she and her children came to Paris to join her husband in 1960, and much of the text describes her attempts to adapt to life in France, the family's struggle to find a reasonable place to live, her difficulties figuring out how to deal with institutions such as her children's school, and the sacrifices made for the house the family is having built in Algeria. Louisa's story, unlike Kerouani's, ends on a note of resignation to the inevitable, to the fact that her immigration has become permanent because of her children's future in France--"la France nous a dévoré nos enfants" (France has devoured our children) (265). As such, her story is a classic account of first-generation parents contemplating the "loss" of their children to their new country yet realizing that France remains "inaccessible" (265) for their own generation who are destined to live "in a state of shabby exile, ignored just as much by Algeria as by France, only eaten away by violent nostalgia" (265).[26]

Ben Jelloun's study of the psychological effects of immigration on "single" men presented in *La plus haute des solitudes* constitutes an interesting variant on collaborative life-writing. As indicated above, Ben Jelloun presents his "psychoanalytical therapy" (23) as a method of treatment for the contemporary form of colonial violence--the erasure of identity due to the exploitation of immigrant workers in a capitalist economic system. Like the other collaborators, Ben Jelloun presents the stories he incorporates into his text as authentic testimonies and does not seek to hide his sympathy for the plight of his patients, indicating very clearly that he is not "a neutral, impartial observer" (14). His objective, then, is to "donner la parole . . . aux travailleurs eux-mêmes" (to give voice . . . to the workers themselves) (17), and the many stories evoked throughout the text combine short profiles presented in the form of notes written by Ben Jelloun with excerpts from his discussions with his patients. While the profiles rapidly sketch out biographical information such as the workers' age, family situation, employment, and living arrangements, the workers' own testimony forcefully brings out the reasons for their psychosomatic illnesses (usually impotence)--isolation, separation from their families, abstinence from sex, humiliation, accidents at work, and unemployment. Their impotence thus reflects their loss of identity, which expresses itself as a form of castration and signifies "le début d'une espèce de révolte passive" (the beginning of a kind of passive revolt) (70). By juxtaposing the stories of many different workers, all attesting to the corporeal inscription of their pain, Ben Jelloun demonstrates how their bodies speak eloquently of their silent suffering and rebellion: "The denunciation of an economic and political system is expressed through the immigrant body" (71).[27]

NOVELS

In addition to the autobiographical narratives, a series of novels, published for the most part in the 1970s, testify to the situation of immigrant workers. The best-known of these are Driss Chraïbi's *Les boucs*, Rachid Boudjedra's *Topographie idéale pour une agression caractérisée*, and Ben Jelloun's *La ré-*

clusion solitaire, but works by writers such as Slaheddine Bhiri, Ousmane Sembène, and Chabane Ouahioune also deal with the same issues. Although the
authors are not uneducated workers themselves, they become their spokespersons in their texts and seek to make the reading public aware of their plight.
While they share this common objective, their novels range in tone from highly
polemical to tragic, and in style from realist to poetic.

Chraïbi's second work, *Les boucs*, was the first novel to portray the
situation of immigrant workers in France. The result of a long period of research
into their working and living conditions, *Les boucs* goes far beyond realist
documentation and creates a nightmarish, often surreal vision of the workers'
lives which serves to denounce the exploitation and humiliation to which they
are subjected. The title, which evokes both the racist terms used to describe
North Africans and their role as scapegoats (*boucs émissaires*), is also the name
of a novel *en abyme* written by the French-speaking Algerian narrator in order to
testify to the suffering of the voiceless workers--"traduire cela en une espèce de
témoignage" (to translate it into a kind of testimony) (71). The narrator's description of himself and his intentions makes him emblematic of all the authors
discussed in this section of the chapter: "Ces 300.000 Nord-Africains, moi par-
lant le français et sachant l'écrire, traduire leurs misères, leurs détresses" (The
300,000 North Africans, and me speaking French and knowing how to write it,
to express their misery, their distress) (71). Like the narrator's manuscript,
Chraïbi's novel is a provocative, polemical cry of revolt which uses images of
violence and recurrent allusions to sacrifice to depict immigrant workers as sacrificial victims. References to recruitment posters in Algeria promising work in
France stand in sharp contrast with the realities of life in France conveyed
through a series of negative images and structures: "pas de travail, pas de gîte,
pas d'aide, pas de fraternité" (no work, no lodgings, no help, no fraternity)
(123). In particular, the self-conscious use of pejorative terms applied to North
Africans--"*Bicot*, disait le vent, *malfrat, arabe, crouillat, sidi, noraf*" (19)--
brings out the central themes of racism and exclusion, which are associated in
the novel with loss of hope and identity. In Chraïbi's racist France, then, the
workers' only possible relationship with society is one of antagonism and anger:
"Our interaction with society expressed itself in the form of insults, theft, or
fights, we ate slept walked saw listened lived... in a state of revolt and hatred"
(20).[28] The *Boucs* themselves, a group of twenty-two of the many North African
workers in France, illustrate the dehumanizing effects of hunger and alienation.
After years of looking for work and eking out an existence on the edge of society, they have become shadowy, ghostly figures living in an old building on a
desolate wasteland in Nanterre: "Formerly they had had a name, a receipt for
their application for a national identity card, an unemployment card--a personality, a presence, a semblance of hope. Now they were the *Boucs*" (28).[29]
Throughout the text, metaphors and vocabulary related to squalor and degradation serve to underscore their abjection, and Chraïbi's denunciation of the treatment of workers is especially apparent in an episode where the hungry, penni-
less *Boucs* murder a racist contractor who refuses to give them work. The killing, which takes the form of a ritual sacrifice in which the French contractor is
stabbed by each of the twenty-two *Boucs*, can be read as a symbolic representa-

tion of the need to put an end to the forces responsible for the exploitation of immigrant workers.

Although published twenty years later, and more postmodern in style, Boudjedra's *Topographie idéale pour une agression caractérisée* has the same hallucinatory, nightmarish atmosphere as *Les boucs* and makes the same indictment of racism and of the treatment of workers. Like *Les boucs*, *Topographie* also contains a symbolic murder, in this case a racist attack on a newly arrived immigrant. The plot of the novel is simple--an unnamed *émigré*, who arrives in Paris on September 26, 1973, spends twelve hours on the metro trying to get from the Gare d'Austerlitz to the Porte de Clichy and is killed a few yards from the metro exit by some hooligans wielding bicycle chains, an attack representative of the murders that took place in the summer of 1973 and caused the president of Algeria to suspend immigration to France. The interest of the text lies rather in its style and structure, which are unusual for texts of the period representing the life of immigrants. The non-linear, labyrinthine structure and the new-novel style fragmented presentation of events are used to convey the increasing anguish of the disoriented immigrant and his underground encounter with an unfamiliar world he is unable to decipher. As he wanders through the metro, his increasingly battered suitcase serves as a central image of his immigrant status, becoming an extension of his body and psyche. At the same time, as the focus of witnesses' comments when a police inspector tries to reconstruct the day's events, it serves to reveal stereotypical prejudices and fears associated with immigrants--other passengers speculate that it contains drugs, a bomb, or stolen money, thus associating the *émigré* with illegal activities. The incorporation into the novel of newspaper articles describing the deaths of victims of racist violence in Marseille in the summer of 1973, and announcing Algeria's decision to stop immigration to France because of this, inscribes the anonymous *émigré*'s experiences into a broader context and brings out the irony of the refrain created by the repetition of the words of the telegram he intends to send to his family as soon as he arrives at his destination: "ARRIVE. STOP. SAIN. STOP. SAUF. STOP" (ARRIVED. PERIOD. SAFE. PERIOD. SOUND. PERIOD) (155). Instead, because of his death, he joins the ranks of the multitude of immigrant workers who are "malmenés, écrasés, assassinés, déportés, ravalés, méprisés, haïs, brimés, exécutés, exacerbés, mutilés, noyés" (mistreated, crushed, assassinated, deported, choked, despised, hated, bullied, executed, aggravated, mutilated, drowned) (81).

Like *Les boucs* and *Topographie*, Ben Jelloun's *La réclusion solitaire* evinces a surreal atmosphere and reads more like a prose poem than a novel. A lyrical evocation of the solitary despair of a twenty-six-year-old North African who left his wife and child to come to France and who now shares a room with three other men, it creates a powerful portrait of a young immigrant worker's experience of exile and alienation. By presenting the text as a kind of inner monologue, Ben Jelloun is able to focus on the psychological effects of immigration such as isolation, nostalgia, and feelings of dispossession. Two recurrent images in particular convey the narrator's state of mind: while the metaphor of an uprooted tree brings out the theme of separation from family and homeland, and portrays North Africa as a land whose forests (men) have been cut down and are dying,[30] the image of the trunk, like the suitcase in *Topographie*, represents the inner world of the narrator's loneliness: "My room is a trunk where I deposit my savings and my solitude" (11).[31] At once a prison and a refuge, the trunk-room both symbolizes the narrator's exile and becomes a protective space in which he conjures up reassuring memories, thereby resisting complete loss of identity. The muted tragic tone is alleviated at the end of the text, however, when the narrator encounters a young Palestinian woman whose "orphanhood" (loss of country) mirrors his own and whose company represents the end of his feelings of uprootedness; with her, "la réclusion ne sera jamais solitaire" (confinement will never be solitary) (129).

     In comparison with the three preceding novels, Sembène's *Le docker noir*, Bhiri's *L'espoir était pour demain*, and Ouahioune's *Les conquérants au Parc Rouge* are more traditional realist accounts of the tribulations and often tragic consequences of immigration. Both Sembène's and Bhiri's texts use the central event of a murder committed by an immigrant worker to explore the topics of racism and injustice. Sembène's very early novel, which was published just one year after *Les boucs*, portrays some of the first black immigrants to France from the West coast of Africa working on the La Joliette docks in Marseille in the 1950s.[32] Sembène thus evokes an important moment of immigrant history, documenting how Senegalese sailors, many of whom worked as coal-trimmers for the French navy, became dockers when they found themselves without jobs in 1945 (Assouline and Lallaoui 32).[33] The novel explicitly refers to the history of the black neighborhood of Marseille--"le petit Harlem marseillais" (the little Marseillais Harlem) (77)--and its rapid increase in size after World War II, describing the different ethnic groups who live there and depicting the difficulties of life on the docks: exhaustion, back-breaking work, long hours, frequent accidents, and competition for jobs. This compassionate portrayal of the black community creates a strong contrast with the racist stereotypes used by witnesses and the press during the trial of Diaw Fall, a docker accused of murdering a well-known French woman writer who had published under her own name a novel (*Le dernier voyage du négrier Sirius*) written by Diaw in the hope of escaping life on the docks. Diaw had entrusted the manuscript to her when she promised to help him find a publisher; when he angrily demands reparation for the theft after she is awarded a prestigious literary prize, a scuffle breaks out during which she falls onto a piece of furniture, a fall which causes her death. Diaw's lawyer refers directly to racism in his defense, and the words of witnesses and the prosecution contain the complete range of stereotypes about blacks, from their indolence and lawlessness to their unbridled sexuality, which leads them to attack white women like a "bête fauve" (wild beast) (67). The juxtaposition of the realistic picture of the dockers' lives with the distorted image of Diaw presented at the trial forcefully brings out the way in which prejudice leads to injustice and blinds people to the fact that a Senegalese immigrant could produce a prize-winning work of literature. Furthermore, the episode in which Diaw is asked to recite a passage from the novel underscores the parallels between his situation as an immigrant worker and that of the slaves during the last voyage of the Sirius, a parallel reinforced by the fact that Diaw is given a life sentence (hard labor). In this sense, the title of the novel *en abyme* applies equally well to Sembène's own text, which ends with a moving plea for an end to the "theft" of the dignity and humanity of workers like Diaw.

Bhiri's *L'espoir était pour demain*, on the other hand, depicts the life of a group of unskilled North African workers in Paris and is structured around the narrator's murder of a French co-worker who had taunted him. Like Sembène, Bhiri focuses on the daily experience of racism, tensions between workers and supervisors, and repressed feelings of violence which, in this case, lead to the crime. In this novel, however, it is ironically the unpremeditated act of killing that gives the narrator (Dine) the impression he exists and that enables him to regain a certain dignity after ten years of humiliation and suffering. In a kind of epiphany in the last pages of the novel, he is able to see his victim (Raoul) as his equal, even his friend, and he welcomes the idea of a death sentence as a form of catharsis and sign of hope. Like *Le docker noir*, *L'espoir était pour demain* thus concludes with a plea for tolerance and understanding, and the final image conveys the desire that the sacrifice of two lives, Dine's and Raoul's, will lead to a change of heart in the future: "From our ashes, a flame, a light, and hope would be born" (157).[34]

Finally, *Les conquérants au Parc Rouge*, the only text in this section published in Algeria, is much lighter in tone than *Le docker noir* and *L'espoir était pour demain*. Events in the novel revolve around the Parc Rouge, a hotel for immigrant workers run by Madame Léon, and Ouahioune's portrayal of the various tenants and the relationships between them creates an affectionate portrait of daily life in an immigrant neighborhood. Tucked away in a side-street in Montreuil, the hotel is home to several generations of men, mostly from the same area of Algeria, and the community they have created is characterized above all by solidarity and mutual protection. Although the text contains references to racial prejudice, and the plot involves some racist incidents, the general atmosphere is less somber than that in many of the other novels, and more space is given to the description of celebrations and small joys in the workers' lives. In similar fashion, a broader range of French characters are presented in a positive light--factory employees participating in an anti-racist demonstration in support of their immigrant co-workers, increasing respect for North Africans in Montreuil, the marriage of Madame Léon's daughter to Farid, and Polly's appreciation for the workers' quiet dignity and the hatred of injustice she has learned from working with them. In addition, in the numerous intrigues related to events at the hotel, emphasis is placed on Madame Léon and the workers helping each other solve problems and on her understanding of what it means to be "the other" in France (152). Unlike many media accounts from the same period, then, Ouahioune depicts first-generation immigrants as men of great dignity whose courage and sense of honor enable them to "conquer" the effects of exile in order to provide support for their families.[35]

SECOND-GENERATION ACCOUNTS

Although the works written by the so-called *Beurs* deal mostly with the concerns of their own generation, they contain many episodes that involve their parents. While the relations between the two generations are for the most part marked by conflict, as the protagonists seek ways to escape the influence of their parents, these narratives nonetheless provide a further perspective on the first generation and constitute another way of giving it a voice. The allusions to the parents' generation range from short passages to lengthy episodes and occasionally form the primary focus of a work. The children are well aware of the silence/voice dichotomy associated with the two generations and allude to it in both their fictional and autobiographical texts: "Our fathers didn't shout, didn't have it out with anyone, they suffered in silence. It is this silence that you are asked to decipher in their children's cries" (Mounsi 17).[36] In the novels, the notion of the children as their parents' voice appears on the thematic level in episodes in which they write letters for their parents (*Béni ou le paradis privé*) and fill out forms or translate the news for them (*Ils disent que je suis une beurette*).

The most common evocation of immigrant life in the second-generation accounts consists of realist descriptions of the environment in which the family lives--shantytowns or various forms of low-income housing--and the parents' difficulties adapting to life in France. Some of the shortest passages refer to hostels for single men: Mehdi Charef's *Le thé au harem d'Archi Ahmed* and Ahmed Zitouni's *Attilah Fakir*, for example, both emphasize the undesirable, peripheral location of such hostels, which they interpret as a sign of exclusion, while Zitouni also foregrounds the prison-like atmosphere and the presence of a manager who used to be in the army.[37] The more extended descriptions involve accommodations for families. Azouz Begag's autobiographical work *Le gone du Chaâba*, in which a large part of the narrative is devoted to the young Azouz's experiences growing up in a shantytown in Lyon, is perhaps the best known example of this type of text. In a similar vein, Brahim Benaïcha's *Vivre au paradis*, which reads like social history, documents every aspect of daily life in the immigrant community of the Nanterre shantytown, from the fathers walking through the mud on the way home from work to the constant battle to keep water out of the shacks. Almost all the other second-generation texts are situated in housing projects on the outskirts of large cities.

In the context of family relations, silence is again portrayed as a defining characteristic of first-generation fathers. They appear in the novels as absent, voiceless figures who are mutilated in both the physical and psychological senses of the term, and are frequently associated with the theme of violence in the home. Yaz's father in Rachid Djaïdani's *Boumkoeur* epitomizes their fate: once "l'esclave qui souffrait en silence" (the slave who suffered in silence) (76) as a construction worker, he is now unemployed, often drinks heavily, and argues violently with his wife. Variants of this figure recur in several other novels in which the father is unemployed because of a work-related accident. Majid's father in *Le thé au harem*, for example, "n'a plus sa tête" (has lost his mind) (41) and has to be looked after like a child, while Malika's father in Ferrudja Kessas's *Beur's Story* seeks solace in alcohol and sometimes becomes violent. Their inability to work thus reinforces the children's impression of their powerlessness and further erases their presence in French society.

Although the children in these texts often display affection or pity for their fathers, they show little real understanding for their lives as immigrants and generally regard them as obstacles to work around as they establish their own life in France. In contrast, Tassadit Imache's *Une fille sans histoire* is one of the first works to present the protagonist's search for her father and his heritage as a central theme. During her father's lifetime, the narrator associated him in traditional fashion with "perpétuelle absence" (perpetual absence) and "mutisme" (complete silence) (109), describing him as "cet homme qui n'ouvrait pas la bouche, qui ne racontait jamais d'histoire" (that man who never opened his mouth, who never told any stories) (14). After his death, however, she realizes that she had not understood him or recognized the suffering behind his silence, and sets out to find and listen to his voice--"son cri" (his cry) (14). In recent years, the desire on the part of second-generation authors to rediscover and to valorize their fathers' lives has become increasingly common. As indicated earlier, Plantade's *L'honneur et l'amertume* is presented as a work intended for young people of immigrant origin "en quête légitime de mémoire" (engaged in a legitimate search for their past) (13), while Benguigui's documentary film sets out to "restituer la mémoire de l'immigration maghrébine" (to restore Maghrebi immigrants' memories) (10), explicitly raising the question of why they have been silenced: "What did you do to my parents to make them so silent?" (9).[38] Leïla Sebbar's fictional work *La Seine était rouge* is in many ways emblematic of this recent trend. Again conceived of as a text for young people who want to learn about the past, it portrays a sixteen-year-old daughter's quest to discover her parents' immigrant history as she retraces the itinerary of the October 1961 demonstration during the Algerian War.[39] The reasons for such a return to the father's generation are explored in Mounsi's autobiographical *Territoire d'outre-ville*. Here, he presents the lives of the two generations as irrevocably intertwined, describing his own adolescent delinquent behavior as an expression of the freedom denied his father--as a gesture intended to empower him. In order to emphasize the importance of rediscovering his father, Mounsi plays on the concept of the Oedipus complex, arguing that, rather than symbolically killing the father, the second generation must give him new life, "ressusciter le père du trépas que la société lui a réservé" (revive the father from the death society reserved for him) (69).[40] By restoring his dignity, Mounsi hopes to provide a corrective vision of the father which will at the same time enable him to find his own path in life. Much of his own writing, as well as Benguigui's film and recent texts such as *Vivre au paradis,* contributes to this rehabilitation of immigrant fathers and constitutes a moving tribute to their lives.

While the most common image of first-generation immigrants is one of resignation and silent suffering, I would like to conclude this chapter by discussing a text which, long before Mounsi spoke of "empowering" his father's generation, portrays what could be called the immigrants' revenge. Published in 1978 by two young writers, Mengouchi and Ramdane's *L'homme qui enjamba la mer* is one of the most unusual portrayals of immigrant workers. Abandoning the social realism and autobiographical approach most often associated with the representation of immigrant workers in favor of a kind of political fantasy, Mengouchi and Ramdane place a workers' hostel in Belleville at the center of their text and describe events there against the apocalyptic backdrop of economic and political crisis and virtual civil war--complete with strikes, barricades, the burning of the Paris mosque, and racist attacks on immigrant workers.

In the midst of the chaos, an array of colorful characters attempt to go about their daily lives: the garbage collectors Tiam and Moussa, Salah the cook, Oncle Slimane the storyteller, and the construction worker Zoubir whose pneumatic drill seems to have become an extension of his own body. Events become increasingly surreal towards the end of the novel where the authors rework and undermine common racist stereotypes by incorporating them into the plot. In particular, they take up the images of the immigrant as a form of contagion and of the Arab as "raton" in their presentation of the city's plan to disinfect the city and prevent an epidemic by quarantining the immigrant population and exterminating all the rats, especially the "type de rongeur venu d'Afrique du Nord, au museau basané et à la moustache frisée" (the North African variety with its swarthy snout and its curly mustache) (196). The transformation of the stereotype and the failure of the plan manifest themselves in the appearance of a mysterious new plant growing through the cracks in sidewalks and on the façades of buildings and whose foliage bears a striking resemblance to the North African rats' hair--with the difference that it now serves as a symbol of hope. The notion that the workers are inscribed in the very fabric of the city recurs in the last pages of the novel in which the paving stones of Paris (*pavés*)--a powerful symbol of revolt--literally come out in support of those who have built the city. In the final section entitled "La prise de pouvoir par les travailleurs immigrés" (Immigrant Workers Take Power) (213), the workers, encouraged by the revolutionary songs of the dead buried in the Père Lachaise cemetery, do battle against the forces of oppression and are presented as a modern version of the Paris Commune. Masters of the city at the end of the novel, they savor their victory under a "swarthy" (*basané*) sun and a sky wearing old blue workers' overalls (221). Although the novel has not received much critical attention, probably because it does not correspond to readers' expectations regarding the depiction of immigrant workers, its call for their contributions to be acknowledged and for them to be recognized as an integral part of French society anticipates the recent emphasis on restoring dignity. As the second generation now takes up this demand for re-evaluation and recognition, it remains to be seen to what extent and in what ways first-generation narratives will be revised and whether the tragic image of defeat will be replaced by one of resilience and triumph over adversity.

NOTES

1. "Je vais te dessiner l'itinéraire d'un expatrié: misère locale--passeport--corruption--humiliation--visite médicale--office de l'émigration--voyage--longue traversée--logement de hasard--travail--métro--la malle--la masturbation--la foudre--l'accident--l'hôpital ou le cimetière--le mandat--les vacances--les illusions--le retour--la douane--l'hôpital--la mort--l'accident--la masturbation--la putain--la chaude pisse--le métro--des images--des images--des images..."

2. "Tu es celui qui viole et qui cache un couteau, jamais celui qui cache un rêve merveilleux dans sa poche et qui a édifié les tours."

3. See, for example, Sylvie Durmelat's "Faux et défaut de langue" in which "le défaut de langue" (the lack of language) is defined as "le silence de ceux qu'on appelle les primo-arrivants" (the silence of new arrivals) (30).

4. See also Ben Jelloun: "la parole de l'immigré n'est pas entendue. Ce n'est pas souvent que l'on l'invite à s'exprimer. De toute façon, la majorité des Français ne manifeste pas un empressement à écouter ce que l'immigré peut lui dire" (an immigrant's words are not heard. He is not often invited to express himself. In any case, most French people are in no hurry to listen to what immigrants might have to say) (*Hospitalité* 130).

5. "cette génération de pères qui ont vieilli avant l'âge porte sur son visage l'histoire de l'immigration, ses méandres, ses blessures et ses espoirs déçus."

6. In addition, a few texts by French writers describe the lives of the first generation; these include, for example, Claire Etcherelli's depiction of a French woman's affair with an Algerian factory worker in *Elise ou la vraie vie* and Thérèse Abdélaziz's account of her life as the wife of an Algerian immigrant in *Je, femme d'immigré*. This chapter will, however, deal only with texts whose authors are of immigrant origin, and it will not examine narratives that deal with temporary forms of immigration such as the lives of students who come to France for a short period of time.

7. See Stephen Castles's analysis of the three phases of immigration in *Here for Good: Western Europe's New Ethnic Minorities*. More recently, Yamina Benguigui has used these three classic stages to provide the structure of her documentary film entitled *Mémoires d'immigrés: l'héritage maghrébin*.

8. See too Ben Jelloun's observation regarding the economic account of immigration: "Capitalism wants anonymous men (one could almost say 'abstract' men), emptied of all desires, but full of strength for work" ("Le capitalisme veut des hommes anonymes [à la limite abstraits], vidés de leurs désirs, mais pleins de leur force de travail") (*La plus haute* 13).

9. In 1973, for example, 32 Algerians were killed in racially motivated attacks, prompting President Boumediene to halt emigration to France (Castles 53).

10. See Mireille Rosello's *Declining the Stereotype* for a description of this stereotype and its transformation into the second-generation version. Ben Jelloun characterizes the racist stereotype of the migrant worker as follows: "brute force, heartless, lacking testicles, feeling no desire, without a family, in short, hardly a man at all" ("une force de travail brute, sans coeur, sans testicules, sans désirs, sans famille, bref à peine un homme") (*La plus haute* 16).

11. This is the title of a chapter in Lejeune's *On Autobiography* (185-215).

12. "toute littérature émergente . . . aura tendance à privilégier, sinon l'autobiographie au sens plein du terme, du moins le témoignage présenté comme 'authentique.' "

13. "tout se passe donc d'abord comme si l'Immigration ne pouvait s'exprimer qu'à travers un analphabétisme affiché, dont l'autobiographie enregistrée apparaît comme le garant" (At first, then, everything takes place as if Immigration could only find a voice through an insistence on illiteracy, and recorded autobiographies constitute the proof of that illiteracy) (205).

14. "par un côté je facilite la lecture et par un autre je l'oriente dans le sens qui m'intéresse."

15. Catani's references to the need to meet deadlines related to his project, and his decision to end his work on Mohamed's story despite the fact that Mohamed himself indicates his desire to rework parts of it, further highlight Catani's influence over the final form of the narrative. See Alec Hargreaves's "Writing for Others: Authorship and Authority in Immigrant Literature" for an analysis of these points.

16. The general indifference to the fate of immigrants is compared to "l'ancienne attitude esclavagiste" (the former attitude of slave owners).

17. "Rose est le dompteur et moi l'animal sauvage en voie de domestication." She also teaches him the French version of Algerian history and instructs him in how to speak, eat, and hold his body in a French way.

18. "Libération s'écrit avec un L, un I, un B, un E, un R, un A, un T, un I, un O, un N! LIBERATION s'écrit avec tous les lettres de l'ALPHABET."

19. This expression ("histoire vraie") is used in the subtitle. The Creole version of the text is followed by the French translation.

20. The translators point out that the Bumidom has been described as a "nouveau négrier" (new kind of slave ship) (12).

21. "l'histoire de Christian est exemplaire en ce qu'elle retrace un itinéraire fréquemment suivi par les Réunionnais" (Christian's story is exemplary in that it traces out an itinerary frequently followed by workers from La Réunion) (10).

22. Françoise Ega's *Lettres à une Noire* will not be discussed here since it is the subject of Patrice Proulx's chapter in this volume.

23. "J'avais l'avantage de parler très bien le français, alors toutes les démarches m'avaient été très faciles" (I had the advantage of speaking French very well, so all the administrative procedures were very easy for me) (146).

24. For an analysis of both these works and of issues related to the autobiographies of Algerian women, see Patricia Geesey's "Identity and Community in Autobiographies of Algerian Women in France."

25. Benguigui describes the same kind of collaboration between herself and those she interviews for her film *Mémoires d'immigrés*.

26. "un exil pouilleux, ignorés tout autant de l'Algérie que de la France, seulement rongés par une violent nostalgie."

27. "la dénonciation d'un système économique et politique passe par le corps de l'immigré."

28. "Notre commerce avec la société s'exprimait sous forme d'injures, ou de vols, ou de coups de poing, nous mangions dormions voyions écoutions vivions... avec révolte et haine."

29. "Jadis ils avaient eu un nom, un récépissé de demande de carte d'identité, une carte de chômage--une personnalité, une contingence, un semblant d'espoir. Maintenant c'étaient les Boucs."

30. "Nous sommes un pays déboisé de ses hommes. Des arbres arrachés à la terre, comptabilisés et envoyés au froid. Quand nous arrivons en France, nos branches ne sont plus lourdes; les feuilles sont légères; elles sont mortes. Nos racines sont sèches et nous n'avons pas soif. . . . Mais que peut un arbre arraché à l'aube de sa vie? Que peut un corps étranger dans une terre fatiguée?" (We are a country cleared of its men. Trees ripped up from the earth, registered, and sent off into the cold. When we arrive in France, our branches are no longer heavy; the leaves are light; they are dead. Our roots are dry and we are not thirsty. . . . But what can a tree do when it is ripped up at the dawn of its life? What can a foreign body do in a tired land?) (56-57).

31. "Ma chambre est une malle où je dépose mes économies et ma solitude."

32. Sembène is also the author of a short story, "La noire de..." in *Voltaïque*, which deals with the exploitation of black women working for families in France.

33. See also Saïdou Bokoum's *Chaîne* for a description of the black immigrant community in Paris in the 1960s and 1970s. Most of the novel deals with a young African's life as a law student, but when he drops out of the university, he sets out to learn about and to help immigrant workers. As the title suggests, the text revolves around the central image of the "chaîne" (chain), with its evocations of slavery and work on the assembly line.

34. "De nos cendres renaîtraient une flamme, une lumière, un espoir."

35. The term "conquérant" (conqueror) is first used in the novel by a taxi driver who equates immigration with invasion: "bientôt ils nous chasseront de France; ils sont bien arrivés à Poitiers une fois" (soon they will chase us out of France; they once got as far as Poitiers) (13).

36. "Nos pères ne criaient pas, ne s'expliquaient pas, ils subissaient en silence. C'est ce silence qu'il vous est demandé de déchiffrer dans le hurlement de leurs enfants."

37. See Charef 77 and Zitouni 94-95.

38. "Qu'avez-vous fait de mes parents pour qu'ils soient aussi muets?"

39. See Anne Donadey's chapter in this volume for a detailed analysis of this event. Another of Sebbar's recent works, *Le silence des rives*, also returns to the subject of immigrant workers. In this lyrical text, which takes the form of an interior monologue, Sebbar portrays the thoughts and memories of an Algerian immigrant who has not kept his promise that he will return home to die.

40. Mounsi also presents this argument in Benguigui's film: "Dans l'Oedipe, il faut tuer le père, mais nous, au contraire, il nous faut le déterrer, il nous faut le faire revivre. Il a été tué socialement par le colonialisme, par les guerres, puis par l'émigration. Au lieu de le tuer, il nous appartient, à nous, les enfants, de le faire revivre, de lui faire redresser la tête, qu'il se tienne fier et droit comme quand il se faisait prendre en photo dans son beau costume pour l'envoyer et rassurer la famille restée au pays" (In the Oedipus complex, one must kill the father, but we, on the contrary, must disinter him, bring him to life again. He was killed socially by colonialism, by wars, and then by emigration. Instead of killing him, it is our role as his children to bring him back to life, to make him hold his head up high so that he will stand proud and tall, as he did when he had his photo taken in his best suit in order to send the picture back home to reassure his family) (Benguigui 163).

WORKS CITED

Abdélaziz, Thérèse. *Je, femme d'immigré*. Paris: Editions du Cerf, 1987.

Ahmed. *Une vie d'Algérien, est-ce que ça fait un livre que les gens vont lire?* Paris: Seuil, 1973.

Assouline, David, and Mehdi Lallaoui. *Un siècle d'immigrations en France: troisième période, 1945 à nos jours*. Paris: Syros/Au nom de la mémoire, 1997.

Begag, Azouz. *Le gone du Chaâba*. Paris: Seuil, 1986.

---. *Béni ou le paradis privé*. Paris: Seuil, 1989.

Belkacemi, Mohamed, and Alain Gheerbrant. *Belka*. Paris: Fayard, 1974.

Benaïcha, Brahim. *Vivre au paradis*. Paris: Desclée de Brouwer, 1992.

Benguigui, Yamina. *Mémoires d'immigrés: l'héritage maghrébin*. Paris: Canal + Editions, 1997.

Ben Jelloun, Tahar. *La plus haute des solitudes*. Paris: Seuil, 1977.

---. *La réclusion solitaire*. 1976. Paris: Seuil, 1981.

---. *Hospitalité française*. Paris: Seuil, 1997.

Bhiri, Slaheddine. *L'espoir était pour demain: les tribulations d'un jeune immigré en France*. Paris: Publisud, 1982.

Bokoum, Saïdou. *Chaîne*. Paris: Denoël, 1974.

Bonn, Charles. "L'autobiographie maghrébine et immigrée entre émergence et maturité littéraire, ou l'énigme de la reconnaissance." *Littératures autobiographiques de la francophonie*. Ed. Martine Mathieu. Paris: C.E.L.F.A./L'Harmattan, 1996, 203-222.

Boudjedra, Rachid. *Topographie idéale pour une agression caractérisée*. Paris: Denoël, 1975.

Castles, Stephen. *Here for Good: Western Europe's New Ethnic Minorities*. London: Pluto Press, 1984.

Charef, Mehdi. *Le thé au harem d'Archi Ahmed*. Paris: Mercure de France, 1983.

Chraïbi, Driss. *Les boucs*. Paris: Denoël, 1955.

Christian. *Zistoir Kristian. Mes-aventures: histoire vraie d'un ouvrier réunionnais en France*. Paris: Maspero, 1977.

Djaïdani, Rachid. *Boumkoeur*. Paris: Seuil, 1999.

Durmelat, Sylvie. "Faux et défaut de langue." *Francophonie plurielle*. Quebec: Hurtubise HMH, 1995, 29-37.

Ega, Françoise. *Lettres à une Noire*. Paris: L'Harmattan, 1978.

Etcherelli, Claire. *Elise ou la vraie vie*. Paris: Denoël, 1967.

Geesey, Patricia. "Identity and Community in Autobiographies of Algerian Women in France." *Going Global: The Transnational Reception of Third World Women's Texts*. Ed. Amal Amireh and Lisa Suhair-Majaj. New York: Garland Press, 2000, 173-205.

Hargreaves, Alec G. "Writing for Others: Authorship and Authority in Immigrant Literature." *Race, Discourse and Power in France*. Ed. Maxim Silverman. Aldershot: Avebury, 1991, 111-119.

Imache, Tassadit. *Une fille sans histoire*. Paris: Calmann-Lévy, 1989.

Kerouani, Dalila. *Une fille d'Algérie éprise de liberté*. Paris: Robert Laffont, 1991.

Kessas, Ferrudja. *Beur's Story*. Paris: L'Harmattan, 1990.

Lejeune, Philippe. *On Autobiography*. Trans. Katherine Leary. Minneapolis: University of Minnesota Press, 1989.

Marimoutou, Jean-Claude. "Trois regards créoles sur la France: Leblond, Kristian, Lorraine." *Littératures des immigrations*. Vol 1. Ed. Charles Bonn. Paris: L'Harmattan, 1995, 103-114.

---. "La faille des origines: de l'autobiographie, du métissage et du secret." *Littératures autobiographiques de la francophonie*. Ed. Martine Mathieu. Paris: C.E.L.F.A./L'Harmattan, 1996, 93-109.

Mengouchi and Ramdane. *L'homme qui enjamba la mer*. Paris: Henri Veyrier, 1978.

Mohamed. *Journal de Mohamed: un Algérien en France parmi huit cent mille autres*. Ed. Maurice Catani. Paris: Stock, 1973.

Mounsi. *Territoire d'outre-ville*. Paris: Stock, 1995.

Nini, Soraya. *Ils disent que je suis une beurette*. Paris: Fixot, 1993.

Ouahioune, Chabane. *Les conquérants au Parc Rouge*. Alger: Société Nationale d'Edition et de Diffusion, 1980.

Plantade, Nedjma. *L'honneur et l'amertume: le destin ordinaire d'une femme kabyle*. Paris: Balland, 1993.

Rosello, Mireille. *Declining the Stereotype: Ethnicity and Representation in French Cultures*. Hanover: University Press of New England, 1998.

Sebbar, Leïla. *Le silence des rives*. Paris: Stock, 1993.

---. *La Seine était rouge*. Paris: Thierry Magnier, 1999.

Sembène, Ousmane. *Voltaïque*. Paris: Présence Africaine, 1962.

---. *Le docker noir*. 1956. Paris: Présence Africaine, 1973.

Zitouni, Ahmed. *Attilah Fakir*. Paris: Souffles, 1987.

WRITERS OF MAGHREBI ORIGIN

Anamnesis and National Reconciliation: Re-membering October 17, 1961

Anne Donadey

Towards the end of the Algerian War, on October 17, 1961, hundreds of the 30,000 Algerians who were peacefully demonstrating in Paris against the curfew imposed on them by police chief Maurice Papon were brutally massacred.[1] Press coverage of this key historical event for North African immigrants living in France was promptly censured by the French government. During the attack, the demonstrators were beaten and shot by police, and dozens were thrown into the Seine and left to drown. Over 11,000 men were rounded up in buses and held in stadiums; hundreds of arrested Algerians were deported to prison camps in Algeria until the end of the war (Einaudi 80). Because of the general amnesty applied to all Algerian war crimes in France, Papon, like hundreds of others, will never have to answer for his participation in the October 17 massacre.[2]

Over the past fifteen years, Franco-Algerian writer Leïla Sebbar's fictional works have highlighted France's uneasy historical relationship with Algeria. Her 1999 text, *La Seine était rouge*, published in a collection targeting young adults, focuses on the October 1961 massacre and its consequences for a series of individuals living in France. Before Sebbar's treatment of this topic, only seven earlier literary texts--all published between 1982 and 1998--had dealt with the massacre; four of them were penned by *Beur* writers. It is important to note that there is a twenty-year silence between the massacre and its earliest literary incarnation, Georges Mattei's *La guerre des gusses*. Sebbar's lengthy dedication inscribes her text in a tradition of rewriting this repressed page of Franco-Algerian history. Her book is dedicated to the Algerian victims of the massacre, as well as to those whose works served as sources for Sebbar's own rewriting. In particular, she mentions four fiction writers, Didier Daeninckx, Nacer Kettane, Mehdi Lallaoui, and Georges Mattei.[3]

Many of the novelists take up the parallel made by historians between World War II and the Algerian War, especially with respect to October 1961. Even before Papon's sordid past was revealed, most accounts drew parallels between the bloody repression of the peaceful Algerian demonstration and Nazi persecutions. Fewer than twenty years after Vichy, French politicians, Jewish personalities, and French supporters of the *Front de Libération Nationale* (FLN) all denounced the French use of the same methods against the Algerians. Soon after the massacre, politician Eugène Claudius-Petit asked for an investigation of the police repression, spoke of racism and drew parallels with Nazism (Tristan 116). Likewise, Claude Lanzmann, who later became famous as the director of the documentary film *Shoah*, wrote a statement signed by many intellectuals in which he equated the imprisonment of over 11,000 Algerian men in the Palais des Sports with the internment of Jews at Drancy, the center from which they were deported to concentration camps abroad (Einaudi 225). The mass imprisonment of Algerian demonstrators was also uncannily reminiscent of the *rafle du Vel d'Hiv*, the July 1942 roundup of over 13,000 Jewish men, women, and children arrested by the French police for deportation.

Historian Henry Rousso's model of the Vichy syndrome is useful in understanding what I call France's Algeria syndrome. Rousso divides the "Vichy syndrome" into four phases, charting a movement from amnesia to obsession: the first phase is one of interrupted mourning (1944-1954); the second (1954-1971), one of repression (forgetting and amnesia), with a reliving of the trauma due to the Algerian War; the third, from 1971 to 1974, a short phase of the return of the repressed and a shattering of established myths about the war; and finally, the last phase (in which we are still engaged), is one of obsession (Rousso 20-21). With respect to the Algerian conflict, France has been moving into the third phase of the Algeria syndrome, that of historical rewriting, since the early 1990s. *La Seine était rouge* represents Sebbar's most recent contribution to this phase, her attempt to piece together an anamnesis (a collective remembrance) of a central but censored historical event of the Algerian War.[4]

Sebbar is not alone in highlighting the importance of October 17, 1961 for immigrant history. Three of the literary texts published before hers refer to the massacre in their opening pages and present it as a landmark event for Algerians living in France. Nacer Kettane's 1985 *Le sourire de Brahim* opens with a chapter entitled "October in Paris." Here, the massacre is presented as one of the first examples of racially motivated violence or *ratonnades* (attacks on Arabs) against Algerians living in France (16). The protagonist's young brother is killed during the massacre, and recounting this event at the beginning of the book both provides the basis of the plot and explains the title (Brahim, the protagonist, loses his ability to smile forever after the loss of his beloved brother). A leitmotif in the novel is that the anti-Maghrebian violence in the 1980s is directly related to a desire on the part of the French to continue the Algerian War.[5] Indeed, both *Le sourire de Brahim* and Tassadit Imache's *Une fille sans histoire* (1989), which focus on the childhood and young adulthood of children of Algerian immigrants in France, highlight the connections between residual traces of the war and the difficulties these youngsters experience in French society decades later.

Like Kettane, Imache opens her novel with references to the October 17 massacre, which occurred when the protagonist was three years old and constitutes her first memory. Her Algerian father is arrested during the demonstration and disappears for three days, and her French mother is interrogated by the police. The title, with its multiple meanings, resonates with this event: part of the young protagonist's malaise is connected to the violent erasure of her history (*sans histoire*). Her French mother is complicit in this erasure as she attempts to protect her daughters from prejudice.

Like Kettane and Imache, Paul Smaïl gives the October 17 massacre foundational status in his autobiographical narrative *Vivre me tue* (1997).[6] He mentions the massacre on several occasions and devotes an entire chapter to it (178-180). The originality of his treatment of the event lies in the fact that the chapter describing the massacre most fully comes right after a description of racist violence in the 1990s. The transition between the two periods is at first made without any indication of a change in the time frame, so the reader at first assumes that Smaïl is still describing the recent violence until the date "1961" appears at the end of the first paragraph, thus blurring the distinction between the two periods. Like Kettane, Smaïl argues that there is a link between the events of 1961 and more recent *ratonnades*; furthermore, both authors explicitly name Maurice Papon as the person who ordered the massacre. In *Vivre me tue*, as in *Le sourire de Brahim*, the narrator loses a family member in the massacre: his Moroccan uncle was killed by the French police when he inadvertently ran into the demonstration on his way to work. Indeed, because of the inclusion of this episode, Farida Abu-Haidar suggests that Smaïl sees the October 17 massacre as a foundational event not just for Algerians but for the entire North African immigrant community. The arrests made in 1961 took on a racist nature as the police relied on physical appearance when making arrests and were not able to distinguish between Algerians, Moroccans and Tunisians. Consequently, the Moroccan embassy in Paris lodged several formal complaints regarding the mistreatment of its citizens (Einaudi 79).

The interpretation of the October massacre as a foundational event for Maghrebians in France is consistent with Mehdi Lallaoui's presentation of it in his 1986 novel *Les Beurs de Seine*. Toward the end of the novel, Kaci, the main character, discusses two landmark historical events for Algerians living in France: the May 8, 1945 massacres in Sétif and Guelma[7] and the October 17, 1961 massacre, which neither Kaci's French girlfriend Katia nor her *Beur* friend Farida had ever heard of before (158-159).

Because such historical knowledge has not been taught in the French school system, there is a need for alternative ways of learning about history, whether through the oral testimonies of participants or through literary rewritings, including those written by people not belonging to the Maghrebian immigrant community in France. One such example is Franco-Belgian writer Didier Daeninckx's 1984 detective novel *Meurtres pour mémoire*, the first literary treatment of the October 1961 massacre to have been widely read in France.[8] Inspired by the then recent revelations that Maurice Papon had been responsible for the deportation of over 1,500 Jews in World War II Bordeaux, Daeninckx wrote in barely veiled fashion about a killer responsible for both events in his *Meurtres pour mémoire*.[9] The novel opens with the epigraph, "If we forget the past, we are condemned to relive it."[10] Although the novel begins with the perspectives of a few Algerian participants in the peaceful demonstration, the rest of the narrative, which takes place twenty years later, centers only on Franco-French characters. The 1961 massacre is soon obscured by memories of World War II atrocities, and the Algerian characters of the first two chapters disappear. However, the crimes committed during the two periods are woven together in Daeninckx's Inspector Cadin's pithy reference to "The Oradour massacre in the heart of Paris" (81), with its implicit comparison between the 1961 pogrom and the infamous killing of 642 Oradour-sur-Glane villagers by SS soldiers in June 1944.[11]

The plot of *Meurtres pour mémoire* centers on re-membering Vichy, as the son of a French historian is assassinated in Toulouse twenty years after his father was mysteriously killed during the October 1961 massacre. During his investigation of the second murder, Inspector Cadin discovers that the Paris prefect of police in 1961, André Veillut, had been responsible for the deportation of hundreds of Jews during World War II. The fact that both father and son die because they have uncovered Veillut's role in the deportation of Jews means that the 1961 massacre remains overshadowed in the plot by events related to Vichy. While Daeninckx's novel deals with the erasure of French memory, it has little to say about immigrant memory and thus unwittingly participates in the continued silencing of the October 1961 massacre.[12]

Like *Meurtres pour mémoire*, Georges Mattei's *La guerre des gusses* (1982) is a fictionalized *roman à clef*. At the end of this historical novel, Mattei provides a detailed account of the massacre and its place in the Algerian War--most of the narrative deals with a French soldier who becomes a deserter and joins the FLN. During the course of the novel, Mattei treats the two foundational events mentioned by Lallaoui: the 1945 Sétif and Guelma massacres in Algeria and the October 1961 atrocities. At the same time, he also foregrounds the well-known 1957 Battle of Algiers, immortalized by Gillo Pontecorvo's 1965 film of the same name. Mattei's descriptions of the October massacre rely on testimonies culled from FLN records as well as from the few accounts extant in newspapers of the time. Like Daeninckx, his narrator expresses his need to remember: "I shall remember this night. . . . I shall be memory" (220).[13]

In *La guerre des gusses*, the identity of the prefect of police is barely disguised: "Marcel Pantobe" bears the same initials and a name sounding quite similar to Maurice Papon's; furthermore, his political trajectory closely resembles that of Papon, and Mattei makes direct reference to 1943 Bordeaux. Since the *Canard Enchaîné*'s revelations about Papon's past had occurred only a year before the publication of Mattei's book, readers would have easily been able to identify the character of Pantobe. Moreover, one chapter begins with a quotation from Papon himself in which he tells the Paris police in 1961 that they would be protected whatever they did (201). These same words are later repeated in the text by Marcel Pantobe (213). Considering Papon's vindictiveness and his predilection for libel suits, this was a courageous act on Mattei's part.

Nancy Huston's *L'empreinte de l'ange* (1998), the most recent novel besides Sebbar's to mention October 1961, also draws these parallels.[14] Most of the events in the novel take place in Paris between 1957 and 1962. In addition to numerous references to the Algerian War, *L'empreinte* also alludes to World War II, and the two wars are compared on several occasions. One of the protagonists, a Jewish Hungarian refugee named András helps members of the FLN organize the October 17 demonstration. The day after the massacre, his German lover Saffie, who has gone looking for him, witnesses bodies being dredged out of the Seine. These events lead András to make the connection between the curfew imposed on the Algerians and Vichy policies against the Jews: "A curfew just for Muslims! Only *twenty years* after the curfew for Jews. It's all the same! The same!" (274).[15]

Taken together, the eight literary rewritings of the October 17, 1961 massacre highlight the intersection of family stories and national history by focusing on the personal ramifications of the historical event for the participants and their children. In every case, the massacre is portrayed as a foundational event of both immigrant and French history. Sebbar's treatment of the massacre in *La Seine était rouge*, which relies on historical and archival documents as well as on the earlier literary rewritings, is the most detailed in French literature to date. Although all the fiction writers discussed above endowed the massacre with symbolic significance for specific constituencies, none of them used it as the main part of their narratives. Sebbar's novel is the only one so far to focus entirely on the memory of October 1961, and to attempt to include the perspectives of all those involved. In Sebbar's rewriting, anamnesis is shown to be a collective endeavor which occurs across generations, genders, political persuasions, and ethnic origins. For this reason, her novel presents the points of view of French police officers, *harkis*, Algerian demonstrators, French *porteurs de valises*, and other eyewitnesses from various walks of life. Several of her characters insist on the partiality of truth and the unreliability of memory, thus highlighting the need for as many forms of testimony as possible if anamnesis is to take place.[16]

Sebbar pays homage to those who came before her and whose activism and testimony afforded her the historical information she needed to write *La Seine*. Besides naming novelists, she also dedicates her novel to a wide range of other figures interested in the massacre: journalist Paulette Péju, historian Jean-Luc Einaudi, writer Anne Tristan, filmmaker Jacques Panijel, photographer Elie Kagan, and editor François Maspéro, as well as the Comité Maurice Audin.[17] Sebbar thus inserts her novel into a four-decades-old tradition of recovery and bearing witness in the face of censorship and silencing. Indeed, of the texts by authors she mentions in the dedication or elsewhere, several were censored and seized by the French government.

Sebbar's novel, written with young adults in mind, highlights how important it is for them to retrieve their history. The action takes place thirty-five years after the October 17, 1961 massacre, and its main characters were all born after 1961. Amel, one of the main characters, is a sixteen-year-old girl of Algerian descent whose grandparents and mother (then a seven-year-old) participated in the demonstration. Omer is a twenty-seven-year-old Algerian journalist who had to leave Algeria and came to France illegally because he feared for his life in the current political climate. Finally, Louis, the twenty-five-year-old son of Flora, a former *porteuse de valises*, is making a documentary film on the massacre. These three central characters are connected through previous generations of women who all fought for the independence of Algeria: Amel's mother

Noria and grandmother Lalla, Omer's mother Mina, and Louis's mother Flora all know each other.

In a way, Amel, Omer, and Louis represent the diverse constituencies (immigrant, Algerian, and French) who have a need for anamnesis as regards both the Algerian War in general and the October 17 massacre in particular. That the process of anamnesis is fraught with difficulties is highlighted by the fact that the three characters often clash in their interpretations of the event and over how it should be memorialized. Tensions arise between Omer and Louis, for example, when Omer uses the word "you" to refer to the French in general. Louis, whose parents were considered traitors during the war for aligning themselves with the Algerian nationalists, is incensed at Omer's historical oversimplifications. Later, Omer also includes Amel in this "you," eliciting a similarly strong response from her. Indeed, Amel and Omer often argue about issues of politics, identity, and history. In these moments, Omer learns that simplistic dichotomies (French versus Algerian) cannot fully account for the events of the Algerian War or for the multiple identities and politics of people of French nationality.

At the same time, each character brings something different but crucial to the process of anamnesis. Due to their lack of knowledge about the October massacre, Amel and Louis set out to unearth information about the past, which Amel's family will not discuss with her--the book begins with the cryptic sentence, "Her mother told her nothing, and neither did her mother's mother" (13).[18] Similarly, Louis's mother is at first reticent to testify about her political commitment as a former *porteuse de valises* (26). This personal silence echoes the general lack of public discourse about the Algerian War in France and highlights the necessity of creating a space for its anamnesis. It is precisely this intergenerational silence about the war that incites Amel and Louis to begin their search for information. Louis's contribution takes the form of a film reminiscent of Jacques Panijel's 1962 documentary on the massacre, *Octobre à Paris*.[19] Although Amel's mother will not tell her daughter about the event, she agrees to bear witness in front of Louis's camera. As for Omer and Amel's contribution, it is expressed through graffiti, often a subversive and fragmentary form of self-inscription favored by the powerless. They write graffiti on well-known monuments to other historical conflicts, thus creating a palimpsest that provides a transgressive response to the lack of official commemoration of the Algerian War in France.

As part of her search, Amel takes Omer on a journey through Paris. Indeed, geography features prominently in the process of reconstructing history, as the characters retrace the itinerary of the 1961 demonstration, from the Nanterre shantytown where Amel's family used to live to the various places where the demonstration was repressed: subway stations, city intersections, major monuments. The names of these locations, together with the names of people who testify, are used as chapter headings, thus foregrounding their importance.[20] From the table of contents on, *La Seine était rouge* presents itself as what Pierre Nora calls a *lieu de mémoire* (site of memory, place of commemoration)--the table of contents brings together the various memories necessary for national reconciliation through anamnesis.

Like other writers, Sebbar draws parallels between the October massacre and the events of World War II. One of the people who had been present at the demonstration speaks to Amel and Omer about it for the first time 35 years later, saying: "The Papon affair stirred it all up again" (103).[21] Similarly, like earlier writers, Sebbar explicitly names Papon as the party responsible for ordering the repression of the demonstration. In addition, as Amel and Omer crisscross Paris, they find themselves in front of several historical plaques referring to France's resistance to the Germans during World War II. The first plaque that Omer and Amel rewrite is located on the wall of the La Santé prison and reads: "High school and university students were incarcerated in this prison on November 11, 1940, because they were the first to rise up against the occupier upon hearing General de Gaulle's call" (29).[22] Next to the plaque, they write in red spray paint, "1954-1962: Algerian resisters were guillotined in this prison because they rose up against the French occupier" (30).[23] The symmetry of the language used in the two sentences--dates, the similar syntax, the use of the words "rose up against," "occupier," and "resistors"[24]--underscores the parallels between the actions of the French against the Algerians during the Algerian War and those of the Nazis against the French during World War II. Omer and Amel's rewriting is all the more subversive since the French are represented as occupiers, even though the October massacre took place in the heart of Paris. In another example, when Omer and Amel find themselves in front of the famous Crillon hotel, they leave behind graffiti that reads, "Here, Algerians were savagely clubbed by Prefect Papon's police force on October 17, 1961" (88).[25] This graffiti is reminiscent of actual words painted on one of the Paris bridges a few years after the massacre--"Algerians are drowned here."[26]

The three main characters' contributions to anamnesis are revealed to be interrelated, as well as being dependent on the testimonies of the earlier generation who witnessed and participated in the demonstration. Interdependence is a prominent theme in the novel and constitutes one of its organizational principles. It is Amel's personal search for the past that inspires Omer, while Louis includes Amel's mother's testimony in his film, and Amel is comforted in her search by Louis's film. Similarly, as Louis is looking for Amel all over Paris, he comes across the various graffiti and includes them in his film. The theme of interdependence is further reflected *en abîme* in Louis's film, which replicates the organizational structure of Sebbar's text, relying as it does on archival documents as well as recent interviews. The structure that divides the story of Amel's mother Noria into six parts which are juxtaposed with other chapters relating to 1961 and 1996 highlights the dialectical movement between past and present that lies at the heart of anamnesis. Every chapter before a section of Noria's testimony ends with the sentence, "Amel hears her mother" or "Amel hears her mother's voice" (32, 40, 57, 83, 111), but before the last installment, the structure of the sentence changes to "*We* hear *the* mother's voice" (126, my emphasis)[27] ("*On* entend la voix de *la* mère"). The new formulation of the sentence, with its use of the generic "on," highlights the way in which the process of anamnesis has widened to include the community at large. Anamnesis occurs when the generation that lived through an event and the next generation come together to find ways to uncover and memorialize it. Through the shift from "her mother" to "the mother," Noria comes to emblematize the mother of all those participating in the process. Sebbar thus suggests that national reconciliation can occur only when the conflicting memories of all those involved in a traumatic event are woven together into a collective narrative of the past. By providing a fictional account of the memories of October 17, 1961, Sebbar engages with French historical amnesia and helps French memory move into the third phase of the Algeria syndrome (shattering established myths).

It may perhaps be said that France fully entered this third phase on June 10, 1999, when the Assemblée Nationale officially recognized that the actions carried out to "maintain order" in 1954-1962 in Algeria actually constituted a war. After 37 years, then, the Algerian War is no longer "a war without a name."[28] This recognition of the Algerian War received little coverage on national television news and in *Le Monde* the next day. The vote was overshadowed by the news of the end of the war in Kosovo that very same day. As the coincidences of history would have it, June 10 also marked the fifty-fifth anniversary of the World War II massacre at Oradour. All of this indicates that France still has a long way to go before entering the phase of obsession, yet it is well into the phase of shattering the silence. That France's official recognition of the Algerian War came only a few weeks after the publication of *La Seine était rouge*, a novel devoted to one of the most occluded events of that war, testifies to how keenly attuned Sebbar is to the French political and social landscape. It is fitting that Sebbar, whose engagement in France's racial, sexual, and cultural politics has remained constant for over twenty years, should once again be at the forefront, this time bringing post-colonial memory into national French history. More than any other writer, Sebbar both highlights the specificity of Algerian immigrant history in France and brings together immigrant, French, and Algerian memories to create a site for national reconciliation through collective anamnesis.

NOTES

1. Papon's collaboration with the Nazis in sending more than 1,500 Jews to concentration camps during World War II was uncovered in 1981; he was found guilty of complicity in a crime against humanity in his 1997-1998 trial and began serving his ten-year sentence in October 1999.

2. For years, the official number of deaths on October 17 was three. The French government's official number of deaths as of May 1999 is now at least 48 (the new report acknowledges the deficiency of some archival documents). FLN estimates range between 200 and 300 deaths.

3. Lallaoui co-edited a three-volume book with David Assouline, *Un siècle d'immigrations en France*, whose third volume includes a short section on October 1961. He also contributed to Anne Tristan's investigative report and picture book on the massacre, *Le silence du fleuve* (1991). Without forcing the issue, Sebbar provides her audience with most of the names necessary for further research on the topic.

4. For a more detailed treatment of the Algeria syndrome, see my "Une certaine idée de la France." For detailed discussions of anamnesis in the post-colonial context, see Françoise Lionnet's *Autobiographical Voices* and my "Between Amnesia and Anamnesis."

5. See especially pages 58, 75, 126, and 142.

6. Smaïl is of Moroccan descent.

7. On May 8, 1945, Algerians demonstrating for independence on the day of France's liberation from German oppression were attacked by the French army.

8. Daeninckx's book was made into a TV movie of the same name by Laurent Heynemann in 1989. More than 100,000 copies of *Meurtres pour mémoire* were sold in the 1980s (Einaudi 282), and the novel was reissued in paperback in 1998.

9. Daeninckx discusses this in an interview in *Ecrire en contre*, 120-121.

10. "En oubliant le passé, on se condamne à le revivre." All translations are my own.

11. "Un Oradour en plein Paris."

12. For an excellent analysis of Daeninckx's novel, see Josiane Peltier's "The Detective as Historian."

13. "Je me souviendrai de cette nuit. . . . Je serai mémoire." Mattei himself was a *porteur de valises*, one of the French people who supported the FLN during the war, and he later provided historian Jean-Luc Einaudi with FLN archival records of the war when Einaudi was writing his history of the massacre (Einaudi 14).

14. Huston and Sebbar have been friends since their involvement in the Paris feminist movement in the 1970s, and published their correspondence on exile, *Lettres parisiennes*, in 1986. The convergence of their interests and concerns is as evident in the late 1990s as it was a decade earlier.

15. "Un couvre-feu rien que pour les musulmans. *Vingt ans* seulement après le couvre-feu pour les juifs. Pareil! Pareil!"

16. See especially pages 17, 26, 29-30, 68-69, 106, 113, 125.

17. See 107, 115, 119-120. The story of Maspéro helping a teenage Algerian boy escape the police is included in Sebbar's book (62) (see also Tristan 67).

18. "Sa mère ne lui a rien dit, ni la mère de sa mère."

19. The film was censured in 1962 (Einaudi 273-274).

20. In her 1982 novel *Shérazade*, Sebbar used the table of contents to provide a cartography of the title character's identity and inner world. In *Les carnets de Shérazade* (1985), the reader follows a similar itinerary as the protagonist retraces the 1983 march against racism known as the *Marche des Beurs*.

21. "C'est l'affaire Papon qui a remué tout ça." Papon is named several times in the novel (37, 42, 88, 101, 103).

22. "En cette prison le 11 novembre 1940 furent incarcérés des lycéens et des étudiants qui à l'appel du Général de Gaulle se dressèrent les premiers contre l'occupant."

23. "1954-1962: Dans cette prison furent guillotinés des résistants algériens qui se dressèrent contre l'occupant français."

24. A word usually reserved for the French who fought against the Nazi occupation.

25. "Ici des Algériens ont été matraqués sauvagement par la police du préfet Papon le 17 octobre 1961."

26. "Ici on noie les Algériens." A picture of this graffiti is reproduced in several books dealing with October 17, 1961 (Assouline and Lallaoui 19; Tristan 99).

27. "Amel entend sa mère"; "Amel entend la voix de sa mère."

28. Raphaëlle Bacqué, "La guerre d'Algérie n'est plus une 'guerre sans nom,' " 40.

WORKS CITED

Abu-Haidar, Farida. "Language, Innovation and Imagery in the Novels of Paul Smaïl." Paper given at the Fifty-Second Annual Kentucky Foreign Language Conference, Lexington, Kentucky, April 1999.

Assouline, David, and Mehdi Lallaoui, eds. *Un siècle d'immigrations en France: troisième période, 1945 à nos jours: du chantier à la citoyenneté?* Paris: Syros, 1997.

Bacqué, Raphaëlle. "La guerre d'Algérie n'est plus une 'guerre sans nom.' " *Le Monde,* June 11, 1999, 40.

Daeninckx, Didier. *Meurtres pour mémoire.* Paris: Gallimard, 1984.

---. *Ecrire en contre: Entretiens*. Vénissieux: Paroles d'aube, 1997.
Donadey, Anne. " 'Une certaine idée de la France': The Algeria Syndrome and Strug-
      gles over 'French' Identity." *Identity Papers: Contested Nationhood in
      Twentieth-Century France*. Ed. Steven Ungar and Tom Conley. Minneapo-
      lis: University of Minnesota Press, 1996, 215-232.
---. "Between Amnesia and Anamnesis: Re-membering the Fractures of Colonial His-
      tory." *Studies in Twentieth Century Literature* 23.1 (Winter 1999): 111-
      116.
Einaudi, Jean-Luc. *La Bataille de Paris: 17 octobre 1961*. Paris: Seuil, 1991.
Huston, Nancy. *L'empreinte de l'ange*. Arles: Actes Sud, 1998.
Imache, Tassadit. *Une fille sans histoire*. Paris: Calmann Lévy, 1989.
Kettane, Nacer. *Le sourire de Brahim*. Paris: Denoël, 1985.
Lallaoui, Mehdi. *Les Beurs de Seine*. Paris: L'Arcantère, 1986.
Lionnet, Françoise. *Autobiographical Voices: Race, Gender, Self-Portraiture*. Ithaca:
      Cornell University Press, 1989.
Mattei, Georges M. *La guerre des gusses*. Paris: Balland, 1982.
Peltier, Josiane. "Didier Daeninckx's *Meurtres pour mémoire*: The Detective as His-
      torian." "(En)quêtes d'identité: Novels of Detection in France and the U.S.,
      1830-1990." Ph.D. Diss., University of Iowa, July 1998, 161-193.
Rousso, Henry. *Le Syndrome de Vichy (1944-198...)*. Paris: Seuil, 1987.
Sebbar, Leïla. *Shérazade. 17 ans, brune, frisée, les yeux verts*. Paris: Stock, 1982.
---. *Les carnets de Shérazade*. Paris: Stock, 1985.
---. *La Seine était rouge*. Paris: Thierry Magnier, 1999.
Sebbar, Leïla, and Nancy Huston. *Lettres parisiennes: Autopsie de l'exil*. Paris: Ber-
      nard Barrault, 1986.
Smaïl, Paul. *Vivre me tue*. Paris: Balland, 1997.
Tristan, Anne. *Le silence du fleuve: ce crime que nous n'avons toujours pas nommé*.
      Bezons: Au nom de la mémoire, 1991.

Balancing Acts: Family and Integration in the Fiction of Franco-Maghrebi Women Writers

Patricia Geesey

I carry this burden, I feel my parents' wounds.[1] (Aïcha, "La messa-gère" 847)

Published in 1993, the collection of essays and interviews edited by sociologist Pierre Bourdieu entitled *La misère du monde* examines numerous issues facing contemporary French society by presenting portraits of recognizable "social actors" (845). The chapter called "La messagère"[2] features an in-depth interview with Aïcha, the eldest of six children in a family that immigrated to France from Morocco. Aïcha was nine years old when she arrived in France with her family; now a graduate student in psychology and sociology, she has devoted her research to the relationship between the home environment and academic success for Moroccan immigrant families in France. In prefacing her own story, Aïcha presents the family as "the critical place in which 'integration' is constantly negotiated" (359).[3] As she describes the forces at home and on "the outside" that have influenced her life (847), Aïcha returns frequently to the concept of negotiation, which might also be described as a kind of balancing or juggling act requiring her to play the role of mediator between the family (inside) and French society (outside). In this context, she defines her role as that of a "garant d'un certain contact avec l'extérieur" (the guarantor of contact with the outside world) and of a "porte-parole" (spokesperson) (852). On one level, Aïcha's studies, her professional life, her decision to marry her non-Muslim French partner, and the fact that she has requested French citizenship can be seen as evidence of her successful integration into French society. On another, she has also served as her family's "messenger" in a more literal sense: even as a young girl she acted as an interpreter and filled out administrative forms for her first-generation immigrant family. Aïcha's experiences are not unusual in the North African immigrant community in France. Many families in which the parents have little knowledge of French must rely on their children to act as a link to the outside world. For this reason, young Franco-Maghrebi women are required to act as messengers or mediators for their families in the same manner as Aïcha. However, and perhaps equally importantly, the young women's role as negotiators also has a symbolic and metaphoric dimension.

This chapter examines the position of Franco-Maghrebi women in the family and their strategies of integration as depicted in novels by women authors of immigrant descent. While many of these novels at first seem to support Florence Assouline's argument that young women of North African origin serve as "un pont entre deux univers *a priori* inconciliables" (a bridge between two necessarily irreconcilable universes) (45), more careful scrutiny reveals that this very notion of cultural mediation is undermined by the strategies of negotiation and integration employed by the female protagonists. The novels often depict characters who attempt to find a personal form of "integration" into French society; in many of the texts, the concept of integration itself is problematic. While French society in general may define the integration of immigrants as leaving the family sphere and merging into a supposedly homogenous French society, many female protagonists find it difficult to challenge parental expectations. Portraying their experiences in fictional form has enabled young women of North African origin to challenge their perceived role as a bridge between two cultures and to explore other forms of integration in their search for balance between the numerous cultural forces in their lives.

The corpus of novels by Maghrebi women, which includes both autobiographical and fictional works, contains frequent critiques of French society's intolerance toward ethnic minorities, as well as criticism of North African cultural patterns that restrict young women's personal freedom. In all of these texts, the complex nature of integration for second-generation North Africans in France plays out on both the symbolic and literal levels. At the heart of the issue of integration for young women is the expectation that they adopt "traditional" roles within the family, roles which often conflict with their desire for more autonomy. In this regard, Camille Lacoste-Dujardin notes that more than any other factor, the relationship between young women and their parents lies at the heart of their "dilemmas" (11) and is fraught with ambiguities and difficulties. Indeed, young women of Maghrebi origin born or raised in France face many pressures within and outside the family--particularly regarding behavior and dress--that are not experienced by young men from the same background. Much of the research on immigrant families, whether from an anthropological or sociological perspective, emphasizes their fear of the consequences of contact between Maghrebi women and French society. In her transcription of a Kabyle immigrant's life story, Nedjma Plantade, for example, documents the common fear among recently arrived North Africans that their wives and daughters will be "contaminated" if they come into close contact with French values and practices (189-190).

Abdelmalek Sayad's essay "Les enfants illégitimes" examines this same fear of contamination and impurity through the notion of legitimacy as it relates to children of Algerian immigrants born in France. He observes, for example, that family members in Algeria often refer to children raised in France as "les enfants de France" (children of France) (197), while the parents themselves often view their French-born offspring as an enigma.[4] The metaphor of illegitimacy is expressed most forcefully in the image of blood and of biological filiation--the notion that the children have become "étrangers de leur sang" (alienated from their blood) (232). The biological link between parents and children becomes suspect when the children raised in France no longer mirror their parent's sense of identity. This symbolic notion of ruptured filiation places great pressure on young women: how can they reassure their parents that they still have a sense of their North African identity while at the same time expressing the desire to live a different sort of life than that of their parents?

The notion of children of Maghrebi immigrants being "illegitimate" is a recurrent theme of both the autobiographical and fictional works. Sakinna Boukhedenna's *Journal. "Nationalité: immigré(e)"* (1987), an autobiographical narrative that presents an indictment of racism and identity politics in both France and Algeria, develops the idea of illegitimacy through Sakinna's experience of rejection: in France, she is defined in terms of her Algerian identity, yet when she visits Algeria, she is perceived as not belonging there either--"I realized that I was only a foreigner to them: a French whore" (91).[5] Algerian men's description of her as a whore from France reveals their prejudices about women's purity and their belief that French society contaminates women. The solution, as the narrator sees it, would be the creation of a third space symbolically located between France and Algeria and which would correspond to the only identity she has in the eyes of others, who define her solely in terms of immigration, that of "Nationalité: immigrée" (Nationality: Immigrant) (74). The title and thematics of Boukhedenna's text thus foreground the notion of the eternal immigrant, which recurs throughout the corpus of texts written by second-generation authors, and the reduction of her identity to her status as immigrant reinforces the impression of her "illegitimate" presence in France.

Similar themes appear in Tassadit Imache's novel *Une fille sans histoire* (1989), which portrays a young protagonist who wishes to reconcile the two sides of her Franco-Algerian heritage. Here, Imache uses different versions of the protagonist's name (Lil, Lila, Lili) to underscore her uncertainty about her identity, in particular her relationship to her Algerian father. In patrilineal North African culture, identity is passed down first and foremost through the father, and the protagonist is therefore given the name Lila, her paternal grandmother's name. However, in order to protect her daughter from racist comments, Lila's French mother truncates her name and transforms it into the French form Lili. The novel recounts Lila's search for her Algerian identity and for her father, and by the end of the text, she has come to terms with her true name, Lila. As she recalls memories of life with her family, she remembers a series of incidents in which the notion of filiation is problematized: the father bemoans the fact that his children will not grow up speaking his language, and the children are embarrassed by symbols of Algeria related to the father. They consider an earthenware pot brought back from Algeria, for example, to be "grossier" (crude) and "incongru" (out of place) (83), even though their father cherishes it as an image of his homeland. The issue of legitimacy is also raised through the thematics of "mauvais sang" (bad blood) (135) and is tied to appearances in that Lila resembles her French mother more than her Kabyle father. Not only is it difficult for the father to pass on his culture to his children born in France to a French mother, but his blood ties are also explicitly questioned when a police officer stops him and asks if he is certain who the girl's father is: "T'es sûr que c'est à toi ça?... Kabyle hein?" (You're sure this is yours?... Kabyle huh?) (30). The officer's racist comments highlight the theme of filiation which symbolizes the problematic relationship between the two generations.

As daughters of Maghrebi families in France become aware of the tension between the two worlds they have to negotiate--home and French society--they must walk a fine line between "legitimacy" and "illegitimacy" as defined by two different cultures. For the female characters in the novels, daily life often represents a struggle to maintain one's sense of balance while negotiating the often contradictory familial and societal expectations. For these women, life at home often reproduces the cultural patterns of North Africa, and consequently becomes "the main arena of conflict between generations" (Ireland 1027). Farida Belghoul's *Georgette!* (1986), a narrative told from the perspective of a young girl who feels torn between her Algerian parents and her French teacher, exemplifies this type of situation. Here, the seven-year-old narrator's father, the representative of family values, stands in direct opposition to the teacher, the emblem of the Republic and the child's main link to successful integration. Belghoul frequently underscores the father's desire that his daughter choose between two worlds he perceives as irreconcilable--home and school--thus placing the child in an untenable situation: "If you don't listen to me...who are you going to listen to? Your teacher? Yeah, listen to her! That's normal: she has a degree and all that. But I've already told you: listen to her, but don't ever believe her. If you do, you'll be buried alive" (129).[6] The difficulties the young girl experiences at school (her refusal to speak, her slowness at writing) are directly linked to her father's admonition. In this sense, although the school system is supposed to be the bridge which will allow immigrant children access to French society, the message she hears at home is that her relationship with her father will be jeopardized if she allows herself to be influenced by the outside world.

Almost without exception, fiction by Maghrebi women in France depicts a difficult family situation in which girls are subjected to parental anger and quite often to physical abuse as a consequence of perceived infractions of accepted codes of behavior, such as talking to a boy who is not a member of the family. In Leïla Sebbar's *Fatima ou les Algériennes au square* (1981), for example, the main character Dalila, who no longer wishes to remain the target of her father's violent temper, locks herself up in her room where she awaits the opportunity to run away from home. Similarly, in the stories told by immigrant women who meet in the small public square of their housing project, violence against women and children is a predominant theme. Fathers and older brothers are most often the perpetrators, but one of the stories also involves a woman from Algeria whose young son is placed in foster care. Overwhelmed by work, poverty, and lack of space, the mother has harmed the child during angry outbursts she cannot control. The responses to violence against women within the family vary but usually depend upon the generation of the victims. Mothers are generally portrayed as resigned to their fate, whereas the daughters react by running away, as in Sebbar's *Fatima ou les Algériennes au square* and *Shérazade. 17 ans, brune, frisée, les yeux verts* (1982) and in Soraya Nini's *Ils disent que je suis une beurette* (1993), a young woman's story of growing up in a housing project. Kabyle singer Djura is forced to take her reaction to violence one step further. Frequently beaten by her father and her brothers, she is condemned by the family for choosing a French partner and is subsequently brutally attacked by her brother and her niece. In retaliation, she not only breaks her ties with the family, but also has to defend herself in a series of legal battles against them, a struggle she recounts in *Le voile du silence* (1990). Other characters resort to suicide as a desperate solution to the relentless violence to which they are subjected, as is portrayed in Ferrudja Kessas's *Beur's Story* (1990).

Father-daughter relations are frequently mirrored in episodes involving sisters and brothers. Unlike their brothers, girls are expected to return home immediately after school and rarely go out at night on dates or to visit friends. Parents generally refuse to grant permission for daughters to participate in school outings or to attend parties with other young people. When girls do leave the home in order to go to school, their elder brothers assume responsibility for ensuring that their sisters' behavior does not dishonor the family. The fictional works, of which Kessas's *Beur's Story* is a typical example, depict the relationship between sisters and brothers as a constant source of resentment for the young women. In *Beur's Story*, Malika is desperately trying to prepare her *baccalauréat* (high-school diploma) while looking after her younger siblings and assisting her mother with the housework; she frequently experiences conflicts with her brothers, who monitor her activities and expect her to leave her homework to serve them. What Malika and her sister Fatima find most objectionable is the narrow-mindedness of brothers, who, like them, have been raised in France but who do nothing to modify their behavior in order to adjust to French cultural norms. Fatima reasons that since they are all second-generation immigrants, there should be greater understanding and assistance between brothers and sisters. However, where the sisters expect to find allies in their brothers, they generally encounter enemies who align themselves with the father: "Instead of reaching out to us, they turn their backs on us! Since they can't be the boss outside, they act as if they are the boss at home" (202).[7]

The same type of problematic relationship appears in *Ils disent que je suis une beurette*, which portrays the difficulties Samia and her sisters have with their eldest brother. The brother is such a violent bully and jealous guardian of his sisters' movements that they call him "KGB" (40) and "l'oeil de Moscou" (the eye of Moscow) (70), terms which clearly associate him with violence and surveillance. In order to protect themselves and to communicate freely with each other without their brother or their parents understanding them, the sisters develop a code they call "la langue 'S,' dite 'de sécurité' " (the "S" language, S for "security") (111).

If fathers and brothers are mainly portrayed in a negative light as strict and authoritative, often to the point of abusiveness, mothers are characterized in a more nuanced and complex manner. For Lacoste-Dujardin, many mother-daughter relationships in Franco-Maghrebi families contain elements that range from total hostility--if the mother is seen as being complicit in maintaining the patriarchal order--to solidarity when the mother is viewed as the primary victim of the father's violence. Lacoste-Dujardin's sociological research shows that with time, and in a manner that reverses the roles in the typical parent-child relationship, many Maghrebi mothers come to depend on their older daughters for emotional and financial support once the latter acquire greater autonomy and become integrated into French society (28-29). In this sense, the daughters become a "bridge" that enables their mothers to move into society, especially when they encourage their mothers to leave the home more often. This pattern is reflected in the fictional works, which often depict an ambivalent mother-daughter relationship. In *Beur's Story*, for example, Malika serves as an interpreter and messenger for her family when she fills out forms for social benefits or writes letters back home. Malika recalls that at the age of eight, she felt unduly burdened by the responsibility of serving as family scribe in matters of correspondence.[8]

When it comes to the authority that mothers have over their daughters, Lacoste-Dujardin notes that the division of duties in traditional Maghrebi families makes mothers responsible for the good conduct of their daughters; this in turn creates a kind of emotional blackmail in which girls are doubly afraid of transgressing paternal authority because the mother too will be punished (31). The theme of mother-daughter solidarity is explored in *Fatima ou les Algériennes au square*, for example. After each episode of violence against her daughter Dalila, Fatima attends to her cuts and bruises, yet is powerless to prevent the brutality in the first place: "Dalila knew her mother didn't approve of her husband's violence, and even though she seemed complicit, she didn't hold it against her" (20).[9] Dalila does not blame her mother because they have shared the experience of listening to the women's stories told in the square, stories that have helped Dalila understand more fully the pressures facing mothers in the immigrant community.

In many instances, when conflicts between mothers and daughters do occur, they concern the question of schoolwork versus housework. A mother may not always understand the desire of her daughter to seek integration into French society by performing well at school. For such mothers, the daughter's future duties will instead center exclusively around home and family. While in some texts the mother encourages her daughters to study so that they will have more opportunities in life, the novels most often portray a more problematic situation in which the characters' attempts to satisfy both their mothers and their teachers lead to exhaustion and identity crises. In Kessas's *Beur's Story*, for example, Malika has difficulty reconciling her mother's demands for help around the house with her own desire to do well at school. For Malika's mother, the situation is simple: as the eldest daughter, Malika "devait se comporter comme une femme" (should act like a woman) (19) and is expected to use the skills her mother has passed on to her, including cooking, sewing, knitting, doing laundry, and cleaning the house. When Malika does not live up to her mother's expectations and accidently burns a meal, her mother insults her with the words: "Sors d'ici, Kahbin! Tu n'es bonne qu'à aller à l'école pour te faire trousser!" (Get out of here, whore! All you're good for is going to school to get laid!) (22). The use of the term "Kahbin" (whore) suggests that Malika's mother equates household incompetence with sexual immorality, thus revealing the deep gulf between her own ambitions for her daughter and Malika's own desire to succeed at school. Furthermore, the expression "te faire trousser" (to get laid), which has negative sexual connotations, reinforces the home-school, inside-outside dichotomy by establishing a parallel between school and impurity.

Nini's *Ils disent que je suis une beurette*, which depicts a mother-daughter relationship in great detail, conveys a more complex picture than *Beur's Story*. In this novel, Samia Nalib, the narrator and sixth of eight children born to an Algerian family living in the south of France, recounts the story of her adolescent years. Like Malika in *Beur's Story*, Samia and her sisters are called upon to help their mother with the numerous household chores required in a family of ten. Samia resents the time spent cleaning at home and recounts her anger and shame at not performing as well as her sisters at school. As she is assigned to remedial classes, her only option for the future will be to take the *brevet* exam to gain entry into a *lycée d'enseignement professionnel* (technical high school). Unlike Malika's mother in *Beur's Story*, Samia's mother refuses to let her abandon her education: "But my girl, you have to, you don't have a choice. You're learning a trade, and that will give you baggage in life. It's like I'm telling you, my girl, baggage" (74).[10] Having such educational "baggage" means her daughter will one day be able to live more independently, and Samia's mother hopes that earning a diploma will afford her daughters more opportunity in life than she had as a girl in Algeria: "You need a job, Samia. You don't want to spend your whole life at home, do you? If my father had educated me, maybe I wouldn't be in this situation" (75)."[11] The text returns insistently to the mother's support of her daughters in their desire for independence and integration, and in this sense, Samia's mother reflects the desire many first-generation immigrant parents have that their children benefit from educational opportunities in France while still maintaining a strong sense of cultural identity that links them to the community of origin.

Samia and her sisters also serve as a direct link to the outside world for their house-bound mother, symbolically becoming "mots de passe" (passwords) (28) and "passeports" (passports) (180) when they act as translators for their mother in administrative offices. In a particularly poignant scene, Samia feels both protective and somewhat ashamed of her mother when an employee is rude to her, addressing her with the familiar "tu" pronoun and scolding her for not bringing the correct forms. While Samia upbraids the employee for her lack of respect, once outside she reproaches her mother for her passivity in the face of an insult. Samia's mother, in turn, scolds Samia for insulting the employee. In this fashion, Samia and her mother embody two different views on how best to cope with commonplace negative attitudes towards North Africans in French society. For Samia, the answer is to react with anger and defiance; for her mother, the solution is patient resignation.

Samia is torn between her desire to protect her mother from humiliation and her refusal to accept some of her cultural practices, believing them to be incompatible with her own sense of identity. In many of the novels, mothers are depicted as maintaining a variety of traditional and even magical beliefs derived from folk practices in North Africa. One episode recounted by Samia reveals the extent to which her mother still clings to some of her traditional beliefs, even though she is the one who ensures that Samia will continue her education. On this occasion, the mother has an elderly Algerian woman (called a "sorcière" [witch] by the girls and their father) come to the house to perform a traditional ritual on the thirteen-year-old Samia and her younger sister to guarantee they remain virgins until their wedding day. During the ceremony, the *sorcière* makes a cut in the girls' thighs while their mother holds them down, and they must then eat a raisin soaked in blood from the cut. Stunned by the experience and by her mother's complicity in it, Samia describes it as "tordu" (twisted), a manifestation of her mother's "délire" (delirium) (127), and she makes a conscious decision to repress the episode. Samia's strategy for survival is thus to compartmentalize her life, to ignore the aspects of her parents' beliefs that do not coincide with her own, in order to focus her energies on succeeding at school. Ultimately, Samia's notion of "baggage" will prove to be different from her mother's since her goal is to leave her family and set off on her own. At the end of the novel, she obtains her diploma, thus bringing home "le bagage de la mother" (the baggage her mother wanted) (279), but the last two pages depict her on the threshold, holding a much more literal form of baggage (her suitcase), as she prepares to walk out of the house. In a symbolic sense, however, Samia is also taking with her the "baggage" of her upbringing and the struggle she has waged in her family to assert her independence in the face of her brother's demands that she be submissive. In this sense, the type of integration Samia achieves at the close of the novel remains ambivalent since it does not correspond to French society's image of a successfully integrated Maghrebi woman.

Samia's experiences at school demonstrate that young Franco-Maghrebi women have problems mediating cultural differences and that academic success does not guarantee they will be integrated. Samia's account of her own balancing acts reveals that the path to integration is much more problematic than many outside observers might realize. French society considers the public school system to be the best possible tool for the integration of immigrants, and many of the novels contain episodes that take place at school. However, they portray it as both a source of possible salvation and an arena in which cultural differences are often the cause of humiliation. Being outside the family and interacting with children of other ethnic and social backgrounds is depicted as an enriching yet intimidating experience for the protagonists of several of the novels under consideration here. Most important, it is at school that girls from immigrant families must come to terms with their socio-cultural differences. As Lila in *Une fille sans histoire* discovers, going to school further problematizes her relationship with her father and raises questions about her Algerian heritage. In particular, her experience encourages her to explore the notions of individual and collective history and to examine why the Algerian war is not discussed in school: "France and Algeria. At one time, she had thought she could find refuge at School, on the other side of the housing project. Where History, when it's unbearable, is not written in textbooks" (123).[12] In other words, school reinforces the tension Lila feels between the two sides of her heritage rather than reducing it. Lila's French mother, in turn, reinforces the message taught at school when she openly attempts to hide the signs of her children's Algerian identity so that they will appear more "French."

Since French school is not experienced as a place where girls encounter tolerance of cultural differences, the protagonists feel they have to employ a variety of strategies to either assert or conceal their "otherness." Several novels, including Belghoul's *Georgette!*, use images related to parts of the body to underscore the young narrator's problematic negotiation of cultural difference. In a telling example, the narrator's perception of a star and a crescent moon that her mother drew on her hand with henna changes radically when she goes outside to run an errand: "Once outside, I didn't like it anymore. I hid in my pocket my hand dirtied by the red earth" (20).[13] Viewed from this new perspective, the traces of henna no longer represent an art form that evokes beauty and celebration, but rather become synonymous with impurity and shame and thus serve as a visible sign of the young woman's otherness when she enters French society. Similarly, in *Beur's Story*, Malika likes to have henna designs painted on her hands during family celebrations, but finds that they call attention to her difference when she is at school. Embarrassed by questions from other students whose reactions range from curiosity to disgust, Malika refuses to use henna when school is in session. The "unacceptable" nature of the designs is reinforced in an episode where the teacher--the official representative of French cultural norms--tells Malika's sister to go and wash her hands: "as the henna didn't wash off, she had sent her to the nurse as if she had the plague" (163).[14] Henna thus becomes the primary signifier of difference, and the teacher's treatment of it as a form of contamination--a potentially contagious disease--highlights the difficulties the girls encounter as they attempt to mediate two conflicting cultural systems.

Other physical and behavioral signs underscore the young women's otherness in the eyes of their majority-culture classmates. For the girls interviewed in Lacoste-Dujardin's study, clothing, hairstyles, make-up, dietary practices, and even smoking are indicators of whether or not the girls from North African families "fit in" with French society or whether they will be labeled "traditional." The traditional ones are easy to identify: "No pants, no pantyhose, no heels, no untied hair, just braids" (50).[15] Similarly, the protagonists use clothing as a form of self-expression and often as a means of challenging their family's behavior codes. In *Ils disent que je suis une beurette*, Samia refuses to dress in the feminine way that her parents prefer--her clothes of choice are baggy jeans, loose sweaters, and thick-soled boots. Likewise, in *Shérazade*, the protagonist and her group of friends are especially adept at dressing in ways designed to confound the expectations of others. Mixing North African scarves and jewelry with flea market purchases, and pairing these with items of clothing borrowed from the trendy boutique where she is employed, Shérazade creates a personal style--"un *look* pas possible" (a really unusual look) (152)--that defies categorization and challenges notions of ethnic stereotyping. These eclectic outfits, often put together to be worn to nightclubs, flaunt conventions and reflect Shérazade's refusal to be classified according to orientalist stereotypes of Maghrebi women. Undermining an erotic photographer's plans to stage a jungle-themed photo-shoot in which Shérazade and her friends would pose as exotic wild animals, the young women dress in an eccentric mixture of chic and primitive clothes and taunt the photographer before threatening him with a fake gun and fleeing his apartment. Their behavior underscores their refusal to conform to the role imposed on them by those who seek to exploit their ethnic identity for their own purposes.

Shérazade's survival as an under-age runaway in Paris depends upon her ability to subvert and to extend the boundaries of a society that seeks to contain her. She lives in a squatt with other young people of similar circumstance, takes part in armed robberies, and shoplifts items she cannot otherwise afford. This adeptness at manipulating conventions, which recurs in many of the novels, enables the adolescents to negotiate cultural differences and to establish their own personal space. A process referred to as "trafiquer" (getting around the system) (105) in *Ils disent que je suis une beurette*, it takes on many forms, ranging from Shérazade's street-wise survival skills to Samia's shortening of her name to the more ethnically ambiguous "Sam." Samia also falsifies her school schedule so that she can remain away from home in the afternoon without raising her brother's suspicions. In all the novels discussed, then, this manipulation of parental and societal expectations represents another form of cultural mediation that allows the young protagonists to express their individuality and forge their own identities.

In conclusion, the novels by young women of Maghrebi origin in France depict integration into French society as a torturous path strewn with obstacles that arise from difficulties within the family and from a lack of acceptance within French society. However, most of the women portrayed in these novels do not wish to break with their families, but struggle to assert their personal preferences, attempting to maintain a sense of equilibrium by creating individual strategies and objectives. In *Ils disent que je suis une beurette*, the ultimate words of wisdom come from a maternal aunt, who explains to Samia's mother that she must accept the fact that emigration to France has brought her children a different destiny: "Your children have grown up here in France, you wanted the best for them, to educate them, to give them what they might not have had if you'd stayed back home, where they would have had another life... You can't take the best and reject the worst for them. They are the ones who will have to choose, you must accept that. How could you think that all this light wouldn't open their eyes?" (135).[16] Here, immigration is aptly described as an "eye-opening" experience: exposed to different models of education, behavior, and dress, the young women seek to incorporate them into their lives, thereby fashioning their own identities. In this sense, their experience as the daughters of immigrants constitutes a veritable balancing act as they attempt to maintain a foot in each world while at the same time carving out a place for themselves in French society.

NOTES

1. "je porte tout ce fardeau, je sens la blessure de mes parents" (Francine Muel-Dreyfus in Bourdieu, *La misère du monde*, 847).

2. Although a young woman referred to as Aïcha is the subject of the interview in "La messagère," Francine Muel-Dreyfus is the author of the chapter.

3. "le lieu critique de la négociation incessante de 'l'intégration.' "

4. Sayad's essay "Les enfants illégitimes" presents an in-depth interview with a young woman named Zahoua who arrived in France as an infant. She describes her father's bewilderment at how different from him his children have become by asking them: "Who are you? We don't know what you are! Where do you come from?" (231). Zahoua suggests that these remarks reveal her father's fear that Algerian children raised in France are somehow "illégitimes" (illegitimate) (232).

5. "J'ai compris que moi, je n'étais qu'une étrangère à leurs yeux: une putain de France."

6. "Si tu m'écoutes pas, moi...Qui c'est qu' tu vas écouter? Ta maîtresse? Oui, écoute-la! C'est normal: elle est diplômée, tout ça. Mais j' te l'ai déjà dit: écoute-la mais il ne faut jamais la croire. Sinon, tu t' fais enterrer vivante."

7. "Et au lieu de nous donner la main, ils nous tournent le dos! Et faute de jouer les caïds dehors, ils les jouent chez eux!"

8. Valérie Dumeige and Sophie Ponchelet's *Françaises* (1999) presents an interview with Naïma, a young woman who arrived in France at the age of five. She too recalls being "burdened" with handling the family's paperwork as soon as she could read and write. Naïma remembers that she had to accompany her mother to banks, offices, and the city hall to fill out forms and speak with employees whose scorn for immigrants was readily apparent. Naïma states that the humiliation of these early experiences has never left her and that now, as an adult, she does not accept any rude treatment: "I react immediately. I'm ready to insult people who are rude to my parents" ("Je réagis tout de suite. Je suis prête à injurier ceux qui parlent mal à mes parents") (164). Even though she acknowledges that serving as an interpreter for her parents builds character, she still feels that these responsibilities are too heavy for a young child.

9. "Dalila savait que sa mère n'approuvait pas la violence de son mari et bien qu'elle parût complice, elle ne lui en voulait pas."

10. "Mais ma fille, tu es obligée, tu n'as pas le choix. Tu apprends un métier et ça te fait un bagage dans la vie. C'est comme je te dis, ma fille, un bagage!"

11. "Il te faut un métier, Samia. Tu ne veux pas rester toute ta vie à la maison? Si mon père m'avait instruite, je ne serais peut-être pas là."

12. "La France et l'Algérie. Un temps, elle avait cru trouver refuge à l'Ecole, de l'autre côté de la cité. Là où l'Histoire, quand elle est insoutenable, n'est pas écrite dans les manuels."

13. "Là, je ne l'aimais plus du tout. Je cachais dans ma poche ma main dégueulassée par la terre rouge."

14. "comme le henné ne partait pas, elle l'avait expédiée chez l'infirmière comme une pestiférée."

15. "Ni pantalon, ni collant, ni talons, pas le droit de lâcher ses cheveux, mais des nattes." For the girls interviewed in Lacoste-Dujardin's study, the label "filles-à-natte" (girls with braids) becomes a euphemism used by Franco-Maghrebi girls to refer to others who come from conservative homes.

16. "vos enfants ont grandi ici, en France, vous avez voulu le meilleur pour eux, les instruire, leur donner ce qu'ils n'auraient peut-être pas eu en restant au pays, où ils auraient eu une autre vie...Vous ne pouvez pas prendre le meilleur et rejeter le pire à leur place. Ce sont eux qui choisiront, il faut l'accepter. Comment veux-tu que toutes ces lumières n'ouvrent pas leurs yeux?" (135).

WORKS CITED

Belghoul, Farida. *Georgette!* Paris: Editions Barrault, 1986.

Boukhedenna, Sakinna. *Journal. "Nationalité: immigré(e)."* Paris: L'Harmattan, 1987.

Bourdieu, Pierre. *La misère du monde.* Paris: Seuil, 1993.

Djura. *Le voile du silence.* Paris: Michel Lafon, 1990.

Dumeige, Valérie, and Sophie Ponchelet. *Françaises.* Paris: Editions du Nil, 1999.

Hargreaves, Alec G., and Mark McKinney, eds. *Post-Colonial Cultures in France.* London: Routledge, 1997.

Houari, Leïla. *Zeïda de nulle part.* Paris: L'Harmattan, 1985.

Imache, Tassadit. *Une fille sans histoire.* Paris: Calmann-Lévy, 1989.

Ireland, Susan. "Writing at the Crossroads: Cultural Conflict in the Work of *Beur* Women Writers." *The French Review* 68.6 (May 1995): 1022-1034.

Kessas, Ferrudja. *Beur's Story.* Paris: L'Harmattan, 1990.

Lacoste-Dujardin, Camille. *Yasmina et les autres de Nanterre et d'ailleurs.* Paris: Editions de la Découverte, 1992.

Muel-Dreyfus, Francine. "La messagère." *La misère du monde.* Ed. Pierre Bourdieu. Paris: Seuil, 1993, 845-858.

Nini, Soraya. *Ils disent que je suis une beurette.* Paris: Editions Fixot, 1993.

Plantade, Nedjma. *L'honneur et l'amertume: le destin ordinaire d'une femme kabyle.* Paris: Balland, 1993.

Sayad, Abdelmalek. "Les enfants illégitimes." *Actes de la recherche en sciences sociales* 25 (January 1979): 61-81.

---. *L'immigration ou les paradoxes de l'altérité.* Brussels: Editions Universitaires De Boeck, 1991.

Sebbar, Leïla. *Fatima ou les Algériennes au square.* Paris: Stock, 1981.

---. *Shérazade. 17 ans, brune, frisée, les yeux verts.* Paris: Stock, 1982.

Translating Immigrant Identities in Mounsi's *Territoire d'outre-ville*

Susan Ireland

In France today, many sensitive issues related to immigration are associated with the suburban areas where large numbers of immigrant families live (*la banlieue*). In an attempt to better understand these issues, "Des légions d'explorateurs de banlieue sont partis à la conquête du secret des cités maudites" (Armies of explorers of the *banlieue* have set out to discover the secrets of the accursed housing projects) (Boubeker and Beau 14), resulting in a proliferation of books, articles, and media reports on these problem areas. The titles of some of the most recent texts--Adil Jazouli's *Une saison en banlieue* and Jean de Boishue's *Banlieue mon amour*, for example[1]--contain intertextual references whose allusions to hell and atomic explosions illustrate the tendency to associate the *banlieue* with apocalyptic images:[2] "People talk about the periphery in terms of safety, housing, and scourges like unemployment or drugs. About culture, they say nothing or virtually nothing" (Mounsi, *Territoire* 99). Although a large number of articles have been devoted to the *banlieue*, the epithets used to describe it in the mainstream media show little variation and generally evoke forms of social disorder: "Haut les mains," "Bout du monde" (Delarue 24), "La poudrière des banlieues," "Banlieue explosive," "Banlieue damnée" (Vieillard-Baron 14).[3] Most recently, the spectre of Islamic fundamentalism has begun to appear in the headlines alongside the *banlieue* and is proving to be "une marchandise journalistique qui se vend bien" (a journalistic merchandise that sells well) (Begag and Delorme 163)--"Les islamistes. France: leur stratégie dans les

banlieues" (L'Express, April-May 1993); "France, terre d'islam. Des banlieues
sous influence" (Le Monde, November 1992); "Banlieues: la tentation islamiste"
(Le Nouvel Observateur, November 1992).[4] Such sensationalist headlines encourage the repetition of negative clichés related to the banlieue and reinforce
the equation "banlieue=immigration=arabes" (suburbs=immigration=Arabs)
(Cesari 38), thus rendering immigrants responsible for the various problems
associated with these areas and suggesting that Muslims in particular constitute
a threat to French national identity.

    Novels and essays written by second-generation immigrants who have
grown up in the banlieue provide a counterweight to the picture painted by the
media. Indeed, many such texts emphasize the idea of being imprisoned within
inaccurate, negative stereotypes: "How many inhabitants have we seen or heard
protesting vehemently against the falsified, deformed images of their lives that
are creating a feeding frenzy for the media?" (Begag and Delorme 21).[5] Taking
up the notion of falsification, the writer and singer Mounsi[6] uses the metaphors
of translation, counterfeiting, and sub-titling to describe his alternative picture of
the banlieue, which calls for a rejection of the stereotypical images that serve to
marginalize immigrants: "The original version of our lives has nothing to do
with the subtitled version we are generally presented with. . . . Because of the
'dubbing' done by French society, foreigners are always poorly translated" (Territoire 18). In Mounsi's "original" version, the banlieue serves both as a strategy
for decentering mainstream definitions of the banlieue and as a means of raising
questions about the place of immigrant writers in relation to French society and
the French literary canon. In this sense, his work constitutes an example of what
Michel Laronde calls "écriture décentrée" (decentered writing), writing that
seeks to undermine the canon from within: "Writing which produces a Text that
establishes linguistic and ideological distance with regard to a centripetal Language and Culture can be called decentered" (8).[7] In order to create such a decentering, Mounsi plays on the notions of "origin" and "originality," makes use
of irony and intertextuality, and reworks the repertoire of topoi related to French
urban literature of the Middle Ages and the nineteenth century. By so doing, he
emphasizes the need for a shift in perspective and seeks to reposition himself in
relation to traditional images of immigrant communities in France.

    Like Boubeker and Beau, Mounsi refers explicitly to the "explorateurs"
(explorers) (Territoire 47) who have ventured into the banlieue in order to interpret its secrets. These explorers--the "translators" of the banlieue--appear in
Mounsi's texts in various satirical guises, including the geographers who examine the banlieue from time to time in La noce des fous and the left-wing Marxist
intellectuals in Territoire d'outre-ville whose forays into the suburbs are presented as a kind of anthropological expedition: "this incongruous juxtaposition
[of the university and the shantytown] was for them an experience similar to that
of an ethnographer discovering a bit of primitive indigenous society, something
like 'the happy dropout' in his jungle. In our company, to be sure, they could get
a taste of a very unusual form of exoticism" (47).[8] Here, the mock-scientific tone
and the ironic use of terms such as "exotisme" (exoticism) and "société indigène" (indigenous population) sets up the parody of anthropological studies
from the colonial period which, through their attempts at cultural "translation,"

contributed to the creation of stereotypes that continue to define those of immigrant descent living in France today.[9] Mounsi's parodic version of the encounter suggests both the perpetuation of such stereotypes and their transposition into a post-colonial metropolitan context ("le zonard joyeux" [the happy dropout]). The use of such rhetorical strategies as *reductio ad absurdum* enables Mounsi to comically undercut the validity of the explorer-translators' conclusions and to ask what has been lost in the translation.

The notion of poor translation is further underscored in Mounsi's references to *verlan* (backslang), in which he reverses the usual associations of the term. While *verlan*, with its reversal of the syllables of a word, is generally interpreted as a symbol of marginality, for Mounsi it is the discourse of the center that constitutes a "monde à l'envers." In particular, he criticizes the recuperation of the term *beur*, the most well-known *verlan* word, and its transformation into a stereotype--into what he calls a "marque déposée" (brand name), which now imprisons second-generation immigrants (*Territoire* 73). In this fashion, he equates the center's use of the term *beur* with the need for retranslation: "Dans ce monde à l'envers, il y a un mot détourné de son origine, un mot qu'il me semble grand temps de remettre à l'endroit" (In this world turned upside down, there is a word that has been diverted from its origin, a word it is high time to turn right side up again) (*Territoire* 73). Playing on the idea of reversal ("l'envers" and "l'endroit"), he expresses the same view as sociologists Azouz Begag and Christian Delorme who have emphasized the negative consequences of the word *beur*: "The 'Beur' label has contributed to creating a narrow characterization of these young people as a homogenous group. In particular, this standardization has served politico-ideological ends intended to designate them as impossible to integrate or to assimilate into national identity" (75).[10] Originally a symbol of potential change, the designation has become yet another ethnic cliché that serves primarily to standardize and to exclude young people of immigrant descent, and Mounsi's call for a further reversal highlights its present role as a form of containment.

For these reasons, Mounsi defines his project as one of renaming and redefining as a means of contesting the center's erroneous interpretation of immigrants and their communities--"Longtemps je fus nommé, aujourd'hui je nomme à mon tour" (For a long time I was named, today I name in my turn) (*Territoire* 20). By equating his own version with the active voice rather than the passive, he presents it as a way of breaking out of the stereotypes that confine "ceux qui sont nommés, définis, circonscrits de mots" (those who are named, defined, circumscribed by words) (*Territoire* 20). Emphasizing the role played by language in creating and perpetuating stereotypes, Mounsi proposes to counter dominant discourses by literally deflecting--decentering--the words used to circumscribe him: "On me jette des mots, je les attrape et les renvoie sur d'autres" (Words are thrown at me, I catch them and throw them back at others) (*Territoire* 20). As he does so, the images of translation and reversal place him in the positive role of innovator, of author of the valorized original, while relegating the center to that of deformer, counterfeiter, and poor translator.[11]

Mounsi employs similar strategies in relation to the version of literary history that relegates *Beur* writers to the margins. Through his use of intertextual allusions, Mounsi inscribes himself into the long line of writers whose work deals with the city and addresses the question of peripheral spaces and social control, a lineage that includes authors such as Charles Baudelaire, Honoré de Balzac, and Emile Zola. Like novelist Mehdi Lallaoui, who explicitly draws attention to this heritage in a description of a strike in *Les beurs de Seine*--"Oh shit, if only Emile Zola had seen that" (121)[12]--Mounsi appropriates urban literature in the name of the second generation and foregrounds the fact that the writers who have most influenced his work are majority-French not North African. Allusions to canonic nineteenth-century authors, especially poets, recur throughout Mounsi's novels and range in form from direct references and partial quotations to passages that echo or parody such works as Baudelaire's "Tableaux parisiens" and *Le spleen de Paris*. Similar echoes of well-known poems by Arthur Rimbaud and Victor Hugo, for example, weave traces of Mounsi's precursors into his own work, thereby opening up a dialogue between his texts and theirs, and claiming the right for authors of immigrant descent to be placed among French writers whose literary merit is universally recognized: "A l'aube, nous nous réveillâmes dans le parc" (At dawn, we woke up in the park) (*La noce* 61); "Demain, à l'aube, je savais que je m'enfuirais" (Tomorrow, at dawn, I knew I would run away) (*La noce* 221).[13] In this fashion, Mounsi demands equal literary citizenship with mainstream French writers and raises questions about literary classification, in particular as it concerns the relationship between the canon and its margins.

Besides alluding to nineteenth-century authors, Mounsi claims as his most influential precursor the medieval poet of urban despair and suffering, François Villon. By presenting himself both as a "fils de Villon" (son of Villon) (64) and as a "fils de l'immigration" (son of immigration) (90), Mounsi makes himself part of two different types of second generation, one literary and one socio-cultural, and places the question of filiation at the heart of *Territoire d'outre-ville*--one of whose main themes is his relationship with his actual Algerian father. At the beginning of the text, the juxtaposition of the epigraph--the famous refrain from Villon's "Ballade des pendus"--with the words of Mounsi's best known song, "Seconde génération," foregrounds the themes of dual paternity and generational change while at the same time undermining traditional notions of what it means to be part of the second generation by portraying the son of an Algerian immigrant as a literary descendent of Villon. In addition, the themes of translation and renewal figure prominently in the epigraphs through Villon's appeal for a change of heart and Mounsi's use of a series of images that transpose traditional orientalist symbols of the Arab world into their modern equivalents:

> For us the Nile is the Seine
> The pyramids are the housing projects
> The Cleopatras of my day
> No longer use snake venom to get high
> Smack is their poison.[14] (11)

The text closes in similar fashion as the refrain from the "Ballade" is quoted a second time and is juxtaposed with a poem entitled "Nostalgérie." The book is thus framed by two references to dual influences, and in the last words of the text, the voices of Mounsi and Villon virtually become one: "And each word slips from my mouth in the same way, I'm sure, as it did from Villon's heart" (124). This emphasis on dual filiation, like the intertextual references, counters attempts to establish a hermetic boundary between the French Villon and the "non-French" Mounsi, and the image of their indistinguishable voices aligns Mounsi with the now canonical, but once marginal, Villon, thereby drawing attention to changing criteria for inclusion in the canon.

In addition to these opening and closing passages, Mounsi's texts point insistently to the parallels between his life and work and those of Villon--prison, delinquency, destitution, life on the streets--and it is the Villon of the "Ballade des pendus," discovered by Mounsi in the prison of Savigny-sur-Orge, who is presented as the successful "translator" of Mounsi's own experience: "What I felt in my own body had finally been translated" (*Territoire* 61). By aligning himself with Villon, Mounsi urges his readers to reexamine the immigrant sub-urbs through the prism of the "Ballade"--"Don't harden your hearts against us" (*Territoire* 124 and epigraph)[15]--rather than subscribing to hostile media images. The link between Villon and the contemporary *banlieue* is underscored in an exercise of naming in which the repetition of the letter V recalls the poet's name:

> V comme Ville
> V comme Vénissieux, Vaulx-en-Velin,
> V comme Vitry,
> V comme Vol, comme Vitrines, comme Violence. (*Territoire* 20)

> (V like town
> V like Vénissieux, Vaulx-en-Velin,
> V like Vitry,
> V like Theft, like Shop Windows, like Violence.)

At the same time, Mounsi's choice of Villon as precursor sets up a more general parallel between the Paris of today and that of the Middle Ages, the period most often associated with the beginnings of anti-Arab prejudice in France:[16] "The strength of anti-Arab prejudice runs from the battle of Poitiers to the battle of Algiers, through the time of the Crusades when the cross and the crescent clashed" (*Territoire* 93). In Mounsi's novels, medieval Paris is fore-grounded in particular in episodes addressing the themes of justice and compas-sion. Like Villon, he refers to specific streets and taverns in central Paris--rue des Lombards, rue Vieille-du-Temple, rue de l'Ecu Doré, "Au Cheval blanc," "A l'Abreuvoir d'or" (*La noce* 80-81)--and his allusions to gallows, charnel houses, and methods of torture highlight the emphasis on justice. These geo-graphical markers, especially the Fontaine des Innocents built on the site of an old charnel house, creates a kind of palimpsest in which Mounsi's Paris is su-perimposed on Villon's: "In Truanderie Street where we used to hang out, there lay the skeletons of thieves that the voracious earth had swallowed up" (*La noce*

80).[17] This setting, with its echoes of Villon's Paris, emphasizes the prejudices and suffering shared by the two periods and further merges the worlds and words of the two writers--"It's the wandering life of lost children, like that of the poet of yesteryear" (*La noce* 82).[18]

In "The Eye of Power," Michel Foucault calls for a greater focus on the relationship between history, space, and power: "A whole history remains to be written of *spaces*--which would at the same time be the history of *powers*" (*Power/Knowledge* 149). Mounsi's depictions of Paris explicitly propose the second generation as a useful example of such a history--"They add history to geography and geography to history" (*Territoire* 90).[19] In *Territoire d'outre-ville*, for example, the Seine, a traditional symbol of Frenchness and of the ad-ministrative and political center of the nation, becomes a geographical reminder of a different past. At once an image of memory and of imagination, Mounsi's Seine is associated with the immigrant laborers of his father's generation who worked at the Renault factory on the river at Boulogne-Billancourt. This Seine, with its barges and its "parfum de Simenon" (scent of Simenon), is also a "fleuve rempli de noyés" (river full of drowned people) (*Territoire* 23)--not corpses in a detective novel, but the Algerians killed in Paris in October 1961 when immigrant workers and their families demonstrated peacefully against a curfew imposed on them by the French authorities. After the demonstration was brutally repressed and many of the dead thrown into the Seine, information on the event was covered up and was not mentioned in many official versions of history.[20] It was this event that taught Mounsi the relationship between history and place--"It is in Paris in October 1961 that I discovered history" (*Territoire* 30)--and both this date and the river recur throughout the text as reminders of the way in which history and geography have been shaped by colonial power structures. Mounsi's evocation of October 1961, along with the allusion to Simenon, creates a powerful contrast between the fictional crimes of Simenon's novels and the actual historical events of 1961, thus suggesting that the latter, too, constitute a crime that needs to be recognized as such--"ce crime que nous n'avons toujours pas nommé" (this crime we still haven't acknowledged).[21] A site of memory for Mounsi, the Seine also serves as a powerful image of his desire to write, and in the resulting text he works to undermine the traditional associations of one of Paris' most well-known geographical markers by appro-priating it as a central image of his immigrant history.[22]

Mounsi's examination of space also suggests how two sets of historical events--France's colonial past and the evolution of Parisian urban planning--have combined to produce current discourses on the *banlieue* by transposing the old colonial geography into images of circularity. Whereas the colonial city was composed of two adjacent but mutually exclusive parts, "the zone inhabited by the colonized" and "the zone inhabited by the colonizers" (Fanon 31), the layout of modern Paris is characterized by rings of suburbs surrounding a central core, the Ile de la Cité on the Seine. The contemporary circular model, portrayed by the media as "un purgatoire circulaire, avec au centre Paris-Paradis" (a circular purgatory, with Paris-Paradise in the center) (Maspero 24), perpetuates the colo-nial order by relegating immigrants to the margins, and the association of this peripheral purgatory with immigration reinforces the colonial notion that one zone is "de trop" (in excess) (Fanon 32), a phenomenon referred to parodically in Tahar Ben Jelloun's *Les raisins de la galère*: "They think that the suburbs are no longer part of the Hexagon, but that this ring has already broken off and drifted away in the direction of the Third World" (125).[23] Like Ben Jelloun, then, Mounsi stresses how the *banlieue* forms part of a "géographie de la peur" (geography of fear) in which fear of the other is configured in spatial terms (Body-Gendrot 60): "People are placed in an area which is declared enemy territory" (*Territoire* 84). His references to urban history point to the changing nature of those associated with the *banlieue* in different periods, and thus draw attention to the way in which the notion of geographical deviance is used to reinforce the stereotypes. By emphasizing the role played by spatial metaphors in maintaining certain groups "hors société, donc hors sens" (outside society, therefore outside meaning) (*Territoire* 90)--terms that recall Albert Memmi's characterization of colonized people as "hors de l'histoire et hors de la cité" (outside history and outside the city) (129)--Mounsi highlights the ways in which imaginary boundaries are inscribed onto the city, and urges us to examine how the city is textualized and read today.

Other spatial images reinforce the notions of containment and incompatability. The concept of a border between two zones is expressed in mock-serious geographical terms in *La noce des fous*--"We were an imaginary line of demarcation, an equator on the circumference of the world" (22)[24]--while the description of Nanterre in *Territoire d'outre-ville* comically underscores the nature of the boundary between center and periphery. Although Nanterre University is located right next to immigrant neighborhoods, the students are associated with the center ("la page de la société") while young people from the housing projects are equated with the periphery ("la marge"): "Entre la page et la marge, il y a le 'bac' des étudiants et le 'background' de la banlieue" (Between the page and the margin, there are the students' diplomas and the background of the *banlieue*) (99). Urban design in Mounsi's Paris thus seems to be dictated by the same criteria as those that govern the Nice described parodically in Nordine Zaïmi's novel *Le tombeau de la folle*. There, Le Grand Thérapeute, who is responsible for the smooth running of the city, creates and guards borders in the manner of a colonial administrator: "The Great Therapist had come up with this spatial configuration a long time ago. He was proud of it: it was designed to prevent contact between people from different races. . . . The quarantining of certain zones that had the reputation of being dangerous nipped the disease in the bud before hybridity and the mixing of races could tarnish the pink complexion of future citizens" (22-23).[25] Like Zaïmi's satirical description, the title of Mounsi's *Territoire d'outre-ville* ironically draws attention to the perpetuation of the colonial geographical model, the expression "territoire d'outre-ville" (territory beyond the city) suggesting both the "territoires d'outre-mer" (overseas territories) and the peripheral status of the immigrant *banlieue* today.

The metaphors of borders are closely linked to the media image of barbarian hordes gathered at the city gates, an image which reflects anxieties about national and cultural identity. This vision of immigration, which Christian Jelen calls "le syndrome de l'invasion" (the invasion syndrome) (161), presents immigrants as invading French territory in a reverse form of colonization. The fear of invasion centers around the emblematic figure of the *loubard* (delinquent) whose transgressive aimless wandering stands in contrast to the potentially subversive, but generally inoffensive, "errance" of the ninteenth-century *flâneur*, a solitary man of leisure with time to stroll around the city. However, while the *loubards'* wandering translates into deviance in the eyes of the media, for the *loubards* themselves it signifies powerlessness, marginalization, and social injustice. In Mounsi's work, the frequent use of the verb "errer" (to wander) and its synonyms foregrounds *errance* as a defining characteristic of the lives of his protagonists: "By roaming in the streets . . . we wandered around, left to ourselves. Our life consisted of roving without purpose" (*La noce* 40).[26]

If *errance* is the first marker of the *loubards'* deviance, the second is "leurs regroupements en bandes, leurs attroupements" (their coming together in gangs, their gatherings) (Barreyre 22). The *bande* (gang), the suburban version of the angry horde at the city gates, features prominently in media reports, where it is associated with delinquency and vandalism, and it plays an equally important role in novels written by Franco-Maghrebi authors. In *La cendre des villes* and *La noce des fous*, for example, groups of suburban youths and police officers engage in a constant battle for the control of territory: "The police officers patrolled the streets to track down the adolescents. . . . From one street to the next, they insulted each other and looked each other up and down" (*La cendre* 74).[27] In these episodes, Mounsi portrays the traditional center as under siege, as the consequences of France's colonial policies are now felt on French soil. Indeed, the closer the *bandes* come to the city center, the more they are associated with transgression and illicit border crossing. In this fashion, young people of immigrant descent are portrayed as encroaching on the heart of the city--"they flocked towards the city from all the surrounding areas" (*La cendre* 75)[28]--in a collective attack whose causes are explained in *Les raisins de la galère*: "We no longer want to live outside the walls, relegated to the suburbs. . . . We're going to go into town" (Ben Jelloun 131-132).[29] "Descendre en ville"--descending on the city center--thus becomes a symbol of the second generation's demand for a legitimate place in French society and of their refusal to remain in the margins.

Mounsi emphasizes the futility of the center's attempts to put an end to these enemy raids by highlighting the determination of his protagonists: "In spite of the middle-class guards and the municipal police, they went there to carry out daring thefts" (*La noce* 80).[30] The metro, which takes the marginalized youths into the city center, serves as an image of their subversion and underground infiltration of space,[31] and the Châtelet-les-Halles area, home of the largest metro station in Paris, represents the invaded center. Here, "A group of shadowy, distorted figures climb out of the underground passageways"[32] to carry out their illicit appropriation of central space: "They pass through Beaubourg like a herd of wild animals shouting and roaring in the streets" (*La noce* 82).[33] Throughout this episode, Mounsi's use of common ethnic stereotypes related to contagion to create the contrast between his own compassion for the group's *errance* and its condemnation by the besieged inhabitants encourages the dislocation of traditional clichés by transposing them into a different register: "The Beaubourg bourgeoisie are terrified and disgusted. . . . The residents of the neighborhood live in constant fear of these pock-marked faces. .... They are afraid that they will one day be infected by these illnesses" (*La noce* 83).[34] It is in this context that Mounsi merges the world of Villon with that of modern Paris in order to create a parallel between the fate of the contemporary "enfants perdus" (lost children) (*La noce* 82) and the life of the medieval poet. The theme of injustice in particular is foregrounded through references to the Middle Ages-- instruments of torture, the Fountain of the Innocents, and the gallows that once stood at the gates of the city. The fact that the Les Halles police station--where the narrator and his friends are sometimes taken--stands on the same spot as one of the gallows encourages readers to ask how today's lost generation is being judged. By presenting such episodes from the perspective of the marginalized narrator, Mounsi underscores his reversal of sensationalist media accounts of similar events and their translation into a tragic vision of wasted lives and social injustice.

A parallel series of images uses clichés involving cleanliness and refuse. In the novels, the descriptions of the wasteland surrounding housing projects emphasizes the presence of trash, as Mounsi takes up the idea of the *banlieue* as the place where the Center dumps its garbage: "Where the gutters are full of stagnant water in which garbage, left-over food, crusts of stale bread, eggshells, bones, chicken carcasses, bottle tops, and rusty supermarket caddies are all piled up together. They [the young people] walk through unspeakable filth, where white linen and the foetuses of dead cats bleed, on the edge of the landfill where rats and evil feed" (*La noce* 77).[35] Such descriptions highlight the idea that in these suburban areas, "Lives are parked like the carcasses of cars" (*La noce* 21),[36] as poor immigrant families are equated with the impurities that must be kept out of the central core of society. Mounsi's insistent use of the parallels between immigrants and refuse, between garbage dump and the figurative wasteland, is again designed to elicit compassion rather than contempt, and to question the urban and social policies that have led to the marginalization of immigrant communities.

References to liquids and odors reinforce the image of the *banlieue* as garbage dump and sewer and are used to further undermine the concept of containment, particularly in relation to definitions of national identity. In a typical example in *La cendre des villes,* "Nadjim was born in the midst of one of these neighborhoods teeming with people whose exhalations smack you in the face. Everything that oozes, dampens, floods" (61).[37] Despite the efforts of Zaïmi's urban administrator (Le Grand Thérapeute), however, "the one who repairs the sewage system, who fixes the water supply by purifying the dirty water" (21),[38] the social sanitation system in Mounsi's Paris does not work well, and its contents constantly threaten to spill out into the city. Impossible to contain, like the contents of the underground sewage system, the young inhabitants of the *banlieue* filter into the fabric of the city and flow ineluctably towards the center: "the sons of immigration are inscribed into the asphalt of the town. They are secreted from the depths of its stones, the children of prophecy" (*Territoire* 90). In Mounsi's work, then, all borders leak, be they geographic, discursive, literary, or purely sanitational, and the margin relentlessly works its way towards the center, constantly shifting and reframing the terms of reference as it goes. For

Mounsi, unlike the mainstream media, this decentering is associated with the positive notion of prophecy rather than with apocalyptic images of destruction, and his vision of transforming the narrative of immigration is presented as both desirable and inevitable.

bell hooks has observed that "the space of refusal, where one can say no to the colonizer, no to the downpressor, is located in the margins" (341). Like hooks, Mounsi links margins, opposition, and renewal: "It is in the margins, in the border zones, that questions related to artistic creation are being raised again" (*Territoire* 83). In his work, the *banlieue* thus becomes synonymous with a textual space from which marginalization can be contested. In this sense, the expression "Territoire d'Outre-Ville" (Territory Beyond the City) also designates the realm of the imagination--"cette contrée de moi-même que je nomme 'Territoire d'Outre-ville' " (that country within myself I call "Territory Beyond the City") (*Territoire* 21). It is from this territory that Mounsi says no to those who seek to exclude him, and it is here that he composes the counter-narrative that stands in opposition to dominant discourses on immigration. For him, then, "Writing is the only act of resistance with the capacity to express my identity: that of a child of the 'peripheral Maghreb' " (*Territoire* 42).[39] He thus acknowledges the subversive potential of language as a means of decentering mainstream discourse: "It is for this reason that a child from the *banlieue* must make the French language his own. . . . We must fight with words to demystify the power of prejudice. Fight to the very end of the alphabet, from one idea to the next, one word to the next" (*Territoire* 80-81).[40] With its emphasis on language and its call for retranslation, Mounsi's work constitutes a powerful example of the ways in which authors of immigrant descent are "writing back" and are "describing empire" in contemporary France.[41] At the same time, Mounsi forcefully suggests what had been lost in the "subtitled" version and proposes a corrective immigrant narrative which envisages a place for the second generation within French society and French literature. As he reminds us, though, it remains to be seen whether the relationships between power, history, and geography will be modified as he hopes: "Only time will tell whether it was an advantage or a tragedy to be a child of immigration" (*Territoire* 41).

NOTES

1. The titles of these works contain intertextual allusions to the film *Hiroshima mon amour* and to Rimbaud's *Une saison en enfer*.

2. Although there are many types of suburb in France, the *banlieue* referred to by Jazouli and the media is always the same--the housing projects (*cités*) inhabited by the urban poor of immigrant origin.

3. "Hands Up," "End of the World," "The Suburban Time Bomb," "Explosive Suburbs," "Damned Suburbs."

4. "The Fundamentalists. France: Their Strategy in the Suburbs"; "France, Land of Islam. Suburbs under the Influence"; "The Suburbs: The Temptation of Fundamentalism." These examples are all cited by Azouz Begag and Christian Delorme in *Quartiers sensibles* (164).

5. "Combien d'habitants n'a-t-on pas vus ou entendus protester violemment contre les images, falsifiées ou déformées de leur vie, livrées en pâture aux médias?"

6. Born in Kabylia in 1951, Mounsi joined his father in Paris at the age of seven and grew up in the Nanterre shantytown. After a turbulent adolescence during which he spent time in prison, he became a singer and composer and used rock music to draw attention to the cause of the immigrant community. Recently, he has turned to writing and is the author of an autobiographical text *(Territoire d'outre-ville)* and several novels *(La cendre des villes, La noce des fous, Le voyage des âmes,* and *Les jours infinis).*

7. "est 'décentrée' une Ecriture qui, par rapport à une Langue et une Culture centripètes, produit un Texte qui maintient des décalages linguistiques et idéologiques."

8. "ce rapprochement incongru fut pour eux une expérience semblable à celle offerte à l'ethnologue découvrant le fragment d'une société indigène primitive . . . quelque chose comme 'le zonard joyeux dans sa jungle.' Près de nous, c'est certain, on pouvait goûter une forme très particulière d'exotisme."

9. In *The Empire Writes Back,* the authors emphasize this aspect of many anthropological accounts: "The danger in 'transcultural dialogues,' such as those represented by some traditional anthropological reports, is that a new set of presuppositions, resulting from the interchange of cultures, is taken as the cultural reality of the Other. The described culture is therefore very much a product of the particular ethnographic encounter—the text creates the reality of the Other in the guise of describing it" (59).

10. "L'étiquette 'Beur' a participé à présenter restrictivement ces jeunes comme un groupe homogène. Cette standardisation a notamment pu servir des desseins politico-idéologiques visant à les désigner comme réfractaires à l'intégration, voire à l'assimilation à l'identité nationale."

11. See Mireille Rosello's *Declining the Stereotype* for a discussion of the ways in which contemporary authors decenter stereotypes.

12. "Ah putain, si Emile Zola avait vu ça."

13. The allusions are to Rimbaud's poem "Aube" and Hugo's "Demain, dès l'aube."

14.   "Pour nous le Nil c'est la Seine
        Les pyramides c'est les HLM
        Les Cléopâtre de mon temps
        Ne se piquent plus au serpent
        La poudre est leur poison."

15. "N'ayez les cuers contre nous endurcis."

16. See, for example, Jocelyne Cesari: "De la bataille de Poitiers, événement mythique, inaugurateur de l'entité Europe, aux Croisades, se bâtit d'abord une vision polémique de l'ennemi politico-idéologique puis de l'hérétique" (13).

17. "Rue de la Truanderie où nous traînions, gisaient les squelettes des mauvais larrons que la terre vorace avait engloutis."

18. "C'est la vie errante des enfants perdus, comme celle du poète du temps jadis."

19. "Ils ajoutent de l'histoire à la géographie et de la géographie à l'histoire."

20. This silencing is highlighted in the title of Anne Tristan's account of October 1961, *Le silence du fleuve.*

21. This is the subtitle of Tristan's account of the events of October 1961.

22. The title of Leïla Sebbar's most recent novel, *La Seine était rouge,* is also an allusion to the events of October 1961.

23. "Ils pensent que la banlieue ne fait déjà plus partie de l'Hexagone, mais que cet anneau-là a déjà décroché et dérivé du côté du tiers monde."

24. "Nous étions une ligne de démarcation imaginaire, un équateur sur la circonférence du monde."

25. "Le Grand Thérapeute avait dessiné cette configuration des lieux il y avait bien longtemps. Il en était fier: il s'agissait d'éviter les contacts entre individus de race

différente. . . . La mise en quarantaine de certaines zones réputées dangereuses tuait dans l'oeuf les foyers d'infection avant que la mixité et le mélange des races ne viennent ternir le teint de rose des futurs concitoyens."

26. "A force de rôder dans les rues . . . nous errions, livrés à nous-mêmes. C'était notre existence que de divaguer au hasard."

27. "Les policiers arpentaient les rues pour traquer les gamins. . . . D'une rue à l'autre, ils s'insultaient et se mesuraient du regard."

28. "de tous les alentours ils affluaient vers la ville."

29. "Nous ne voulons plus vivre hors les murs, rélégués dans les banlieues. . . . Nous allons descendre en ville."

30. "Malgré la garde bourgeoise et la police municipale, ils venaient y opérer des vols audacieux."

31. See Rosello's *Infiltrating Culture* for a discussion of "the way in which infiltration as a metaphor can be used to resist power" (xii).

32. "C'est un cortège de formes indécises, distordues, qui grimpent des boyaux souterrains."

33. "Il passe à travers Beaubourg comme un troupeau de bêtes sauvages qui crient et rugissent dans les rues."

34. "Les bourgeois de Beaubourg sont épouvantés de dégoût. . . . Les résidents du quartier vivent dans la hantise de ces faces grêlés. . . . Ils craignent que ces maladies ne les infectent un jour."

35. "Là où coulent dans les caniveaux les eaux pourries où s'entassent les détritus, les amas de débris de ripailles, croûtons de pain rassis, coquilles d'oeufs, os, carcasses de poulet, tessons de bouteilles, caddies rouillés des supermarchés. Ils vont parmi les immondices où saignent des linges blancs et des foetus de chats morts, au bord de la décharge où se nourissent les rats et le mal."

36. "Les vies sont garées comme des carcasses de voitures."

37. "Nadjim était né dans les exhalaisons que ces quartiers grouillants vous lâchent au mufle. Tout ce qui suinte, humecte, inonde."

38. "celui qui restaure le système des égouts, qui refait les adductions d'eau en purifiant les eaux sales."

39. "Ecrire est le seul acte de résistance capable d'affirmer mon identité: celle d'un enfant du 'Maghreb périphérique.' "

40. "C'est pour cette raison qu'un enfant de la banlieue doit faire sienne la langue française. . . . Nous devons nous battre avec les mots pour démystifier la force des préjugés. Nous battre jusqu'au bout de l'alphabet, d'une idée à l'autre, d'un mot à l'autre."

41. The expressions "writing back" and "de-scribing empire" are from the titles of Bill Ashcroft, Gareth Griffiths, and Helen Tiffin's *The Empire Writes Back: Theory and Practice in Post-colonial Literature* and Chris Tiffin and Alan Lawson's *De-scribing Empire: Post-colonialism and Textuality*.

WORKS CITED

Ashcroft, Bill, Gareth Griffiths, and Helen Tiffin. *The Empire Writes Back: Theory and Practice in Post-colonial Literature*. London: Routledge, 1989.

Barreyre, Jean-Yves. *Les loubards: une approche anthropologique*. Paris: L'Harmattan, 1992.

Baudelaire, Charles. *Les fleurs du mal*. Paris: Garnier-Flammarion, 1964.

---. *Le spleen de Paris*. 1869. Paris: Livre de Poche, 1964.

Begag, Azouz, and Christian Delorme. *Quartiers sensibles*. Paris: Seuil, 1994.

Ben Jelloun, Tahar. *Les raisins de la galère*. Paris: Fayard, 1996.

Body-Gendrot, Sophie. "Fantasmatique de la ville dangereuse." *Urbanisme* 286 (January-February 1996): 58-60.

Boishue, Jean de. *Banlieue mon amour*. Paris: Table Ronde, 1995.

Boubeker, Ahmed, and Nicolas Beau. *Chroniques métissées*. Paris: Alain Moreau, 1986.

Cesari, Jocelyne. *Faut-il avoir peur de l'Islam?* Paris: Science Po, 1997.

Delarue, Jean-Marie. *Banlieues en difficultés: la rélégation*. Paris: Syros/Alternatives, 1991.

Fanon, Frantz. *Les damnés de la terre*. Paris: Maspero, 1961.

Fein, David A. *François Villon Revisited*. New York: Twayne, 1997.

Foucault, Michel. *Power/Knowledge: Selected Interviews and Other Writings, 1972-77*. Ed. Colin Gordon. New York: Pantheon, 1980.

hooks, bell. "Marginality as Site of Resistance." *Marginalization and Contemporary Culture*. Eds. Russell Ferguson, Martha Gever, Trinh Minh-Ha, and Cornel West. Cambridge: MIT Press, 1992, 357-366.

Jazouli, Adil. *Les années banlieues*. Paris: Seuil, 1992.

---. *Une saison en banlieue*. Paris: Plon, 1995.

Jelen, Christian. *Ils feront de bons Français*. Paris: Robert Laffont, 1991.

Lallaoui, Mehdi. *Les Beurs de Seine*. Paris: L'Arcantère, 1986.

Laronde, Michel, ed. *L'écriture décentrée*. Paris: L'Harmattan, 1996.

Maspero, François. *Les passagers du Roissy-Express*. Paris: Seuil, 1990.

Memmi, Albert. *Portrait du colonisé*. Paris: Pauvert, 1966.

Mounsi. *La noce des fous*. Paris: Stock, 1990.

---. *La cendre des villes*. Paris: Stock, 1993.

---. *Territoire d'outre-ville*. Paris: L'Harmattan, 1995.

---. *Le voyage des âmes*. Paris: Stock, 1997.

---. *Les jours infinis*. La Tour d'Aigues: L'Aube, 2000.

Rimbaud, Arthur. *Oeuvres*. Paris: Garnier, 1960.

Rosello, Mireille. *Infiltrating Culture: Power and Identity in Contemporary Women's Writing*. Manchester: Manchester University Press, 1996.

---. *Declining the Stereotype: Ethnicity and Representation in French Cultures*. Hanover: University Press of New England, 1998.

Sebbar, Leïla. *La Seine était rouge*. Paris: Thierry Magnier, 1999.

Tiffin, Chris, and Alan Lawson. *De-scribing Empire: Post-colonialism and Textuality*. London: Routledge, 1994.

Tristan, Anne. *Le silence du fleuve*. Bezons: Au nom de la mémoire, 1991.

Vieillard-Baron, Hervé. *Les banlieues françaises ou le ghetto impossible*. La Tour d'Aigues: L'Aube, 1994.

Zaïmi, Nordine. *Le tombeau de la folle*. Paris: L'Harmattan, 1995.

Voices of Change: Interlanguage in Franco-Maghrebi Texts

Farida Abu-Haidar

The main character of Rachid Djaïdani's novel *Boumkœur* (1999) describes the language used by his friend Grézi as being a mixture "du gitan, de l'arabe, du verlan et un peu de français" (of gypsy language, Arabic, backslang, and a little French) (45). He links this type of language to marginalization and to a particular generation: "Grézi's generation has invented such a complicated dialect that is almost impossible for me to understand it. Young people nowadays have become ghettoized with their hybrid speech" (45). This hybridity is also apparent in the intermingling of cultures in the areas of French cities where large numbers of immigrant families live, such as Barbès, the part of Paris described in Paul Smaïl's three novels: *Vivre me tue* (1997), *Casa, la casa* (1998), and *La passion selon moi* (1999). Smaïl's description of multi-cultural Barbès, where he grew up, strongly resembles Djaïdani's characterization of Grézi's speech as a mixture of diverse influences: "un semblant de New York, un bout d'Afrique, un peu de France" (resembling New York, a bit of Africa, a little of France) (*Casa* 27). In the texts to be examined in this chapter, language constitutes a central element of the immigrant experience, as different generations are portrayed coming into contact with French language and culture. Through their presentation of different types of language, Djaïdani and Smaïl explore the relationship between mainstream French and the "peripheral" forms of speech associated with immigrant communities. Most important, their self-conscious language practices highlight the desire of those relegated to the margins of society to make their voices heard and to legitimate their presence within French society and the French language.

Smaïl and Djaïdani are two of the most recent authors of Maghrebi origin whose work addresses the in-between position of immigrant communities in France. Djaïdani is himself of Sudanese and Algerian origin, while Smaïl is of Moroccan Berber descent, as is the narrator of his three novels, also called Paul Smaïl. Like most Franco-Maghrebi writers, Smaïl and Djaïdani "feel inhabited by two conflicting identities" (Ireland 1027). This is reflected in their texts through their use of a series of linguistic codes, many of which are typical of the hybrid "youth-speak" of the Parisian suburbs, a mixture I will refer to in this chapter as "interlanguage." While Smaïl combines colloquial French with Moroccan and literary Arabic expressions, as well as some German and Spanish terms, Djaïdani does not use much Arabic, but incorporates French and occasionally English words into his novel.

Interlanguage was initially defined as a discursive phenomenon, particularly in situations where forms of minority speech come into close contact with majority languages. For David Crystal, interlanguage is "a language system created by someone who is in the process of learning a foreign language. This intermediate state contains properties of both the first and the second language" (190). Pierre Goudaillier applies the same term--*interlangue*--to the "linguistic mosaic" of French urban areas, describing this hybrid language as including Maghrebi Arabic and Berber expressions (6).[1] In a similar move, Michel Laronde examines what he calls "intertitralité" (55), the presence of intertextual allusions in the titles of *Beur* novels. By extension, he looks at the significance of mother-tongue words in titles from this corpus, noting, for example, that *Le gone du Chaâba* (Begag, 1986) announces the hybrid nature of the protagonist and the text by combining the word "gone" (lad), a slang term from Lyon, with the Arabic term "Chaâba" (of the people), the name of a shantytown inhabited by members of the Maghrebi immigrant community.

Through their use of interlanguage, these recent authors of immigrant descent inscribe themselves into a literary tradition in which foreign words are introduced into a text written in French. Ever since Maghrebi literature written in French appeared in the 1920s, writers have been experimenting with the French language by introducing into it terms and expressions from their mother tongue. Such experimentation has often been described as a response to colonization and to the imposition of French as an official language. Najib Redouane, for example, argues that when mixed with terms from the native language, the use of French ceases to be problematic: "the mixture of languages noticeable in the writings of Maghrebian authors leads one to believe that, by repeatedly intruding into the text, the mother tongue is getting its own back" (87).[2] In the case of second-generation immigrants who were born and educated in France, the same strategies serve to foreground the hybrid nature of their identity and to make the French language their own. The importance of this move is evident when one considers that the French spoken by young people today contains a large number of Arabic terms, which testifies to the presence of the Maghrebi community in France.[3]

Interlanguage in Franco-Maghrebi texts has not received the attention it deserves. In her study entitled "Faux et défaut de langue," Sylvie Durmelat, for example, observes that its importance has not been sufficiently emphasized (29). Indeed, Begag's *Le gone du Chaâba*, discussed by both Laronde and Durmelat, constitutes one of the earliest and best examples of the use of interlanguage. This semi-autobiographical work, narrated by the young Azouz, who has the same name as the author, portrays the arrival of the Begag family and their gradual adaptation to life in France. Throughout the novel, Begag carefully re-produces the forms of speech used by first-generation Maghrebi immigrants, which include Arabic, French which is incorrectly pronounced, and a mixture of the two. The spellings used in the text convey the problems the parents in par-ticular have speaking French: "l'icoule pour li zafa" (school for the children) and "la fisite" (the visit) (240). However, as recent immigrants, their children too make mistakes in French. When asked by his teacher what his father did in Algeria, Azouz replies that he was a "journaliste" (journalist) on a farm, when he should have said "journalier" (day worker) (211), thus revealing his cultural and linguistic confusion. Similarly, Azouz thinks that some everyday Arabic words are in fact French. Answering questions in class about bathing, he says he uses "un chritte et une kaissa" (98). When the teacher does not understand, he explains: "C'est quelque chose qu'on met sur la main pour se laver" (It's some-thing one puts on one's hand while bathing) (99). On other occasions, mention of his parents or other older relatives seems to trigger switches to Arabic, par-ticularly when reported speech is involved: "Labaisse, labaisse, répond ma mère" (Fine, fine, my mother replies) (145).[4]

Other Franco-Maghrebi writers who use Arabic words in their texts as well as backslang and non-French terms include Akli Tadjer. His novel *Les ANI du "Tassili"* (1984) is a good example of a text in which interlanguage--colloquial French, and Arabic and English terms--occurs in the dialogue. The novel, which describes a Mediterranean crossing from Algiers to Marseilles aboard the Algerian ferry the *Tassili*, brings together a group of passengers who represent a range of positions on Franco-Algerian relations. One member of the group is an Algerian immigrant who, like Azouz's father, mispronounces French words, and Tadjer uses the same type of transcription as Begag to convey his difficulties with the language. He therefore writes "boulicier," "icoute," and "mon z'affaires," for example, instead of "policier" (policeman) (56), "écoute" (listen) (186), and "mes affaires" (my business) (186). In order to emphasize his hybrid identity as a second-generation immigrant, the narrator portrays himself as a "kabylo-parigot" (60) speaker, a self-description that underscores his intercultural and interlanguage skills. Although he is perfectly comfortable speaking French, he often uses Arabic words such as "zaama" (I presume) (59) and "redjla" (manly pride) (91). At the same time, he demonstrates his familiar-ity with the culture and language of the majority ethnic group: describing the passengers forming a line, he comments: "They've all come, they're all there, even the little Redhead, the accursed son" (99).[5] Here, he rephrases the opening lines of Charles Aznavour's song "La Mamma," substituting "Petit Rouget" for "Giorgio" and thus revealing his ability to manipulate French linguistic and cultural codes. Tadjer also displays a penchant for anglicisms, which he incorporates into French phrases, creating such expressions as "*son* speech" (his speech) (115), "*tout sera* clean" (everything will be clean) (134), and "*c'est pas ma* cup of tea" (it isn't my cup of tea) (134). This ludic international word-play further underscores the theme of interlanguage and presents the protagonist in a positive light, as a creator of new linguistic forms rather than as a poor translator.

The same emphasis on the immigrant writer as linguistic innovator appears in Smaïl's work. Arabic and other non-French terms appear throughout his three novels, recreating the polyglossic "youth-speak" of Parisian multi-ethnic suburbs. The interlanguage he uses mixes French street jargon with Maghrebi Arabic and the Anglo-Americanisms of Western youth culture. Smaïl draws attention to his use of popular terms through an intertextual reference to a dictionary of French slang, *Comment tu tchatches! Dictionnaire du français contemporain des cités* (1998), imagining that the cover of the dictionary refers to additions made to include "une dizaine d'entrées des exemples tirés de: *Vivre me tue*, de M. Paul Smaïl" (about a dozen entries of examples taken from *Vivre me tue* by Mr. Paul Smaïl) (*Passion* 139). Like Tadjer, Smaïl thus emphasizes the creativity of second-generation immigrants and their transformation of the French language to make it reflect their hybrid identity.

The setting of Smaïl's three novels is predominantly the densely populated north Parisian neighborhood of Barbès whose multi-racial inhabitants are compared to the "United Colors" of Benetton and are portrayed as "tous frères" (all brothers) (*Vivre* 41). The immigrant origins of this community are underscored in the description of its members as including Beurs, blacks and "zantilles, un Feuj... Et même un Français de souche aux yeux bleus" (and West Indians, a Jew... and even a real Frenchman with blue eyes). The setting thus reflects the multiplicity of cultures and identities that are part of the protagonists' daily lives and emphasizes that theirs is "un moi multiple et polyvalent, issu de la rencontre de cultures différentes les unes des autres" (a multiple and varied self born of the meeting of different cultures) (Delvaux 685). The multi-ethnic nature of Barbès is reinforced in the novels through the many allusions to historical events in Algeria and Morocco, to French and Arabic literature, and to popular music. Both Anglo-American pop songs and Algerian raï--"le raï, le vrai raï, pur et dur" (raï, authentic raï, the real thing) (*Casa* 28)--are quoted in the text, and many singers and other artists are referred to by name--the North Africans Cheb Khaled, Lounès Matoub, and Cheb Mami, and singers of Maghrebi origin born in France such as Rachid Taha, whose songs have immortalized Barbès; and Faudel, who was born in Mantes-la-Jolie and whose songs represent a form of interlanguage since they are "émaillées de mots français" (studded with French) (*Casa* 54) although written mainly in Arabic. Each novel also has an international dimension: Hamburg in *Vivre*, Casablanca in *Casa*, and Madrid and Toledo in *Passion*. However, although the narrator feels a close affinity with Spain because of its Arab history, it is Barbès which most corresponds to his sense of home. For him, Barbès is a "médina," an Arab city within Paris (*Casa* 98), and his examination of the consonants contained in the word Barbès links it to "Rebeu" (*Beur*) and "Berbère" (Berber) (*Passion* 48)--designations of Algerian identity from both sides of the Mediterranean. Furthermore, Barbès rhymes with the Maghrebi Arabic word *labès* (OK), and the narrator's word-play underscores the parallels between language and place: "Labès, labès, Barbès" (*Passion* 135), suggesting that the narrator is in his place (OK) in this area of Paris.

In Smaïl's work, interlanguage is particularly in evidence in expressions combining French and English or French and Arabic words. These recur frequently in all three novels: "bad boys dans les feuilletons" (bad boys in soaps) (*Vivre* 20), "je suis live" (I'm live) (*Vivre* 38), "par moi, myself" (by me, myself) (*Vivre* 180), "Half une patate" (half a potato) (*Casa* 15), "Huit hundred" (eight hundred) (*Passion* 23), and "Je te call un taxi" (I'll call you a taxi) (*Passion* 91). French and Arabic combinations include: "Je suis accueilli en mansour" (I was received as a victor) (*Casa* 33), "il veut jouer avec moi au moul dar?" (Does he want to play the role of owner of the house with me?) (*Casa* 88), "les cadeaux l'drari" (presents for the children) (*Casa* 174), "Des f'tours" (meals breaking the fast) (*Passion* 33), and "une vieille jadda" (an old woman, a grandmother) (*Passion* 78). Unlike Begag, however, Smaïl does not often give explanations or translations of the non-French words he uses, forcing the reader who is not familiar with Arabic to guess their meaning from the context. This serves to defamiliarize the French expressions, and new meaning is created through these transgressive combinations.

In addition, Smaïl's innovative style is characterized by alliteration, rhyme, punning, and general word-play. His rhymes, some of which recur as refrains, occasionally use words from only one language, but most often combine languages and cultural references: "Sueur, sciure, cire, cuir" (sweat, sawdust, wax, leather) (*Casa* 117), "mélange de sueur, de sciure, de cire, de cuir" (a mixture of sweat, sawdust, wax, leather) (*Vivre* 32), "la Ménara, la Médersa, la Médina... la merde, quoi!" (the Minaret, the School, the City... shit) (*Casa* 137). Even the word "humour" itself becomes a trigger for word-play, leading to the alliterative exclamation "l'humour, l'honneur, l'horreur!" (humor, honor, horror) (*Passion* 106). Like the rhymes, the puns and word-play reveal Smaïl's skill at manipulating language: "trois coups de fil sur son sans fil" (three calls on his cordless phone), "Smile Smaïl" (*Vivre* 12). In similar fashion, he sometimes uses a word from one language to imply a meaning in another, as when he turns the word for Shiite into an expletive--"Chiite" (*Casa* 84)--or playfully incorporates swear-words from different languages: "ouald al qahba!" (son of a bitch) (*Passion* 100) and "*hijo de puta!*" (son of a bitch) (*Vivre* 44) as well as the standard French "putain" (bitch), which recurs throughout the novels. The same playfulness appears when Smaïl extends the concept of inversion which characterizes *verlan* words to the structure of short sentences: "Toi chez? Moi chez?" (Place your or place mine?) (40), "Et ta famille revoir, jamais cherché tu as" (And your family, to see them again, never looked you have) (47). All three novels thus demonstrate the pleasure the narrator derives from playing with words and highlights his appropriation of the linguistic tools he needs to express his personal voice.

Like Begag and Tadjer, Smaïl combines sardonic humor with serious social and political commentary. In particular, the frequent code-switching in his novels creates a style that changes suddenly from the colloquial to the sentimental, from the humorous to the polemical. His often subversive word-play creates much of the social criticism. He coins words from King Hassan's and former Algerian president Zeroual's names, for example, in order to denounce their regimes--"Je suis hassanée," which implies harassment, and "Zero... ual," which emphasizes incompetence (*Passion* 35). Similar linguistic play is used to create the scathing criticism of racial and cultural prejudice, and of all those who consider themselves superior to others, including the French press, which, when Smaïl's novel was well received, immediately classified him as a writer from the *banlieue,* thus reinforcing the stereotypical distinction between mainstream authors and writers from the immigrant margins.[6] In order to demonstrate how this stereotype functions, Smaïl plays on both geographic and linguistic codes, pointing out that Barbès is in fact located within Paris while Neuilly is part of the *banlieue*: "Ces banlieusards de Neuilly, qui se croient Parisiens, pensent que Barbès est en banlieue! Khra!" (Those suburbanites from Neuilly, who believe they are Parisians, think that Barbès is in the suburbs! Shit!) (*Casa* 43). Here, the use of alliteration, and the sudden shift to the Arabic expletive "khra" rather than its French equivalent "merde," reinforces the sense of defamiliarization and the undercutting of traditional categories.

Smaïl employs similar strategies to denounce those who treat him and his Maghrebi friends with condescension. As in the previous example, he often does so by using Arabic insults such as "Haloufin!" (Pigs!) (*Passion* 90). On other occasions, when describing people he does not hold in esteem, he uses *verlan* terms like "chetron" (face) (*Vivre* 37), "loilpé" (naked, undressed) (*Vivre* 165), "n'importe oiq!" (it doesn't matter what) (*Passion* 65), "Pas de houdoûd pour oim" (no boundaries for me) (*Passion* 138), and "fiassepou" (prostitute) (*Passion* 152). Likewise, in *Vivre,* he mocks those who think that the young are not racist, and draws attention to the racial intolerance that sometimes occurs among young people from ethnic minorities. In this context, the use of words from different languages highlights the differences and possible tensions between the various groups: "white" (in English in the text), "Les Blackos" (Africans), "les Niaqs" (Vietnamese), and "des Francaouis" (majority French) (27). In one episode in particular, he lashes out at those who conceal their racist attitudes under a veneer of politeness. When the narrator's employer at a bookshop patronizingly gives him novels by Maghrebi authors, assuming this is the only type of literature he is likely to read, he responds angrily, shouting: "Mais vous, vous pouvez pas oublier deux secondes que je suis d'origine... C'est une obsession chez vous!" (But can't you forget for two seconds that my origin is... It's an obsession with you!) (*Vivre* 93-94). By purposely not naming his roots, he counts on the reader's ability to fill in the gap and foregrounds society's obsessive interest in designating immigrant origins. In this fashion, intercultural issues and interlanguage are inextricably linked throughout Smaïl's work and serve to undermine clichés about those of immigrant descent.

Although the world of Smaïl's novels is mainly bicultural, he uses references to other languages and cultures to reinforce his depiction of the multicultural nature of contemporary language. In *Vivre,* he incorporates phrases and words in German into the chapters set in Hamburg, and when talking about the Spanish boxing-trainer Luis, he uses Spanish expletives and imitates the Spaniard's speech in the same way that Begag represents the accents of first-generation Maghrebi immigrants: "Il soutient que 'la psyholochie, y est un truc de maricon, por les gonzesses, por les pédés' " (He maintains that "psychology is a matter for queers, for effeminates and gays") (*Vivre* 33). Here, Smaïl's transcription of Luis's French reproduces his accent--"psyholochie"--and his vocabulary errors (the Spanish "por" instead of the French "pour") and uses synonyms from the two languages: the Spanish "maricon" (queer) together with its French equivalent "pédé." Through its realistic depiction of an immigrant negotiating two languages, Smaïl's use of interlanguage in this episode both reinforces the comic tone and provides an element of authenticity. Indeed, Smaïl self-consciously draws attention to his use of interlanguage and other marginal forms of speech throughout his work, evoking it alongside allusions to literary and educated French: "le français de Barbès et le bon français, le français littéraire, le français des Marocains éduqués, le français de Marcel Proust" (the French of Barbès and good French, literary French, the French of educated Moroccans, the French of Marcel Proust) (*Casa* 60). In so doing, he highlights the ways in which language is used and encourages the reader to consider the place of his work in relation to that of Marcel Proust.

Djaïdani's *Boumkoeur* resembles Smaïl's novels in many respects, particularly as regards subject matter, setting, and the use of interlanguage. The novels written by both authors are all examples of self-referential fiction: the narrator of *Boumkoeur* (Yaz) is in the process of writing a novel and often comments on its progress, while Smaïl's main character, Paul, is the author of a text entitled *Vivre me tue* and often alludes to the critical reception of his work. Besides this fundamental resemblance, the two protagonists are both badly shaken by the death of a much-loved younger brother from an overdose of drugs, and both were inspired by the fantasy worlds of classic children's stories--*Treasure Island* and *Moby Dick* in Paul's case, and *The Jungle Book* in Yaz's. Furthermore, both narrators describe how difficult it is for children of immigrants to find employment, a situation which forces some of them to turn to illegal or demeaning work. Daniel, Paul's brother, takes up body-building in order to earn a living, exhibiting his body in backstreet nightclubs, while Yaz's sister sometimes resorts to prostitution, and his older brother, who makes money on the black market, was once a drug-dealer.

Although *Boumkœur* lacks the humor of Smaïl's works, it too uses colorful, innovative language to depict the world of a second-generation immigrant living with his parents on the periphery of French society in the kind of housing project most often associated with the *banlieue*--"a neighborhood where the tower blocks are so high that the sky seems to have disappeared. There are no leaves on the trees, everything around me is all gray" (9). His portrayal of his neighborhood is both realistic and disturbing, and quickly evokes the stereotypical, unpleasant atmosphere of the protagonist's environment: "urine and blood are discharged here like mushrooms. A pig couldn't live here without being afraid of swallowing nasty germs" (20).[7] Djaïdani uses fairly standard French when setting the scene, as Smaïl does when describing serious events such as the death of the narrator's father and brother, but as soon as he begins the narrative, he adopts the youth-speak of the neighborhood. The narrator's older brother, Aziz, for example, is described as someone who regularly "s'évapore de chez nous . . . il part vivre chez des meufs" (flies the coop . . . he goes to live with some chick) (12), and the narrator introduces himself in similar fashion: "J'ai stoppé l'école à seize piges, maintenant j'ai vingt et un hivers" (I quit school when I was sixteen, and now I'm twenty-one) (10). His explanations of why he is unable to find a job, in particular his lack of previous work experience, use colloquial expressions and play on the similarities between the French slang term "bosser" and the English word "boss"--"je n'ai pas vraiment eu l'occasion de bosser, pas assez d'expérience comme disent les boss" (I never really had the chance to work, not enough "experience," as the bosses say) (10). The colloquial language thus serves to highlight social problems and is used in this fashion throughout the novel.

Besides the youth-speak, many other characteristics of Smaïl's language recur in *Boumkoeur*, from the French-English hybrid expressions to the use of rhyme. Djaïdani frequently uses combinations of French and English to emphasize the influence of popular culture on contemporary colloquial French: "j'aurais bien aimé l'avoir comme brother, ce killer" (I would have loved to have had him as a brother, that killer) (44), "mes shoes" (my shoes) (81), "un sourire de welcome" (a welcoming smile) (54), and "un voyage aux States" (a trip to the States) (105). Although he does so less often than Smaïl, Djaïdani sometimes uses rhyme-- "mon seule arme fut les larmes" (tears were my best weapon) (14)--and *verlan* words such as "oinjs" (joint) (21), "reupe" (father) (69), "mirdor" (to sleep) (113), "ouam" (I) (113), and "tisgra" (free) (113) occur throughout the text. The characters themselves refer to their use of *verlan* and associate it with drinking and certain states of mind: "l'alcool crache mieux le verlan" (alcohol spits out *verlan* better) (21); "quand je suis énervé il réinvestit ma langue" (when I'm agitated it takes hold of my tongue) (58). Most importantly, *verlan* is presented as a form of language that should be readily understood as a variant of mainstream French: "si tu comprends pas ce que je te dis, moi je vais pas te parler à la Molière pour te dire que j'ai tué un mec" (if you don't understand what I am saying, I'm not going to speak Molière's French to tell you that I killed a guy) (45). The linguistic world of contemporary youth culture is further reinforced by the narrator's creation of colorful expressions relating to drugs and sex which range in tone from entertaining to vulgar: "il . . . dealait ses poèmes contre des orangeades glacées" (he . . . traded his poems for ice-cold orange drinks) (83); "le collègue s'est sodomisé les orifices avec des écouteurs qui éjaculent des lyrics explicites" (my friend sodomized his ears with a headset which ejaculated explicit sexual lyrics) (58). Finally, Djaïdani adapts well-known French sayings to the immigrant context, and his creation of intercultural proverbs, like much of Smaïl's word-play, foregrounds his adaptation of French to his own needs. In this fashion, the expression "L'habit ne fait pas le moine" (clothes don't make the man) becomes "C'est pas l'habit qui fait l'imam" (clothes don't make the imam) (26).

Like Smaïl's narrator, Yaz refers to the context in which his novel is written, alluding in particular to the majority culture's interest in suburban culture and the media images associated with it, and inviting the reader to reflect on the place of *Boumkoeur* in relation to this phenomenon--"en ce moment, c'est à la mode, la banlieue, les jeunes délinquants, le rap et tous les faits divers qui font les gros titres des journaux" (right now, the suburbs, young delinquents, rap, and all the incidents that make the headlines in the papers are really in fashion) (13). In this regard, he refers specifically to the film *La Haine* (21)--which was not made by a producer of Maghrebi origin but which uses the same kind of interlanguage and colloquial French as Djaïdani's novel--as an example of the way in which outsiders cash in on the world of the *Beurs*. These references echo Smaïl's ironic comment on media interest in *Beur* culture--"Basané frisé: succès assuré" (Dark-skin and curly hair guarantees success) (*Passion* 45).

In the work of all the authors discussed in this chapter, word-play and transformations of standard French constitute a form of subversion, a "prise de parole et de pouvoir" (Durmelat 29), through which writers of immigrant origin take control of a language they know well and shape it to make it their own. They are thus able to propose their own definition of themselves rather than allowing others to define them. In this sense, their novels portray a generational shift in which interlanguage moves from representing the difficulties immigrants have learning a new language to expressing the second generation's creation of new linguistic forms. By imitating their parents' incorrect pronounciation of French words, writers such as Begag draw attention to a generation that has been denied a voice in France. The parents in both Begag's and Djaïdani's novels are good representatives of this "génération du silence" (the silent generation), as Yaz remarks when he describes his father as "l'esclave qui souffrait en silence" (the slave who suffered in silence) (76). Their children, on the other hand, have claimed a voice and have become the spokespersons of both their generation and that of their parents. Their innovative use of language, the incorporation of their parents' speech patterns into their work, and their use of words from their parents' mother tongue is their way of valorizing a culture that has long been denigrated in France, while at the same time demonstrating their command of the French language. Their work thus testifies to the "overlapping territories and intertwined histories" that Edward Said sees as a defining characteristic of postcolonial societies and identities (720). In their novels, this intertwining manifests itself primarily in their ingenious use of an innovative, composite language whose vitality gives the immigrant voice a new vibrancy.

NOTES

1. Scholars such as Anne Donadey have pointed to the similarities between interlanguage and intertextuality: just as intertextuality designates a relationship between one text and another, interlanguage incorporates expressions from different languages.

2. "Le mélange des langues repérable dans les écrits des écrivains maghrébins permet de croire que, par des intrusions répétitives, la langue maternelle prend sa revanche."

3. See for example Farida Abu-Haidar's "Arabic Terms in Contemporary French: The Algerian Contribution" and Pierre Goudaillier's *Comment tu tchatches! Dictionnaire du français contemporain des cités*.

4. On the recommendation of the publishers, Begag has provided glossaries of French regional terms, Sétifian expressions, and words mispronounced by Azouz's father "as a reassuring gesture aimed at French readers" (Hargreaves 39).

5. "Ils sont venus, ils sont tous là, y'a même Petit Rouget, le fils maudit."

6. The term *banlieue* designates the suburbs where large numbers of immigrant families live.

7. "la pisse et le sang se déchargent ici comme des champignons. Un porc ne pourrait vivre là sans avoir à craindre de se gober un mauvais microbe."

WORKS CITED

Abu-Haidar, Farida. "Arabic Terms in Contemporary French: The Algerian Contribution." *Awraq* 13 (1992): 141- 155.

Begag, Azouz. *Le gone du Chaâba*. Paris: Seuil, 1986.

Crystal, David. *A Dictionary of Language and Languages*. Harmondsworth: Penguin, 1994.

Delvaux, Martine. "L'ironie du sort: le tiers espace de la littérature *beure*." *The French Review* 68.4 (March 1995): 681-693.

Djaïdani, Rachid. *Boumkœur*. Paris: Seuil, 1999.

Donadey, Anne. "The Multilingual Strategies of Postcolonial Literature: Assia Djebar's Algerian Palimpsest." *World Literature Today* 74.1 (Winter 2000): 27-36.

Durmelat, Sylvie. "Faux et défaut de langue." *Francophonie plurielle*. Quebec: Hurtubise HMH, 1995, 29-37.

Goudaillier, Pierre. *Comment tu tchatches! Dictionnaire du français contemporain des cités*. Paris: Maisonneuve et Larose, 1998.

Hargreaves, Alec G. "Writers of Maghrebian Immigrant Origin in France: French, Francophone, Maghrebian or Beur?" *African Francophone Writing*. Ed. Laïla Ibnlfassi and Nicki Hitchcott. Oxford: Berg, 1996, 33-43.

Ireland, Susan. "Writing at the Crossroads: Cultural Conflict in the Work of *Beur* Women Writers." *The French Review* 68.6 (May 1995): 1022-1034.

Laronde, Michel. *Autour du roman beur: immigration et identité*. Paris: L'Harmattan, 1993.

Redouane, Najib. "La littérature maghrébine d'expression française au carrefour des cultures et des langues." *The French Review* 72.1 (October 1998): 81-90.

Said, Edward. *Culture and Imperialism*. London: Vintage, 1994.

Smaïl, Paul. *Vivre me tue*. Paris: Balland, 1997.

---. *Casa, la casa*. Paris: Balland, 1998.

---. *La passion selon moi*. Paris: Robert Laffont, 1999.

Tadjer, Akli. *Les ANI du "Tassili."* Paris: Seuil, 1984.

The Post-Colonial Writer between Anonymity and the Institution: Inscriptions of the Author in Chimo and Paul Smaïl

Michel Laronde

After the author as social worker, the author as preacher! the author as saint! the author as Christ! the author as prophet! In truth, I tell you, this is Allah's promise... But it's a novel I wrote, an autobiographical novel, but a novel nonetheless![1] (Smaïl, *La passion selon moi* 61)

If Jesus Christ wanted the Gospels published today, he would not find a publisher. Hadj Chester Himes.[2] (Zitouni, *Attilah Fakir* epigraph)

The question of the place occupied in French culture by an author whose ethno-cultural roots lie partially outside the national boundaries of France has been an institutional issue since *Beur* literature first appeared in the 1980s. Several recent novels point to an evolution of the representation of the author in contemporary Arabo-French fiction.[3] In particular, new representations of writers of Maghrebi origin are being developed in the work of two authors writing under pseudonyms, Chimo and Paul Smaïl. Chimo's novels, *Lila dit ça* (1996) and *J'ai peur* (1997), constitute two complementary steps in this process--the inclusion of paratextual references to the circumstances of the publication of the first novel in the second contributes to the portrayal of an author figure. By inscribing himself in *J'ai peur*, Chimo, an author figure, counters a stereotype propagated by the Institution (the publisher and the media) in the paratext of *Lila dit ça.* This first novel demonstrates how the Institution has used a specific kind of discourse to control and--as seems to be the case here--to dismiss Arabo-French literature. A close examination of the framing of the novel, which takes the form of an "avertissement de l'éditeur" (note from the publisher),[4] reveals the way in which the Institution manipulates the image of the author. In an attempt to counter and to reappropriate the stereotypical image of a post-colonial immigrant author, the writer incorporates the figure of the author of Maghrebi origin, Chimo, into the second novel. In similar fashion, the publication of Paul Smaïl's *Vivre me tue* in 1997 marks the beginning of a trilogy[5] completed with *Casa, la casa* (1998) and *La passion selon moi* (1999), a trilogy which again contains a socio-cultural and political (self)-representation of the author by a writer who takes on a post-colonial angle. This is accomplished through a *mise en abyme* of the figure of the author that is given increasing prominence in each successive novel.

The work of both writers is also characterized by systematic references to the realities of the publishing world and the press associated with the publication of the novels. These five novels, therefore, can be viewed as seminal texts in the sense that they bring together two types of discourse: the one generated by the Institution, which restricts the literature of immigration to the domain of political writing[6] whose only referent is an actual ethnic and socio-cultural situation, and the other constructed by the immigrant writer in response to the former, which is an attempt to subvert, if not to completely erase, the Institution's image of a *Beur* or "immigrant" author to the benefit of the writer and his writing. Paul Smaïl's tactic, then, is to incorporate into his fiction, especially into the second and third novels, authentic paraliterary comments from the large number of newspaper articles generated by the advertising campaign that surrounded these works. Many of the articles use a sensationalistic style to raise questions about the nature of the novels and the identity of their author. This appropriation of real life comments and situations takes on sociological and political significance in that it constitutes one of the main techniques used by the writer to oppose the stereotypical representation of post-colonial immigrant authors promoted by the Institution with his own antinomic representation.

Bringing together these two authors in particular can also be justified from a sociological perspective: they are, to my knowledge, the only two anonymous authors in post-colonial literature in France. In addition, the fact that the five novels were published during the same period may herald a new form of positioning of Arabo-French authors within French culture. Borrowing Roland Barthes's metaphor of the death of the author, I would like to suggest that Chimo's and Paul Smaïl's novels are part of a discourse located at the intersection of the "death"[7] and subsequent "return" of a specific kind of author who has tried to carve out a niche for himself within French literature over the past two decades. The title of Chimo's second novel, *J'ai peur*, already contains an allusion to death and even to "a fear more intense than death" (196). In similar fashion, the textual matrix for the title of Paul Smaïl's first novel, *Vivre me tue*, which states "living kills me," is in fact the first line of a novel that was never written: "Today, I can only remember the first sentence: *living kills me* [*vivre me tue*]. However, I did not get much further than the first line. In three words, in fact, I had said it all" (140). This second comment in particular highlights the question of the author in relation to the theme of death. Given this shared emphasis on the nature of the author, then, investigating representations of the author, their manipulation, and their political and aesthetic value takes on major significance. Furthermore, the two writers have in common their portrayal in their first novel of a narrator in the process of becoming a writer, while their next novels depict this same character "experiencing" the professional and cultural status of being an author. In this sense, these works are coming-of-age novels in which the protagonist first learns how to write, then is faced with the role of the individual as author. In *Lila dit ça*, the first Chimo novel, the reader follows the narrator step by step as he writes the novel one is now reading--a familiar process for readers of twentieth-century fiction. At this stage, the comments of the writer-protagonist inscribed in the text are concerned with the writing process exclusively. In *J'ai peur*, however, the writer-protagonist also appears as the author-protagonist of *Lila dit ça*, and the narrative abounds in comments on both the writing process itself and on the function and status of the author. This material grounds Chimo's criticism of the Institution in the fiction. Similarly, Paul Smaïl's *Vivre me tue* presents a protagonist who is in the process of writing what he hopes will become a novel. Here again, comments on the writing process recur throughout the text and contribute to its structural organization. In the next two novels, the narrator's discourse on the Writer and the Author (considered now as entities rather than individuals)[8] permeates the text to the extent that political, cultural, and literary commentaries predominate over the purely descriptive quality of the text, especially in the last novel, *La passion selon moi*. The commentary incorporated into the fiction allows the writer to denounce the stereotype constructed *from the outside* by the publisher and the press in the paratext of *Lila dit ça*, and to reinscribe the oppositional figure of the author of immigrant origin *from the inside*, through the writing process.

INSTITUTIONAL ANONYMITY

> Who am I?
> Paul is my first name--a nasrani name, my father wanted it that way and I thank him for it every day--, Smaïl, my pen name, the name I have chosen for myself. In homage to Melville.
> My war name?
> In homage to Cervantes, Sidi Ahmed Ben Engeli.[9] (Paul Smaïl, *La passion selon moi* 173)

In the first novel attributed to Chimo, *Lila dit ça*, the anonymous author is first referred to in a "note from the publisher" where Olivier Orban, the director of Editions Plon, warns that the author, Chimo, "wishes to remain anonymous" and that he himself has "never met" him and does not know "anything about him." This paratextual space on the margins of the fiction allows the Institution to orchestrate a representation of the post-colonial author. Since the note indicates that the name of the author "is in the text," Chimo-the-protagonist becomes the figure around which the anonymous author, Chimo, is imagined.

This paratextual commentary, which fueled the controversy over the author (both this particular author and the post-colonial Author as a figure) created by the news media when the novel was first published, is centered around one fundamental uncertainty: Chimo's ethnic identity. Indeed, the pseudonym is disguised so well that it gives no clue as to the specific ethnic origin of the author. While it is clear that Chimo is not a typical "French" name, it is not typically Arab either; it resembles a nickname that sounds like a first rather than a family name, and it does not suggest any specific cultural references, although it does in some sense seem foreign. The numerous press releases that appeared at the time of publication clearly make use of the anonymous status of the author in order to construct *from the outside* an authorial figure that conflicts with that of a canonical French author. The publisher's decision to frame the text with this paratextual commentary further reinforces the stereotype of the writer of Maghrebi origin through an outrageously schematic analysis of the style of the novel. The debate over the author's identity thus revolves around an opposition set up by the media as a means of distinguishing between two contrapuntal images of the author: is he well-known or unknown, a professional or an amateur? To borrow the terms used in the "note," "are we dealing with an established author or with the first novel by a talented new writer?" These choices are reiterated when the "note" concludes that, because of the text's "stunning literary quality," the author must be "an established author," a statement reinforced on the back cover of the book where *Lila dit ça* is described as the work of "such a gifted unknown writer," or "a well-known writer wearing a mask." In an interview in *Le Monde* entitled "Chimo, a mysterious novice writer or a literary hoax?" (April 27, 1996), Olivier Orban returns to the established writer theory when he states: "[t]he structure and the beautifully crafted metaphors are not the work of an amateur but point to an experienced writer"--which leads to the now predictable conclusion that the novel is an elaborate hoax, a form of "mystification." Subsequently, in the French edition of *Flair* (July 8), Olivier Orban clarifies what he means by this: "If tomorrow someone told me that a young *Beur* wrote it, I would be the first to be surprised, even though this is not impossible. But personally, when I read the book, I said to myself right away that it was the work of an established writer." His syllogistic logic finally concludes that the author cannot be Arabo-French since the style of the novel *does* have aesthetic value. Following the same line of reasoning, it can be argued that since . the value of the novel as a sociological document is being questioned--novels by writers of immigrant descent are generally read as such--therefore it cannot possibly have been written by an Arabo-French author.[10]

Even at this early stage of my discussion, I am tempted to suggest that the publisher's framing of *Lila dit ça* in terms of authorial identity has two potential political effects. It could be considered as the first attempt by a publisher, and by the press following his lead, to polemically (symbolically) exclude post-colonial authors from inclusion in contemporary French literature. This attempt at erasure uses a rhetorical strategy that manipulates the anonymous author in two ways: on the one hand, the post-colonial dimension of the author is effaced when the aesthetic worth of his style is recognized, since the reading public is reminded that Arabo-French authors are not capable of producing works of aesthetic value; concomitantly, the press also deplores the novel's lack of documentary value that has traditionally been identified as the hallmark of *Beur* writing. In this sense, the Institution signs the "death warrant" of Arabo-French authors by rendering them anonymous--and here, I am using "death" in the sense of obliterating the Individual by making him invisible.

The second political effect is a corollary of the first: while the institutional framing of *Lila dit ça* causes the figure of the Arabo-French author to literally "disappear," it paradoxically resurfaces unchanged in its original 1980s form, as if the question of its very *existence* was again being raised. At that time, the corpus of what was then known as *Beur* literature was generally labeled "ethnographic"--in order to gain recognition, *Beur* authors had to restrict themselves to the narrow path of being *ethnographes de banlieue* (inner-city ethnographers). Indeed, the presence of a *Beur* author in the literary world is deemed "natural" only when his or her text can be classified as an authentic sociological document akin to autobiography in both its style and content. Since institutional rhetoric portrays Chimo's work as devoid of these qualities, he appears as a figure of a non-canonical non-French author. Because the media expect rigid adherence to an "autobiographical pact," where the space between author and writer is obliterated, *Beur* texts are almost always classified as forms of autobiographical writing: confessions, life stories, diaries, and testimonies. Expecting authors of immigrant origin to conform to this image means they are made to fit a predefined mold which determines and limits the way their texts are read. For the Institution, then, the Author-as-Person takes precedence over the writer, who is seen as a mere reflection of the Author-as-Person. This privileging of the author as real person over the writer has important consequences for post-colonial authors, and for their literary production. It effectively bars from Franco-French literature an entire corpus of texts which are evaluated in terms of their autobiographical content (the Author-as-Person) rather than on the aesthetic merits of the text (the role of the writer). The nature of this discourse both explains and justifies post-colonial writers' reversal of institutional rhetoric as a counter-strategy. In *La passion selon moi*, the author-protagonist Paul Smaïl summarizes this dialectics of authorship in concise formulaic fashion: "Si je rate mon livre, je suis rebeu, si je le réussis, écrivain français... Ou le contraire? Question" (If my book is a failure, I'm a *rebeu*, if I do a good job, I'm a French writer... Or is it the reverse? Who knows?) (156). Smaïl's formula, with its play on institutional logic and its two complementary propositions, opens up the possibility of a "third space" somewhere between *Beur* and *écrivain français*, which could perhaps be designated by the median term "Arabo-French." In this sense, I would suggest, the contemporary post-colonial author--part *rebeu* and part *francaoui*--may prove to be a very successful "parasite."[11]

FROM WRITER TO AUTHOR: A PARADIGM OF INSCRIPTION IN THE TEXT

> I reread the last lines:
> I congratulate myself for choosing exile, and silence. Three publishers were fighting over my book, and I quickly understood the risk I ran: that of becoming the token Beur, the fashionable Beur, the good Beur! So I signed on with the one who guaranteed me my anonymity and gave me enough money to live here and start writing again.[12] (Paul Smaïl, *Casa, la casa* 146)

The post-colonial author writing from within French culture now faces the task of breaking the autobiographical pact that binds the Author to his Work. In order to create a place for the process of writing (*Ecriture*), the writer must open a space between the Author and his Work. His task, therefore, is to reverse the causal relationship suggested by the Institution which asserts that the Author *is* the Work and that the Work does not go *beyond* the Author. If the inscription of the Author in the novels under consideration does indeed respect the equivalence between Protagonist, Writer, and Author required by the auto-biographical pact, then it would confirm the institutional argument and would not constitute a counter-discourse. On the other hand, if the self-representation establishes a distance between Protagonist, Writer, and Author, who all appear as distinct entities, then the writing process may move to the forefront and take on a new dimension, thus signifying a shift--in terminology as well as in ideol-ogy--from "*Beur* novels" to "Arabo-French literature," and thereby creating a type of counter-discourse.

In order to circumvent the autobiographical Author-as-Person con-structed by the Institution, Chimo appropriates the figure created in the paratext of *Lila dit ça* and incorporates it into his writing. Each novel has a role to play in this two-step process: the first step, which I described above, consists of the publisher's setting up a figure of the author *outside the text*, thus creating a stereotype, while in the text itself, Chimo appears as a writer-protagonist, a fig-ure of the writer in the process of writing a novel. This inscription of the writer stands in direct opposition to the representation of the author constructed in the paratext. The situation shifts in the second novel, *J'ai peur*. Here, the figure of the Arabo-French author which the Institution grafted onto the first novel is reappropriated in the form of a narrator--again called Chimo--who is portrayed as both the author of the earlier novel and the writer of the second. The same tech-nique is used in Smaïl's first two novels. His first text presents a writer-protagonist called Paul Smaïl who is in the process of writing *Vivre me tue*. Since there is no external paratextual commentary, however, no counter-discourse is conveyed in this first novel alone. The second step, which occurs in *Casa, la casa*, consists of the creation of an inscribed author-protagonist who reappears in the third novel, *La passion selon moi*, as a process of *mise en abyme*.[13]

In rhetorical terms, both writers adopt the same dialogical strategy of using an inscribed author in order to decenter the figure constructed by the me-dia. The post-colonial writer initially manifests his presence in the first novels, *Lila dit ça* and *Vivre me tue*, in the form of a writer-protagonist. In the later novels, the role of the writer figure expands to include that of author-protagonist, thus generating a discourse on the representation of the Author and engaging in a critique of the literary Institution. This suggests the following paradigm for the empowerment of post-colonial authors:

real world	*fictional world*	*real world*
the writer→	[writer-protagonist→author-protagonist]→	the author-as-person

The originality of the strategy is not so much that it inscribes the fig-ure of the author of the first novel into the narrative of the second in combina-tion with that of the writer, but rather that the figure is used to filter the institu-tional discourse on the Author. In this sense, Chimo's writing reaches its high-est rhetorical potential in the second novel when it appropriates the figure of the author created by the Institution in the paratext of the first. The first chapter of

J'ai peur refers explicitly to the media attention surrounding the publication of *Lila dit ça*, alluding to its sensational success in France and abroad, using the real name of the publisher to underscore the role Plon editor Olivier Orban played in the controversy, discussing the questions raised about the identity of the author, and recalling the accusations of plagiarism.[14] Although it does not occupy the conventional position of a paratext, this first chapter functions as one since it contains the kind of commentary traditionally found in a paratext and is all the more rhetorical because of its ambiguous status. By serving as a *mise en abyme* of *Lila dit ça*, it gives the later novel an ironic dimension which decenters the institutional representation of the author. While Smaïl's *Vivre me tue* is not framed by a "note from the publisher," his second novel contains similar material of a paratextual nature, with the difference that it is not concentrated solely in the first chapter, but is disseminated throughout the text. Like *Vivre me tue*, *Casa, la casa* contains references to the institutional discourse surrounding the publication of the first novel, including press commentaries, exchanges between the author and the publisher, and media assumptions as to who the anonymous author might be.

At this point, it is tempting to associate the strategy used by these two post-colonial writers with that deployed by Luis Borges in "Borges and I"[15] when he establishes a series of distinctions between the real Person, the private "I," and the first-person narrator, on the one hand, and the Author, the public "I," Borges, on the other. It also recalls Roland Barthes's tactic in *roland BARTHES par roland barthes*,[16] in which he distinguishes between Roland Barthes-the writer and the Roland Barthes who is the subject of the narrative. In this context, the author-protagonist Paul Smaïl expresses this same duality: "I was... how should I put it?... detached. It was me and it was not me. I was looking at myself doing it. I was becoming double. Just as in boxing: me, and the one who is fighting, you see? Or like a novelist, if you prefer: me, and the hero of the novel. Two men in one" (*Passion* 21).[17] And also, in a still vague manner, I wonder if the role Mikhaïl Bakhtine attributes to the locutor in the novel, the one of "a *social individual,* historically concrete and defined," who is "always, on different levels, *an ideologist,*" who "always represents a special point of view on the world,"[18] would not open up a distinction between Author and Writer. By adopting the strategy of categorizing the Author as the physical and social individual, and the Writer as the private and creative side of the person who writes, the post-colonial writer may be able to develop an authorial dialectics that counters the one proposed by the Institution and that allows him to displace the all-powerful presence of the Author without necessarily proclaiming his "death." To a certain extent, in Chimo's and Paul Smaïl's novels, the place given to the writer figure recalls Barthes's notion of the *scripteur*, but whereas this "scriptor" plays a somewhat passive, mechanical role in the writing process, the post-colonial version is active and his role is political.[19]

"Being" an author, then, is a status that depends on the function of "being" a writer. Without the pivotal function of writer, there is no author, only a Person with no status. It is by active empowerment through writing that the writer is able to create the author. The author is an individual who has found a *status* and only the *function* of writer can give him that status. The writer inscribes himself as a figure through self-representation(s) in the writing, and representation(s) of self as a function reverberate(s) onto the figure of the author as

"Person" (which recalls Roland Barthes's "Individual"). Rather than a direct cause-effect relationship where the author, "being" the writer and "creating" the works, is "present" *ipso facto* as a figure in the writing, a chain is established between the author and the writing, a chain which necessarily originates in the writer who generates it. Producing writing at one end of the chain, the writer is also able to produce the figure of the author at the other end. Without a writer, there is no writing and no author. The figure of the author "resurfaces" in the text through the act of the writer. Therefore, in the act of writing, a paradigm opens up between the two poles marked by writer and author in the real world, and it accounts for the dialogic position occupied by the writer-protagonist. Because its function is creative, the writer-protagonist is the one to comment on the author-as-Person whose function is social. And since the author-as-Person is a reality twice removed in post-colonial literatures in France, because its position in the writing process is tropological, it will play an original and primary role as a support for a critique, or at least for an ideological decentering, of the French literary Institution, and consequently of the literary canon as well. (This would require another study centering not on the author-protagonist but on the writer-protagonist.[20])

In conclusion, the anonymity of the inscribed authorial figure, which is used to question the stereotypical representation of post-colonial authors, signals a new direction for literature by post-colonial authors and suggests a move towards reexamining the familiar theme of the Institution's refusal to recognize Arabo-French writing as having aesthetic value. The two authors discussed in this chapter both exploit the space at the intersection of anonymity and biography to counter the Institution's classification of their work as social documentation. Chimo and Smaïl make reference to ethno-cultural origins in order to complement biographical information on the anonymous author and use it as a means of debunking stereotypes and of creating a counter-discourse. In this fashion, the "return" of a non-canonical, non-Franco-French author opens up a potential space for dialogue and introduces a new type of text which could be called ethnobiography.

NOTES

1. "Après l'auteur en animateur socioculturel, l'auteur en prédicateur! l'auteur en saint! l'auteur en Christ! l'auteur en prophète! En vérité, je vous le dis, c'est la promesse d'Allah... Mais c'est un roman que j'ai écrit, un roman autobiographique mais un roman!" All translations are my own.

2. "Si Jésus-Christ voulait publier les Evangiles aujourd'hui, il ne trouverait pas d'éditeur. Hadj Chester Himes."

3. To those readers who may object to the designation *arabo-français* for the same reasons as they might object to the term *Beur*, I will respond with a quotation from one of Paul Smaïl's novels wherein the protagonist, who also dislikes the term *Beur* but continues to use it, describes Lili Boniche's songs in *La passion selon moi* as: "Du judéoaraboandaloufrancaouitzigane" (167). My choice of *arabo-français* (Arabo-French) rather than *beur* is intended to underscore the evolution of a type of literature, not of an ethnic or social group. Furthermore, the term Arabo-French creates a parallel with "Afro-French" (*afro-français*), as one might say Afro-American and "Franco-French" (*franco-français*), and takes on cultural rather than ethnic connotations. For a discussion of the value of these terms, see Michel

Laronde's "Les littératures des immigrations en France: questions de nomenclature et directions de recherche."

4. Here the *éditeur* is both the publisher of Editions Plon and editor of the text; in the *avertissement*, he explains how the text was edited.

5. A fourth novel by Paul Smaïl is announced in the text of the third: "I will write other books: an idea for a novel came to me last night, when I saw the outline of a body marked in chalk on the asphalt in front of Les Sables d'Or. And a title: *H'Nana*" (*Passion* 168). What leads me to read this comment as real information is that the fourth novel is listed under the title *H'Nana* in a section of the paratext called "By the same author" and under the designation "To appear." As I try to illustrate my reflections on the tensions and elasticity between Institution and post-colonial author, text and paratext, fact and fiction through literary, editorial, and journalistic data, details such as this should not necessarily be considered insignificant.

6. I am using the word "political" in the same sense as Roland Barthes in *Le degré zéro de l'écriture* to describe a type of writing "whose role is to connect in one go the reality of actions with the ideality of ends" (22).

7. See Roland Barthes's "La mort de l'auteur." My reference to "return" is an allusion to Sean Burke's title *The Death and Return of the Author*.

8. I will use capitals with terms like "Author," "Writer," and "Person" when I perceive them as representations rather than individual entities. This is important, for example, when one wants to locate the possible presence of a stereotype. As for the term "Institution," I see it here as a symbol of control and power.

9. "Qui suis-je?

Paul est mon prénom--un prénom nasrani, mon père l'a voulu ainsi et je l'en remercie chaque jour--, Smaïl, mon nom de plume, le nom que je me suis choisi. En hommage à Melville.

Mon nom de guerre?

En hommage à Cervantès, Sidi Ahmed Ben Engeli."

10. For a critical study of the paratext in *Lila dit ça*, see Michel Laronde's "La littérature de l'immigration et l'institution en 1996: réflexions à partir du paratexte de *Lila dit ça*."

11. The words *rebeu (beur), francaoui (français)*, or "parasite" are not used here with any intention of disparaging post-colonial authors. I am using the term "parasite" in the same sense as Michel Serres does, as a type of osmosis where fusion takes place between heterogeneous elements that come into contact with each other and are modified in the process. This phenomenon is evident in the way in which the modification of the designations *français* and *arabe* have given rise to the term *beur*, and more recently *beur* and *français* have been transformed into *arabo-français*. (See Michel Serres's *Le parasite*.)

12. "Je relis les dernières lignes:

Je me félicite d'avoir choisi l'exil, et le silence. Trois éditeurs se disputaient mon livre, et j'ai compris très vite ce que je risquais: devenir le beur de service, le beur à la mode, le bon "beur"! Alors j'ai signé avec celui qui me garantissait l'anonymat et me donnait assez d'argent pour vivre ici et me remettre à écrire."

13. The *mise en abyme* continues as a projection towards the future, with the announcement of a novel to come, *H'Nana*; the announcement is made both in the novel itself and by the publisher in the list of works by the author. The references to *Vivre me tue* as an aborted novel and as the title of the novel one is actually reading constitutes another form of *mise en abyme*. Various forms of *mise en abyme* are at the heart of post-colonial counter-discourses.

14. "Others said I had copied someone else's work, my lawyer even says there will be a trial" (Chimo, *J'ai peur* 11). The references to plagiarism are not as clear in *Casa, la casa*, but it is suggested, for example, in the following allusion to

"the rats who have doubted my existence or, at least, the fact that I was able to write my book alone" (23). Plagiarism is a "crime" that several post-colonial authors, especially in France, have been accused of in recent years.

       15. Jorge Luis Borges's *Dreamtigers*. See also Sean Burke's *The Death and Return of the Author*.

       16. See, for example, "Moi, je" (170). Barthes's title also plays with typography and capitalization to create the same effect.

       17. "J'étais… comment dire?… détaché. C'était moi et ce n'était pas moi. Je me regardais faire. Je me dédoublais. Comme à la boxe: moi, et celui qui se bat, tu vois? Ou comme pour un romancier, si tu préfères: moi, et le héros du roman. Deux hommes en un."

       18. Mikhaïl Bakhtine, "Le locuteur dans le roman," 153. The italics are in the text.

       19. See Barthes's "La mort de l'auteur" and "Ecrivains et écrivants." The post-colonial writer figure also resembles the *écrivant*, who Barthes defines as belonging "to a new group, the owner of public language" (148). However, neither concept adequately describes the post-colonial writer. The hybrid *écrivain-écrivant* (author/writer) comes closest to doing so: "We want to write something, and at the same time, we just write. In short, our time is giving birth to a bastard figure: *l'écrivain-écrivant*. His function is necessarily paradoxical: he both provokes and exorcises" ("Ecrivains et écrivants" 153).

       20. Ahmed Zitouni's *Attilah Fakir* would have to figure prominently in such a study. The protagonist of the novel is poised in the ambiguous position of a writer who has just published a novel and must accept or refuse the social function of being an Author: he has been invited to appear on a television show that promotes new authors, and the novel spans the five days that lead to his appearance on the show.

WORKS CITED

Bakhtine, Mikhaïl. "Le locuteur dans le roman." *Esthétique et théorie du roman*. Paris: Gallimard, 1978, 152-182.

Barthes, Roland. "Ecrivains et écrivants." *Essais critiques*. Paris: Seuil, 1964, 147-154.

---. "Ecritures politiques." *Le degré zéro de l'écriture*. 1953. Paris: Seuil, 1972, 18-24.

---. *roland BARTHES par roland barthes*. Paris: Seuil, 1975.

---. "La mort de l'auteur." *Le bruissement de la langue*. Paris: Seuil, 1984, 63-69.

Borges, Jorge Luis. "Borges and I." *Dreamtigers*. 1964. Austin: University of Texas Press, 1998.

Burke, Sean. *The Death and Return of the Author*. Edinburgh: Edinburgh University Press, 1992.

Chimo. *Lila dit ça*. Paris: Plon, 1996.

---. *J'ai peur*. Paris: Plon, 1997.

Laronde, Michel. "Les littératures des immigrations en France: questions de nomenclature et directions de recherche." *Le Maghreb littéraire* 1.2 (1997): 25-44.

---. "La littérature de l'immigration et l'institution en 1996: réflexions à partir du paratexte de *Lila dit ça*." *Etudes francophones* 14.1 (Spring 1999): 5-25.

Serres, Michel. *Le parasite*. Paris: Grasset, 1980.

Smaïl, Paul. *Vivre me tue*. Paris: Balland, 1997.

---. *Casa, la casa*. Paris: Balland, 1998.

---. *La passion selon moi*. Paris: Robert Laffont, 1999.

Van Renterghem, Marion. "Chimo, mystérieux écrivain débutant, ou supercherie
    littéraire?" *Le Monde,* April 26, 1996.
Zitouni, Ahmed. *Attilah Fakir.* Paris: Souffles, 1987.

Le jeu de piste: Tracking Clues to the Emergence of Maghrebi-French Literature in Farida Belghoul's *Georgette!*

Mark McKinney

CLASSIFYING AN EMERGENT LITERATURE

Maghrebi-French fiction is difficult to classify, mainly because of a general tendency to group literary works according to an author's nationality or ethnicity, and because of uncertainties regarding the ethnic and national identities of the authors. The difficulty stems in part from the complexity of classifying fiction about emigration/immigration from a formerly colonized nation. For example, does a text belong to the national literature of the ancestral homeland or rather to the country to which the author or her/his parents migrated? These problems of classification become apparent when one considers the following two examples. First, adopting the backslang term *Beur* (from "Arabe") to refer to the Maghrebi-French and their fiction is an oblique way of referring to their North African origins without saying "Maghrebi," "North African," "Muslim," or "Arab," designations which have become stigmatized in France through colonial and neo-colonial usage. Secondly, when Alec Hargreaves adopted the term *Beur* in order to define a literary category, his use of a variety of criteria (ethnicity, social class, cultural influences) excluded from *Beur* fiction works by Maghrebi authors whose formative early years were not spent in France or Belgium (Driss Chraïbi, Leïla Sebbar, and Ahmed Zitouni, for example), arguing that they produced fiction of a very different nature from that of *Beur* writers.[1] In both these cases, a radical distinction is made between certain Maghrebi communities and cultures in France and those in North Africa. While not wishing to abandon this often useful distinction altogether,[2] I would like to question its strict either/or logic, and propose instead the alternative term "Maghrebi-French," along with a more flexible continuum that combines North African and French components, as well as allowing for other influences. In this chapter, I will analyze the problematic categorization and critical reception of this body of ethnic minority fiction through a reading of Farida Belghoul's novel *Georgette!*, which was well-received by reviewers in France and won a literary prize, both because of its literary value and of its perceptive treatment of such issues surrounding the emigration of Algerians to France as the colonial roots of emigration and contemporary anti-Maghrebi racism, the injustices resulting from state-sponsored French assimilationism, and problems related to gender existing in an Algerian-French immigrant milieu.

Gilles Deleuze and Félix Guattari's *Kafka: Toward a Minor Literature*, has been an influential theoretical model for categorizing and analyzing literature by minorities (colonized people and immigrants, for example) who write in the dominant group's language. Indeed, in an article entitled "La littérature issue de l'immigration maghrébine en France: une littérature 'mineure'?," Hargreaves argues that one of Belghoul's public statements[3] raises the possibility that fiction by French writers of North African heritage constitutes a "minor literature," in Deleuze and Guattari's sense of the term (27).[4] His analysis of *Beur* texts, however, determined that this was not in fact the case, mainly because he discerned no signs of radical Maghrebi alterity in them. However, surprising new evidence warrants reopening the debate and suggests that defining Maghrebi-French fiction along strict national and ethnic lines is problematic when it minimizes the cultural hybridity of the texts and thereby obscures its potential affinities with other literary formations.

Georgette! is the story of the narrator, an unnamed seven-year-old French girl of Algerian descent who lives in Paris with her family. Her father cleans streets for the city of Paris, for which he started working during the Algerian War, and her mother has an unspecified job outside the home. The novel, which covers one school day, is told in the first person and is composed of three sections--the first two are set mainly in a public school, whereas the third describes the narrator's flight from school and her teacher, towards home. The narrator never reaches home, however, but is run over by a car as she crosses a street. The final sentence of the novel, which is not followed by any punctuation, appears to leave the ending open to interpretation.

A CHILD'S PERMISSION TO NARRATE

In her novel, Belghoul successfully confronts what Deleuze and Guattari term "the problem of immigrants, and especially of their children, the problem of minorities" (19) who express themselves in a "dominant" language that feels foreign. By injecting the minor languages of Maghrebi and French oral cultures into the dominant language of the French novel, she disrupts the conventional patterns of written literary expression, thereby creating a sophisticated means of self-expression--"a deterritorialized language, appropriate for strange and minor uses" (Deleuze and Guattari 17) such as subverting hegemonic cultural norms. The narrator, a young girl, resembles the author in several ways:

both are working-class Maghrebi-French of recent immigrant background who use story-telling to convey a marginalized perspective on French society; both narrator and author occupy a vulnerable position and, according to the logic of the unidirectional communication model associated with assimilationist ideology, neither has "permission to narrate" (Said 1984). In *Georgette!*, however, the narrator's ability to tell stories--to narrate--serves as a potent weapon as she attempts to work out an autonomous position between her teacher and father, who represent an intractable opposition between French and Algerian cultures and national identities.

The narrator's story-telling technique is part of her quest for autonomy, because it lets her interpret school events and attitudes in terms of her home experiences and values, thus creating an interface between her "milieu de contre-référence" (Maghrebi culture) and her "milieu d'adoption" (mainstream French society) (Belghoul, interview 32-33). The constant movement back and forth between her recollections of earlier incidents at home and events in the present at school as her day unfolds underscores her negotiation of the two "milieux,"[5] as she desperately tries to create an interface between what she learns at school and what she learns at home. For example, she mentally compares learning to read, orally summarize, and write about stories in French at school with learning to write and recite Koranic verses in Arabic at home, and this comparison suggests she is weighing the egalitarian ideology, individualistic competition, and secularism learned at school against the patriarchal hierarchy, communal cooperation, and religious piety she observes at home. When finally confronted with her teacher's determination to exclude Maghrebi culture from the public sphere, though, the narrator rebels and runs away from school.

Although learning to write in French is ultimately revealed as culturally alienating,[6] the girl does progressively hone her ability to tell stories and read culture, which becomes her principal survival technique. A crucial dimension of her narrative skill is her use of traditional tales about ogres told on both sides of the Mediterranean. The narrator's brother first speaks of ogres while the two children wait for their mother to meet them. When the boy tells his sister that no ogre would want to eat her because she has "cuisses de grenouille" (frog's legs) (92) and is therefore too meager a morsel, she says ominously that as frogs both she and her brother would constitute potential food for ogres. Having learned that the "others" (European-French) eat frogs, she believes that she and her brother are in danger of being eaten. However, the narrator is not yet able to answer her brother's question: "Qui c'est les autres?" (94). The novel's play on ethnic insults (the French as frogs), culinary traditions, and idiomatic expressions conveys the narrator's attempts to make sense of her position as a member of an ethnic minority.

In the third section of the novel, when the girl has left school and is running home, the ogre theme recurs in two passages where the narrator describes her teacher in metaphorical terms. In the first, she imagines her teacher as a cannibal--another incarnation of the ogre--who here eats frogs, including the narrator.[7] The upshot of this, in the narrator's mind, is that she will not be buried as a Muslim--which can be interpreted to mean a loss of cultural identity. Instead, she will remain forever alienated from Maghrebi-Islamic cultural traditions, which are often not accommodated by dominant French institutions such as schools, which are described as cannibalistic.[8] In the second passage, the narrator imagines the teacher as a dog-ogre driving through the streets of Paris looking for her prey (the little girl): "That woman at the wheel is a bulldog/ball-of-an-ogre. She's a big dog who likes to cook frogs" ("Cette femme au volant c'est un boule-d'ogre. C'est un gros chien qui adore cuisiner les grenouilles") (140).[9] In this passage, the narrator uses the word-play characteristic of children's oral culture (*boule-d'ogre*/*bouledogue*) to describe her own fierce resistance to an oppressive situation: by referring to the teacher as a *boule-d'ogre*, she both presents her as a fearsome figure of authority and insults her. Indeed, in *Georgette!* and in several public statements by Belghoul, cannibalism and ingestion represent "political absorption" (Douglas 4), cultural dissolution or assimilation, and the loss of autonomy and subjectivity. Belghoul herself experienced these kinds of alienation at several points in her life: as a child in a neighborhood with few other North African immigrant families, as a university student under pressure to conform to ethnic majority norms, as a political activist defending the rights of working-class immigrant groups, and as a novelist able to write only in French. In this sense, Belghoul's use of the language of cannibalism to characterize her experiences resonates with Jan Nederveen Pieterse's observation that "Africans and Third World peoples generally have often experienced and described western domination as a form of cannibalism" (120).[10]

The narrator's play on words also mimics the methods used in teaching children to read, since *boule-d'ogre* may be thought of as a compound word composed of *boule* and *ogre*, or as a word that is sounded out and broken into its component parts. A similar example of this type of word-play appears in the narrator's use of the word "analphabète" (illiterate) (147), which she first employs correctly and then transforms into the expression "âne-alpha-bête" (first-class dumb-ass), an insult she imagines her father accusing her of having applied to him (151). These two hybrid terms constitute striking examples of the narrator's increasing sophistication in intertwining the cultural codes she has learned at school and at home in order to describe her life experiences in her own terms and to articulate a response to the strong pressures placed on her by her teacher to conform to French cultural norms and by her father to avoid conforming to them.[11] Belghoul inscribes within her novel the motifs of French and Maghrebi traditional tales about ogres and lost children as a way of disrupting the clichéd, received ways used by the mass media to depict immigrants and their offspring. When discussing the representation of immigrants and their children in films, for example, Belghoul speaks of the need to go beyond the *seuil du témoignage* (threshold of testimony) imposed by dominant cultural institutions if one is to avoid being devoured by them (Belghoul, interview by Gilles Horvilleur).[12] In *Georgette!*, she accomplishes this by representing assimilation as a form of cannibalism, by having her young Maghrebi-French characters respond to and insult those with authority over them (teacher and father), and by encoding ethnic references in terms unfamiliar to most ethnic majority readers.

THE TRACKING GAME: HUNTING FOR CLUES TO POST-COLONIAL ETHNIC IDENTITY

In a review of Mehdi Charef's *Le thé au harem d'Archi Ahmed*, Belghoul argues that by presenting a conventional image of a multi-ethnic immigrant community in a working-class neighborhood, Charef has tailored his film to the expectations of outsiders, and she calls his approach "Big Brother's eye" in the sense that it makes the viewers voyeurs (32-33). Belghoul herself attempts to avoid becoming another Big Brother by refusing to gloss certain ethnic markers in her novel. In this fashion, she creates for the reader a kind of tracking or orienteering game (*jeu de piste*) with hidden clues, which mirrors a serious game the immigrant family members play in the novel. In order to set up the game, Belghoul interweaves the character types and symbolic logic of traditional tales with the experiences of a working-class, North African immigrant family living in Paris--for example, its members sometimes experience public space as dangerous either because they are marked as racially inferior and could be attacked, or because they cannot understand cultural markers. A good example of this interweaving can be seen in one of the passages analyzed above: because she is illiterate, the mother has trouble finding her way in the subway system; consequently, when she is late in arriving, her children imagine that an ogre has eaten her and may eat them too. From the father's perspective, the game tests the ability of his wife and children to return home without getting lost or going astray, a competence he views as proof of the family's cohesiveness in a foreign (French) environment, and of his wife and children's allegiance to an Algerian identity and submission to his authority.

In the third section of the novel, the narrator plays the risky orienteering game as she tries to find her way home safely. For her, the urban space between school and home resembles the dangerous liminal territory of traditional tales (like the forest in "Little Red Riding Hood" and "Tom Thumb") through which an assimilationist ogre, the teacher, is driving a car in order to track her down.[13] To cross the liminal space and win the game, the narrator must retrieve the information that will guide her home safely. However, as in the traditional tales on which Belghoul draws, the signs and helpers the child encounters are sometimes untrustworthy and test her ability to interpret, just as the author tests the reader's knowledge.[14] The narrator meets one such potential helper in a park, an old lady in black walking her dog Moustique. A type of orphan, because her grown sons have abandoned her, the old lady writes them letters which she reads to her neighbors, and she now suggests that the narrator assume the identity of her estranged sons by answering her letters to them. The girl immediately imagines her father's reaction to her writing under a French name: "Most of all, he yells: 'I send you to school to sign your name. In the end, you come up with other catastrophic names. I didn't think my daughter would do that. . . . And would ya look at that: she's called Georgette!' " (147–148).[15] For this reason, the narrator refuses to occupy this alienating discursive position, since doing so would be equivalent to assuming the one already offered her by the teacher, who links cultural assimilation to learning how to read and write in French. The girl thus concludes that it would be mad for her to take on such a foreign identity in order to please either the old woman or the teacher. She therefore runs away from the park and avoids the trap the old lady represents, but soon thereafter is run over by a car that we assume is driven by the teacher:

> I run a red light and cross the street. Happiness is in...
> The wheel of the car is on my belly.
> I've ripped my clothes. I'm completely naked, like a
> dirty thing. I'm bleeding on the street. I took my chances: no dice.

I'm suffocating at the bottom of an inkwell [no final period][16]
(163)

Readings of this open-ended conclusion have varied, but hinge on the crucial question of how the reader fares at unearthing the clues related to ethnicity buried throughout the novel.[17] An initial clue appears when the narrator escapes from the old lady in black, and is contained in the woman's words: "Oh, oh, oh... But I recognize you! You're the one who kicked Mosquito!" ("Bô, bô, bô... Mais je te reconnais! C'est toi qui a botté Moustique!") (148). Our recognition of the fact that "Bô, bô, bô" is a *Pied-Noir* exclamation of surprise or strong emotion brings out the full significance of the narrator's situation: she is being asked to assume the identity of a former colonial settler's sons.[18] What could be more alienating, especially in the Algerian father's eyes?

Another clue is Belghoul's choice of the name "Georgette" rather than another girl's name. The author has indicated that she had "deliberately chosen the name as the most alien she could think of in Arab ears" (Hargreaves, *Immigration and Identity* 38). At the same time, the name also contains the letters "o," "g," "r" and "e" and therefore conceals the word "ogre,"[19] or even the diminutive or feminine "ogrette," and rhymes with "marionnette," suggesting a loss of freedom.[20] A final crucial clue takes the form of the author's Arabic name, Belghoul, which means "son of the ogre" and suggests the French expression "belle goule."[21] Belghoul believed she was engaged in an unequal contest against French institutions and the dominant ethnic group--in the novel, this conflict is often expressed in allusions to the struggles between cowboys and Indians found in westerns. She therefore felt it necessary to shun the use of Islamic or Maghrebi names in her novel, explaining that "Muslim names do not attain universal dimensions in the universe of contemporary French" (personal interview 1992).[22] Indeed, except for one minor slip at the end of the novel,[23] Belghoul avoids naming the novel's Maghrebi characters, because, as her narrator says, "[t]he Indians' identity card is a secret of war" in their struggle to avoid being annihilated by the cowboys, the equivalent of the ethnic majority in France (72).[24] The only name Belghoul could not avoid divulging, except by publishing her novel anonymously, was her own on the front cover.

Belghoul, then, as cannibalistic ogress, has devoured her own offspring, the narrator, who is the literary representation of her younger self. Consequently, the final period of the text is missing because the child was gobbled up on the run and had no time to finish her sentence. By writing her novel in French, the language of the former colonizer, Belghoul has adopted the discursive position held out to her narrator by the old lady, who serves as the schoolteacher's double in her role as assimilationist: in this sense, Belghoul is indeed "Georgette." The exclamation point gives the title the force of a bitter proclamation and prefigures the disgusted reaction of the father as imagined by the narrator. Indeed, Belghoul has stated that writing her novel in French rather than in Arabic meant metaphorically killing and burying "la fille Belghoul" (the Belghoul girl/daughter) (Hargreaves, *Immigration and Identity* 142). As such, the "I" who drowns at the bottom of the teacher's inkwell in the final words of the novel is both the narrator and, by extension, the author herself. The cover of the book thus represents a kind of death certificate, the simple illustration depicting a blood stain or inkspot suggesting the cause of death is writing. Why, then, does Belghoul write, if writing can be seen as a form of suicide? Possible reasons include the sense of despair she felt after the apparent failure of Convergence '84, the national demonstration against racism she had helped lead, and her anger at the pervasive influence of the dominant cultural institutions of French society. In this fashion, her work also functions as a cautionary tale for Maghrebi-French young people about the dangers of discrimination and assimilation--after all, warning children is a primary function of traditional stories. In this regard, Belghoul has also stated her belief that because literature has no national identity in the same way as authors do, it holds the promise of nondiscriminatory treatment and fair evaluation ("Témoigner d'une condition" 25). This brings us back to the issue of how to define Maghrebi-French fiction.[25]

BELGHOUL: TOWARD THE EMERGENCE OF MAGHREBI-FRENCH LITERATURE

If we now return to Deleuze and Guattari's description of a "minor" literature as one characterized by deterritorialization and in which everything has political and collective value (16-17), its relevance to *Georgette!* soon becomes apparent. "Deterritorialization" is a polysemic term suggesting both the movement of emigration (leaving a territory) and the belief that alienation expressed in language can be productive and even revolutionary. The language of *Georgette!* is deterritorialized by its interwoven multi-cultural references--to French, Maghrebi, and majority and minority cultures in the United States--which make any attempt to classify the novel problematic. To take but one example, the ogre figure also appears in fiction by mainstream French authors such as Michel Tournier and Maghrebi-French writers like Leïla Sebbar. In addition, as Winifred Woodhull observes in *Transfigurations of the Maghreb*, the ogress motif recurs frequently in francophone North African fiction where its role is to evoke the "making and unmaking of identities" (72). In *Georgette!*, the ogre helps both to make and unmake the narrator's identity, but at the same time raises questions about the nature of Maghrebi-French fiction, especially the difficulty for its Maghrebi referents to emerge and "attain universal dimensions" in contemporary French society (personal interview 1992).

The collective and political aspects of a minor literature are omnipresent in *Georgette!* and include the ways in which the novel addresses its readers. Whereas Hargreaves argues that in *Georgette!* "[t]he complicity of the author and reader is, in a very real sense, built behind the back of the immigrant community" (*Immigration and Identity* 143), we have seen that the reverse is in fact true: it is built behind the backs of readers unfamiliar with Maghrebi cultures. It is based on the premise of a shared ability to interpret the codes of French fiction, and in addition, to recognize the narrative patterns and symbols of French *and* Maghrebi traditional tales, and to decipher ethnic references drawn from *both* cultures and from their shared, bitter history. As Michel de Certeau lucidly argues, immigrants and their offspring are proficient cultural translators, who smuggle in pieces of their dismembered cultures of origin and embed those relics into the already composite host culture (248-268). These fragmentary relics "transgress assimilation" (268), scandalously so when brought from cultures regarded as inferior or frighteningly different--which is how working-class Maghrebi cultures are generally viewed in France. Relatively little attention has been paid to these relics in the study of Maghrebi-French fiction, but they are important if one is to accurately categorize it and understand its affinities--or lack thereof--with other "minor" literary formations such as African-American, black British, and francophone North African. In this regard, Samia Mehrez's observation about Abdelkebir Khatibi's *Amour bilingue* applies equally well to *Georgette!*: it "is a text that challenges our competence as readers/translators capable of a global reading in this postcolonial world" (135). In Belghoul's novel, the demand to be heard and understood is made in the voice of a child--a minor[26]--whose narrative presents the marginalized points of view of formerly colonized immigrants and, above all, of their offspring. However, hers is not a "minor"[27] but a radical minoritarian demand for an equitable share of power in French society. Satisfying this demand will require major changes, including how we read and understand Maghrebi-French fiction.

NOTES

Warmest thanks to Valérie Dhalenne, Alec G. Hargreaves, Philip E. Lewis, and Jonathan Ngaté, who kindly read and commented on earlier versions of this chapter and to Patrice J. Proulx and Susan Ireland for their helpful editorial input.

1. Hargreaves recently dropped the term *Beur*, but has not altered the definition of his original category.
2. This distinction is especially useful in defending the rights of the Maghrebi-French in France.
3. See Belghoul's interview by Gilles Horvilleur.
4. In *Kafka: Toward a Minor Literature*, Deleuze and Guattari define a "minor literature" as one in which: "language is affected with a high coefficient of deterritorialization . . . everything . . . is political . . . everything takes on a collective value" (16–17).
5. Hargreaves, for example, has analyzed this movement (*Immigration and Identity* 163-164.)
6. See also Sylvie Durmelat's "L'apprentissage de l'écriture dans *Georgette!*," and Hargreaves's *Immigration and Identity*.
7. See Bouloumié's "L'ogre dans la littérature" on ogres and cannibalism, including the motif of parents eating their children in European myths. North African traditional stories about ogresses in Khemir's *L'ogresse* contain themes woven into *Georgette!*: daughters given by their father to an ogress (7–10), an ogre-like dog (47–54), and a trickster outwitting an ogress into eating her daughter (81–84).
8. See Hargreaves's *Immigration and Identity* (38, 77) for a discussion of the narrator's name. On obstacles to Muslim burial in France, see Bencheikh's *Marianne et le Prophète* (101, 125–127).
9. On the teacher as a dog-ogre, see also Hargreaves (*Immigration and Identity* 162).
10. See also Mark McKinney's "Haunting Figures in Contemporary Discourse and Popular Culture in France."
11. My interpretation diverges from that of Hargreaves, who argues that the puns may be unintended malapropisms formulated by a naïve and confused narrator (*Immigration and Identity* 162–164). I believe that throughout the third section of *Georgette!*, she struggles to master a syncretic narrative mode, to describe a world that exerts increasingly unbearable and contradictory pressures on her.
12. "Seuil de témoignage" is a neologism that ironically plays on the racist pseudo-scientific concept of a "threshold of tolerance" (*seuil de tolérance*) to people defined as foreigners.

13. The themes of assimilation through schooling and of the cultural division of space are common in Maghrebi-French novels, as Hargreaves shows (*Immigration and Identity* 50–53).

14. My analysis of traditional tales is informed by Propp's *Morphologie du conte* (see 51–55 on helpers and tests, for example).

15. "Surtout, il gueule: 'j' t'envoye à l'école pour signer ton nom. A la finale, tu m' sors d'autres noms catastrophiques. J' croyais pas ça d' ma fille. . . . Et r'garde-moi ça: elle s'appelle Georgette!' "

16. "Je grille un feu et je traverse. Le bonheur est dans...
La roue de la voiture est sur mon ventre.
J'ai déchiré mes vêtements. Je suis toute nue comme une saleté. Je saigne sur la rue. J'ai joué ma chance: manque de pot. J'étouffe au fond d'un encrier"

17. The verses quoted on pages 127 and 163 ("Le bonheur est dans...") are from Paul Fort's poem *"Le bonheur"* (*Ballades françaises* 202). Valérie Dhalenne suggested Paul Fort as the probable source. Belghoul kindly praised the discovery of this French source, which was previously unknown to her, but cautioned that I had not yet been able to discover other allusions, because I did not have the cultural references.

18. The expression is written *"Poh! Poh! Poh!"* and *"Pah! Pah! Pah!"* in A. Lanly's *Le français d'Afrique du Nord* (160–161). Roland Bacri gives its origin as Arabic: *"Ya baba!"* meaning "Oh my father!" (*Trésors des racines pataouètes* 144). The girl may not understand that the old lady is a *Pied-Noir*.

19. This was Aurélie Bordet's excellent suggestion during my graduate seminar on Maghrebi-French fiction (Miami University, Fall 1997).

20. The name Georgette may also refer to Minister of Social Affairs Georgina Dufoix, whom Belghoul confronted and criticized during a conference on anti-racism in March 1984 ("L'antichambre des prétendants" 40).

21. Warmest thanks to Susan Van Deventer and Mohammed Malih who brought this to my attention. The *Petit Robert* defines "goule" as a "[s]orte de vampire femelle des légendes orientales." The word comes from the Arabic *"ghul,"* as D. B. Macdonald and C. Pellat explain: "In popular language *ghul* (*ghula, kutrub,* etc.) is frequently used to indicate a cannibal, man or demon, and this ogre is often invoked as a threat to naughty children; it also appears in many stories and has even passed into French and English" (1079). Van Deventer suggested this source. For clues to "Belghoul" as a nickname (*laqab*), see Annemarie Schimmel (53) and P. Marty (398). Regarding the influence of French colonial law on the transformation of Algerian *laqab* into family names, see Anna Parzymies (113) and Schimmel (80).

22. "[D]ans l'univers de la langue française actuelle, des noms musulmans n'atteignent pas de dimensions universelles."

23. The name "Bendaoud" (162). Belghoul said that I first alerted her to the slip (personal interview 1992).

24. "La carte d'identité des indiens est un secret de guerre."

25. On literary emergence, see Bonn.

26. See Hargreaves's "La littérature issue de l'immigration maghrébine en France" (18-19).

27. In this sense, Deleuze and Guattari's term *"minor* literature" can be misleading.

WORKS CITED

Bacri, Roland. *Trésors des racines pataouètes*. Paris: Belin, 1983.

Begag, Azouz, and Abdellatif Chaouite. *Ecarts d'identité*. Paris: Seuil, 1990.

Belghoul, Farida. "La différence entre dominant et dominé." *Bulletin de l'agence IM'média* (May–June 1984): 19–21.

---. Review of *Le thé au harem d'Archi Ahmed* by Mehdi Charef. *Cinématographe* 110 (January 1985): 32–33.

---. "L'antichambre des prétendants." *IM'média Magazine* 2 (Spring 1985): 17–18, 40.

---. Interview by Gilles Horvilleur. *Cinématographe* 112 (July 1985): 32–33.

---. *Georgette!* Paris: Bernard Barrault, 1986.

---. "Témoigner d'une condition." *Actualité de l'émigration* 80 (1987): 25.

---. Personal interview. Paris, July 3, 1992.

Bencheikh, Soheib. *Marianne et le Prophète: l'Islam dans la France laïque*. Paris: Grasset, 1998.

Bonn, Charles. "Un espace littéraire émergent." *Littératures des immigrations*. Vol. 1. Paris: L'Harmattan, 1995, 11-14.

Bouloumié, Arlette. "L'ogre dans la littérature." *Dictionnaire des mythes littéraires*. Ed. Pierre Brunel. Paris: Editions du Rocher, 1988, 1071–1086.

Certeau, Michel de. *La prise de parole et autres écrits politiques*. Ed. Luce Giard. Paris: Seuil, 1994.

Deleuze, Gilles, and Félix Guattari. *Kafka: pour une littérature mineure*. Paris: Minuit, 1975.

---. *Kafka: Toward a Minor Literature*. Trans. Dana Polan. Foreword by Réda Bensmaïa. Minneapolis: University of Minnesota Press, 1986.

Douglas, Mary. *Purity and Danger: An Analysis of the Concepts of Pollution and Taboo*. London: Routledge, 1991.

Durmelat, Sylvie. "L'apprentissage de l'écriture dans *Georgette!*" *L'écriture décentrée: la langue de l'autre dans le roman contemporain*. Ed. Michel Laronde. Paris: L'Harmattan, 1996, 33–54.

Fort, Paul. *Ballades françaises: choix 1897–1960*. Paris: Flammarion, 1963.

Hargreaves, Alec G. "La littérature issue de l'immigration maghrébine en France: une littérature 'mineure'?" *Littératures des immigrations*. Vol. 1. Ed. Charles Bonn. Paris: L'Harmattan, 1995, 17–28.

---. *Immigration and Identity in Beur Fiction: Voices from the North African Immigrant Community in France*. Oxford: Berg Publishers, 1997.

Khemir, Nacer. *L'ogresse*. Paris: Maspero, 1975.

Lanly, A. *Le français d'Afrique du Nord: étude linguistique*. Paris: PUF, 1962.

Macdonald, D. B., and C. Pellat. *"Ghul."* *The Encyclopaedia of Islam*. Vol. 2. Ed. B. Lewis, C. Pellat, and J. Schacht. Leiden: E. J. Brill, 1965, 1078–1079.

Marty, P. "Folklore tunisien: l'onomastique des noms propres de personne." *Revue des études islamiques* 10 (1936): 363-434.

McKinney, Mark. "Haunting Figures in Contemporary Discourse and Popular Culture in France." *Sites* 1.1 (Spring 1997): 51–76.

Mehrez, Samia. "Translation and the Postcolonial Experience: The Francophone North African Text." *Rethinking Translation: Discourse, Subjectivity, Ideology*. Ed. Lawrence Venuti. London: Routledge, 1992, 120–138.

Nederveen Pieterse, Jan. *White on Black: Images of Africa and Blacks in Western Popular Culture*. New Haven: Yale University Press, 1992.

Parzymies, Anna. "Noms de personnes en Algérie." *Folia Orientalia* 20 (1979): 107-118.

Propp, Vladimir. *Morphologie du conte*. Trans. Marguerite Derrida. Paris: Seuil, 1970.

"Quand nos parents nous ont perdus: un déjeuner débat au F.I.C." *Cahiers F.I.C.* (March 1984): 34–47.

Said, Edward. "Permission to Narrate--Edward Said Writes about the Story of the Palestinians." *London Review of Books* (February 16–29, 1984): 13–17.

Schimmel, Annemarie. *Islamic Names*. Edinburgh: Edinburgh University Press, 1997.

Woodhull, Winifred. *Transfigurations of the Maghreb: Feminism, Decolonization and Literatures*. Minneapolis: University of Minnesota Press, 1993.

On Natives and Narratives from the *Banlieues*

Sylvie Durmelat

> My topic is my neighborhood. Got to take advantage of it, right now the banlieue's trendy--young delinquents, rap music and all the news that makes the headlines. (13) (Rachid Djaïdani, *Boumkoeur*)

In the 1960s and 1970s, a new type of housing, the so-called "grands ensembles" (tower blocks), was built on the periphery of large and medium-size cities both to meet the pressing demand for lodging left unresolved after World War II and to eradicate shantytowns. These newly built housing projects were intended to provide the working masses and migrant populations with the benefits and comforts of modern life (such as running water and electricity).[1] The utopian ideal underlying this massive construction effort assumed that a new society and a new way of life would emerge from this new functional architecture.[2] However, in the narratives written by children of the North African immigrants who were some of the pioneers and test subjects of life in the *Habitations à Loyer Modéré* (low-income housing), old dichotomies resurface. Representations of peripheral urban spaces in France have traditionally been structured around underlying binary oppositions[3] that define them in opposition to the city per se, heir to the latin "urbs," which was considered to be the heart of the civilized world. Even though these suburban spaces have gone through some significant changes in terms of their size, inhabitants, and administrative status, the same type of clichés persist in the way they are defined. From the "faubourgs,"[4] to the "banlieues rouges," to the contemporary "cités" (housing projects) or "quartiers sensibles," the same paradigm is perpetuated, opposing center to periphery, cleanliness to filth, civilized to savage, native to foreign, and historical heritage to disquieting modernity.[5]

Narratives by Maghrebi-French authors show the other side of modernity, as the material wonders of urban planning and social engineering are viewed as a new form of containment, and the utopian vision of a new type of urban dwelling is slowly replaced by the dystopia of the ghetto. The ironic depiction of the HLMs as paradise in these stories provides a subtle yet derisive corrective to the earlier optimistic version of progress. In the early 1980s, Mehdi Charef's description of Madjid's *cité* in *Le thé au harem d'Archi Ahmed* sets the tone for other texts to follow. There are no flowers in "la Cité des Fleurs" (the *Cité* of Flowers) (24), and the dominant odor in the alleys is that of urine. In similar fashion, Soraya Nini's *Ils disent que je suis une beurette* starts with the following words: "I was born in Paradise and apparently I am 'a beurette,' which means 'a daughter of immigrants.' . . . I live in the tower block called 'My Paradise' " (9).[6] Samia, the narrator, condenses the expression "the tower block called 'My Paradise' " into the word "Paradise" at the very beginning of the novel to highlight the contrast between the name and the nature of the housing project. As she guides a journalist through her neighborhood, along with her readers, she observes: "Next, we arrive in the garden of Paradise. Then Sylvie looks at me, wide-eyed, and asks: 'Where is the garden? There are no trees, no flowers, no lawns here?' "(11). At this point, the journalist realizes that this is a Paradise without an Eden, a Paradise where excrement thrown from the rooftops by a group of adolescents rains down on the *cité*. The ironic title of Brahim Benaïcha's *Vivre au paradis: d'une oasis à un bidonville* offers the same derisive and disenchanted view of peripheral spaces.

But is this fall from "paradise" to ghetto as automatic and inevitable as it seems? Isn't conforming to this entropic vision of progress and modernity gone awry yet another way to blame immigrants for the gradual degradation of their habitat? Indeed, the now dominant stereotype of the *banlieue*-turned-ghetto seems to be another way of erasing the immigrant presence and experience from French urban spaces. Certainly, the HLMs were rapidly and cheaply built and have aged faster than expected. In order to "regenerate" peripheral urban spaces and to rid society of the tensions and conflicts that have emerged in these suburban areas, the new urban planning policies of the 1990s advocated the demolition of some of these hastily built apartment complexes--a form of destruction that appears to be both a dismissal and a denial since it is accompanied by the obliteration of the stories and the landscapes, the habits and the memories of the communities that created new identities for themselves in these places while making them into their home. This destruction is possible because the *banlieues* are often considered to be non-places or empty spaces, rather than ones that are inhabited. One can thus argue that HLMs are an unlikely monument to working class and immigrant histories as well as an unacknowledged repository of France's colonial past. As such, they can be thought of as a site of memory, a place of pilgrimage, or even a museum, since shantytowns have been eliminated and no museum dedicated to immigration has yet been created.

Given the inflammatory discourses on and negative perceptions of the *banlieues* which predominate today, one can ask how Maghrebi-French authors portray the suburban places where they have grown up. How, for example, do their novels deal with stereotypical images of the *banlieues*? Do they manage to counter them by showing other aspects of life on the periphery or do they tend to reproduce them? How can they avoid dwelling on the sordid side of life and the self-stigmatization this often entails? Finally, what sort of negotiations are at work in their depictions? In answer to these questions, it can be observed that their narratives display a wide variety of attitudes and positions. Most of the better-known texts focus on the perceptions of young male protagonists, but they also give us access to the experiences and everyday practices of other members of their families. In these narratives, the *banlieues* are not only associated with delinquency and degradation, but are also a place where people cook, have daily contact with their neighbors, and can be happy.

In addition, narratives by Maghrebi-French authors generally maintain a certain ambivalence between various positions on the *banlieues*. As such, they are part of the ongoing negotiation process, of the tensions and conflicts that are related to this social question. On the one hand, one finds a dominant dystopic and self-disparaging discourse, frequently coupled with the denunciation and criticism of the social processes that make the *banlieues* a space of exclusion. On the other hand, a more defensive yet affectionate personal identification with the places where the authors grew up, and often still live, is apparent. For this reason, narrators and protagonists struggle to reconcile their everyday experiences in their place of residence with the predominantly negative media representations that are also part and parcel of daily life in their neighborhood.

Sociologist Didier Lapeyronnie, author of several books on young people from the *banlieue*, remarks that the images that researchers and the media produce about Franco-Maghrebi youths mediate the ways in which they think of themselves while at the same time turning them into objects of study. Once the youths internalize these confining images, they have a harder time defining or reinventing themselves. In this fashion, they are silenced instead of being empowered by the knowledge produced about them. However, since Lapeyronnie is himself a researcher in the social sciences, there is an additional level of complexity in his analysis of the potential silencing effect of such work on the youths: could one not argue that his own work as a sociologist is yet another way of not listening to their voices?

In "La vision médiatique," sociologist Patrick Champagne makes the same argument: "Rather than speaking, [those who are dominated] are spoken, and when they address those who dominate they tend to use a borrowed discourse, the very discourse that those in a position of dominance formulate about them" (68).[7] He observes, for instance, that young people interviewed on TV programs devoted to the *banlieues* tend to talk about themselves using the "third person": "The adolescents, they want their own place to meet" (68).[8] It thus appears as if these youths are robbed of their own voices and agency as interpreters of their own experiences. This sociological analysis and paradigm of "youths-deprived-of-their-voices-as-they-speak" is another dominant construct that ultimately silences them. The assumption underlying this construct is that there is an "authentic voice" somewhere, but it is not theirs.

Similarly, Maghrebi-French authors who have grown up and lived in the *banlieues* do not necessarily offer the "untainted," "authentic" narratives we wishfully and naively think they might produce in their role as native informants. By this, I do not mean to deprive these authors of agency and the ability to interpret and decode their own experiences and surroundings, but rather to underline the fact that their narratives grapple with the very same tensions and conflicts that underlie other discourses on the *banlieue*. Their status as "natives" does not exempt their narratives from these tensions. Their struggle to represent their experiences, and the conflicting interpretations one finds in their accounts, demonstrate that the term *banlieue* does not merely designate a peripheral urban space. Rather, it is a discursive mode, and as such it can take on the values of any other discursive mode, depending on its context and use. The concept of the *banlieue* thus signifies the way one relates to urban space, and it is constantly shaped and reshaped by ongoing negotiations and power relationships. Taken together, these authors show us that an "authentic" narrative on the *banlieues* does not exist in and of itself, but becomes authentic only as a result of the discordance and play of difference that take place between and within their narratives, a discordance that is usually absent from television shows and news programs on the *banlieues*.

Mounsi's autobiographical essay *Territoire d'outre-ville* illustrates the complexity of this discursive mode. The polysemous title, with its coining of the expression *territoire d'outre-ville*, extends the borders of the notion of the *banlieue*:

My life will have found its meaning on the fecund wasteland of the *banlieue*, where, paradoxically, the city ends. . . . It took me thirty years to move from the news-in-brief section to the literary section of the newspaper. My memories force me to take a sinuous path in order to find myself in this inner land I call "*Territoire d'outre-ville*" [Territory beyond the city], that for me is "*Outre Seine*" [Beyond the Seine]. And the river continues its silent, secret movement within me. (21)

The title of the text thus designates peripheral urban spaces beyond the city limits. At the same time, it alludes to an unacknowledged geographical and historical space through its reference to the Territoires d'Outre-Mer (French Overseas Territories)--remnants of the French colonial empire. Mounsi's play on words highlights the filiation between overseas colonies and French suburbs, the latter acting as a repository of France's colonial and post-colonial legacies. In this fashion, the *Territoire d'outre-ville* becomes an autobiographical space, a multi-layered site of memory that Mounsi incorporates into the literary representation of his self, as the suburban spaces he has inhabited now haunt him; it also functions as a mythical space connected to the great beyond. The Seine, which is compared to the Styx (41), allows him to descend into the world of the dead, where he attempts to recover through his writing both the figure of his dead father and the victims of violence drowned in the Seine in October 1961.[9]

The allusions and the play on the word "outre" contribute to an unusually complex depiction of the *banlieues* as a social, historical, autobiographical, and mythical space. At the end of the book, Mounsi describes his visit to les Quatre-Mille, an infamous *cité* in la Courneuve: "I went there, sent by a newspaper, trying to establish contact with the youths who hang out between the tower blocks" (102). Even though he mentions that the *cités* are diverse in nature and can be relatively happy places, his report on the Quatre-Mille is singularly gloomy, desolate, and one-sided; with its focus on male adolescents and on instances of drug trafficking and delinquency, the *cité* he describes is a place of social anomie and fragmentation. Because he explores the *banlieues* as an autobiographical space, he tends to project his own tormented experience onto them, thus creating a rather apocalyptic portrait of La Courneuve. For this reason, his article, intended for an audience of outsiders, seems to perpetuate traditional stereotypes about the *banlieues* instead of defusing them. One might reasonably wonder to what extent his outlook on life at La Courneuve is informed by the fact that he goes there as a journalist to write an article. Mounsi, like other journalists, calls attention to young adolescent males who are already stigmatized as violent and unlawful, while other inhabitants such as mothers and children go unmentioned.

The coexistence of these two veins in his narrative--one that highlights the rich complexity of the *banlieues* while the other stresses its dystopic nature-- shows that even within a single book the *banlieues* are not portrayed in a monolithic fashion. Rather, their representations are subject to negotiations between various characters and are dependent on their situations. Even though most accounts of the *banlieues* revolve around the malaise of adolescent characters and their feelings of imprisonment, glimpses of the everyday life of other members of their families provide a corrective to the dominant bleakness. These alternative portrayals show that the *banlieues* are a site where social interaction takes place--not a social void. In *Le thé au harem d'Archi Ahmed*, for example, Madjid's mother has developed close relationships with some of her neighbors. Azouz Begag's *Béni ou le paradis privé*, suggests a similar picture of the *banlieue*. Here, Begag describes the Lyonnais suburb of La Duchère where the protagonist has just moved with his family after leaving the centrally located and run-down immigrant district of Le Pont. Begag's narrative illustrates how the various members of Béni's family adapt to their new environment, describing in particular the difficulties experienced by his mother, who at first misses the warmth and solidarity between women fostered by life in the shantytown and still very much present in Le Pont. Despite spending her days obsessively cleaning the apartment, she does not feel at home until she finally meets an Algerian compatriot at the local open-air market and then creates a network of acquaintances and friends in her new neighborhood: "From one market day to the next, she ended up in the midst of a group of Algerian women, and each time she cleaned up the apartment, it was no longer to kill time but to prepare for their visits. . . . My mother had adapted for good. My father followed suit and met the respective husbands" (57-58).[10] The story of Béni's mother, however rapidly sketched out in the novel, shows that the *banlieues* are not condemned to a state of social anomie--they are not *non-lieux* (non-places). In the *cité*, Béni's mother and other Algerian women are able to create a new form of sociability both within and outside of their HLM apartments, one that does not completely replicate the rules for social interaction of their country of origin and relies on the agency of women.

The play of differences and the negotiation at work in representations of the *banlieues* are epitomized in Rachid Djaïdani's first novel, *Boumkoeur*, published in 1999. This book sets out to denounce both the dominant vision of the *banlieues* and the producers and outsiders from the entertainment industry who seek to capitalize on it. The narrator, a young man named Yaz, decides to write a story that will recount the everyday events and "nonevents" of his *cité*. His self-proclaimed and seemingly contradictory aims are both to "bear witness" (17) and to make money: "I'm going to tell all these adventures to make money galore, to make things change. Since it's always guys from the outside who collect the dough by telling stories or making movies, I also feel *hate, ma cité va craquer* [my housing project is going to explode], and it's not by using a *raï* tune that I'll make my *état des lieux* [inventory]" (17-18, my emphasis).[11] Indeed, the author was in many ways successful--his book on the urban and social margins of society was a best-seller, and he was invited to be a participant on Bernard Pivot's famous TV show "Bouillon de culture," a major "center" of French culture. It seems, then, that Djaïdani wants to beat the media at their own game and that he is upping the ante. In the quotation above, the author creates a sentence using the titles of four fairly recent movies[12] which came to be known as *banlieue* films[13] after the box-office success of *La Haine.* The movies cited contain scenes of violent riots, uprisings, and confrontations with the police, and most of them focus on young male adults and adolescent characters. Through his playful appropriation of these movie titles, the author shows that the *banlieue* has become a spectacle for the masses and also emphasizes that since the appearance of these films in the 1990s, it has become difficult to conceptualize urban spaces other than through the prism of these movies.

Djaïdani seems to condemn this situation while at the same time trying to take advantage of it. His novel includes a scene in which a journalist, who has come to the *cité* to stage a scoop by asking the usual questions--"Who of you owns a weapon? Who deals drugs?" (21)--is being manipulated by a group of youths who initially agree to answer his questions, but eventually they beat up the journalist and steal his camera: "The setting they chose was not very original; the interview took place in the bowels of a high-rise building. The youths, who were worried about their image, had hidden their faces with hoods so that only their eyes showed, as if they had metamorphosed into the poster of the movie *Hate*" (21). To a certain extent, this quotation supports Lapeyronnie and Champagne's analysis of the silencing of dominated youths by television and the media. Here, the young inhabitants of the *cité* project an image of themselves borrowed directly from the movie *La Haine.* However, there is a certain degree of manipulation on both sides. The journalist wants to obtain his scoop, and the youths give him what they know he wants. In the end, the only way they can escape from this masquerade is by violently attacking the journalist who has contributed to creating this image of them (which they reproduce in order to attract him) and by stealing the camera that freezes this image. Djaïdani thus denounces the common stereotype that *banlieues* are a dangerous place because of the youths who live there by attributing the responsibility for having created it to journalists: the *banlieue* is a dangerous place, he suggests, because journalists portray it as such. In so doing, it seems that the author produces what could be called a "second-generation" stereotype, or a stereotype about a stereotype. For Djaïdani, the youths are vindicated in their actions against the journalist because he is promoting a distorted image of the *banlieues* (and here there is another reference to a scene in *La Haine* in which journalists are being chased out of the *cité* because they are trying to get a scoop). However, by turning the journalist into a scapegoat, the youths end up reinforcing the earlier stereotype that depicts them as violent and delinquent. In the end, they do steal the camera, but cannot or are not willing to produce images different from those in *La Haine*. Indeed, they finally throw the camera away.

Likewise, because of the media attention the *banlieues* have been receiving, Djaïdani knows that these themes are likely to attract readers, as they do journalists. It is therefore difficult to assess to what extent he is manipulating his readers and feeding them the usual stereotypes, or in what sense he is himself the victim of the discourse that he, perhaps unknowingly, reproduces--at times he is able to dissociate himself from it, while at others he seems to be incapable of doing so. Yaz, the narrator of *Boumkoeur*, is a native of the *cité* who also acts as a journalist of sorts. He has asked Grézi, an adolescent from the neighborhood, to help him collect stories and anecdotes about their *cité* and to serve as a primary informant; he will write the story, hoping that they will share the profits generated by the sale of the book. It turns out, however, that Grézi makes up stories in order to lure Yaz into the cellars, or the infamous "caves" of the tower blocks (hence the title that refers to a bunker). Unbeknownst to him, Yaz is held hostage there by Grézi, who pretends he is hiding from the police after killing a young man who "dissed" him. Fooled by this friend/informant, Yaz agrees, out of friendship and solidarity, to remain with Grézi for four days until the latter surrenders to the police after his upcoming eighteenth birthday. Meanwhile, Grézi asks Yaz's parents for a ransom. In the end, Yaz--who nearly dies--recovers his freedom, and Grézi is sent to jail where he eventually writes the anecdotes he promised as well as an account of life in prison which he sends to Yaz.

The very fact that Yaz uses an informant, a guide to the *cité* (Grézi), tends to present the *banlieue* as a foreign country. In addition, Djaïdani frequently uses *verlan* (backslang), the now popular and widely studied language associated with youths from a working-class, immigrant background--his narrator positions himself as the translator of Grézi's masterful *verlan* into "standard" French for neophyte readers. In such instances, Yaz gives the readers the original *verlan* and then offers a translation, or vice versa. The insistence on *verlan* is, as Marie-Claude Taranger emphasizes, one of the most common yet clearest ways of designating otherness (65). In this respect, *Boumkoeur* seems to constitute an example of the ethnographic vein typical of much *Beur* literature, as Alec Hargreaves has observed in "Une littérature à la croisée des chemins." Indeed, in his presentation of the *banlieues*, Yaz has internalized the common views of the mainstream French readership for whom the book seems to be tailored. Providing translations reinforces the idea that such translations are necessary if one is to understand the *banlieues*.

However, this story offers an original twist on the common ethnographic trait of so-called *Beur* literature, because the primary informant turns out to be unreliable and the would-be ethnographer is trapped, deceived, and almost killed. Furthermore, the structure of the novel is such that readers occupy the same position in relation to Yaz as Yaz does to Grézi. Both the readers and Yaz feel cheated in their quest for "authentic" information, since most of the story is revealed to be bogus. The readers, like Yaz, rely heavily on informants from the *banlieues* whose trustworthiness is doubtful, just as

Djaïdani's might be. If we are expecting a reliable account of life in the *banlieues*--a testimony, as the narrator calls it at one point--we will be disappointed. *Boumkoeur*, then, can be read as an indirect cautionary tale. It teaches us that when it comes to the *banlieues*, there is no such thing as a straightforward account: texts dealing with this subject[14] should be read as participating in the production of an imagined reality which is constantly being reconstructed.

Djaïdani's text confirms that the *banlieues* are not only a peripheral urban space, but can also be said to constitute a complex discursive mode. Narratives on and by "natives" of the *banlieues* demonstrate that their place of residence is not an empty, chaotic space but an inhabited, social space. Due to the pervasive negative stigmatization of suburban spaces and to ongoing debates concerning their representation, the natives portrayed in these narratives constantly have to find new ways and new tactics with which to reterritorialize the places they inhabit, whether it be through a simple system of invitations and visits from one apartment to another, as in the case of Béni's mother, through the literary fictions of an unreliable native informant, as in *Boumkoeur*, or through the infinite mimicry and mirroring of images taken from the media.

NOTES

1. For an analysis of paradoxes and misgivings concerning modernization in France, see Mireille Rosello's article "North African Women and the Ideology of Modernization: From *Bidonvilles* to *Cités de Transit* and *HLM*."

2. See Boyer and Lochard, 58-80.

3. See Boyer and Lochard's *Scènes de télévision en banlieues, 1950-1994* for a synthetic historical overview of peripheral suburban spaces in France.

4. *Faubourgs* are inner suburbs to which marginal populations were relegated in the sixteenth century. During the Industrial Revolution, working-class residents settled there and on the outskirts of cities. In the early twentieth century, members of the socialist and communist parties established themselves successfully in these peripheral spaces, hence the expression "banlieues rouges," which refers to their political "colors." The expression "quartiers sensibles" (sensitive neighborhoods) emerged in the late 1980s and designates the perceived instability and volatility of the young population of the *banlieues* who are described as prone to rioting. The medical metaphor suggests these areas are potentially unhealthy and diseased.

5. See Susan Ireland's "Les banlieues de l'identité: Urban Geography and Immigrant Identities" for a detailed description and analysis of these dichotomies and the criticism of them in the works of Maghrebi-French authors.

6. "Je suis née au Paradis et il paraît que je suis 'une beureutte,' ça veut dire 'une enfant d'immigrés.' . . . J'habite la cité HLM 'Mon Paradis.' "

7. "[les dominés] sont parlés plus qu'ils ne parlent et lorsqu'ils parlent aux dominants, ils tendent à avoir un discours d'emprunt, celui que les dominants tiennent à leur propos."

8. "Les jeunes, ils veulent un local pour se réunir."

9. See Anne Donadey's "Anamnesis and National Reconciliation: Remembering October 17, 1961" in this volume.

10. "De jour de marché en jour de marché, elle finit par se retrouver au milieu d'un groupe de femmes algériennes, et à chaque fois qu'elle briquait l'appartement, ce n'était plus pour pousser le temps mais pour préparer leur arrivée

lors des visites. . . . Ma mère s'était définitivement acclimatée. Mon père suivit le mouvement et fit la connaissance des maris respectifs."

    11. "C'est toutes ces aventures que je vais raconter, pour me faire des tunes à gogo, pour que ça change. Comme c'est toujours les mecs de l'extérieur qui prennent l'oseille, en racontant des histoires, ou en faisant des films, moi aussi j'ai la haine, ma cité va craquer et ce n'est pas sur un air de raï que je ferai mon état des lieux."

    12. *La Haine* by Mathieu Kassovitz (1995), *Ma cité va craquer* by Jean-Louis Richet (1998), *Raï* by Thomas Gilou (1996), and *Etats des lieux* by Richet (1995).

    13. See Thierry Jousse's "Le banlieue-film existe-t-il?" and Yann Tobin's "Etat des (ban)lieues."

    14. This novel is also representative of a recent trend in books on the subject of immigration and suburban cultures, a trend which includes Chimo's and Paul Smaïl's novels. Until this point, the literary value of *Beur* novels had been questioned, since they were considered to be thinly veiled autobiographies. The recent novels are still autobiographical in nature but are recounted by narrators whose reliability is immediately put into question. Furthermore, Chimo's and Smaïl's books are rumored to be hoaxes--the identity of both these authors remains unknown and is used as a marketing ploy; both books were best-sellers.

WORKS CITED

Begag, Azouz. *Le gone du Chaâba*. Paris: Seuil, 1986.
---. *Béni ou le paradis privé*. Paris: Seuil, 1989.
Begag, Azouz, and Abdellatif Chaouite. *Ecarts d'identité*. Paris: Seuil, 1990.
Benaïcha, Brahim. *Vivre au paradis: d'une oasis à un bidonville*. Paris: Desclée de Brouwer, 1992.
Boyer, Henri, and Guy Lochard. *Scènes de télévision en banlieues, 1950-1994*. Paris: L'Harmattan, 1998.
Champagne, Patrick. "La vision médiatique." *La misère du monde*. Ed. Pierre Bourdieu. Paris: Seuil, 1993, 61-79.
Charef, Mehdi. *Le thé au harem d'Archi Ahmed*. Paris: Mercure de France, 1983.
Djaïdani, Rachid. *Boumkoeur*. Paris: Seuil, 1999.
Hargreaves, Alec G. "Une littérature à la croisée des chemins." *Hommes et Migrations* 1170 (November 1993): 7-9.
Ireland, Susan. "Les banlieues de l'identité: Urban Geography and Immigrant Identities." *French Literature Series* XXIV (1997): 171-188.
Jousse, Thierry. "Le banlieue-film existe-t-il?" *Cahiers du cinéma* 492 (June 1995): 37-39.
Lapeyronnie, Didier. "Pour un autre regard sur la banlieue." *Observatoire des politiques culturelles* 16 (Fall 1998): 36.
Mounsi. *Territoire d'outre-ville*. Paris: Stock, 1995.
Nini, Soraya. *Ils disent que je suis une beurette*. Paris: Fixot, 1993.
Rosello, Mireille. "North African Women and the Ideology of Modernization: From *Bidonvilles* to *Cités de Transit* and *HLM*." *Post-Colonial Cultures in France*. Eds. Alec G. Hargreaves and Mark McKinney. London and New York: Routledge, 1997, 240-254.
Taranger, Marie-Claude. "Télévision et 'western urbain': enjeux et nuances de l'information sur les banlieues." *Cahiers de la cinémathèque* 59/60 (February 1994): 59-71.
Tobin, Yann. "Etat des (ban)lieues." *Positif* (September 1995): 28-29.

CARIBBEAN IMMIGRANT NARRATIVES

Negotiating the Metropole: Patterns of Exile and Cultural Survival in Gisèle Pineau and Suzanne Dracius-Pinalie

H. Adlai Murdoch

In a certain sense, questions of self-definition have haunted French visions of the nation since before the establishment of the Compagnie des Iles d'Amérique and the colonization of Guadeloupe and Martinique in 1635. France is a nation shaped by a political fragmentation and ethnic and cultural pluralism it has continually sought to deny, from its origins in such epochal events as the conquest of Languedoc in the mid-thirteenth century, through the acquisition of the duchy of Brittany in the late Middle Ages, to the return of Alsace-Lorraine by the Treaty of Versailles in 1919. Historically, it has been a nation constructed from shifting, diverse fragments, paradoxically made up, at least in part, of elements of its "others." As Fernand Braudel writes, "France is not one society, then, but many societies" (72), a multi-cultural melting pot upon which the idea of the French nation was perhaps forcibly imposed rather than simply being allowed to emerge. It is from the intersection of this idea of the nation and the ways in which the values and practices of the colonial *mission civilisatrice* came to impinge upon it that the parameters of this chapter will take shape.

Such intersections may be traced to the moment of the emergence of the modern nation, a product of the phenomenon of modernity that arguably finds its beginnings in late eighteenth-century Europe. But it is with the mass social movements of the nineteenth century, coinciding as they did with the peak of the colonial "scramble for Africa" and its corollaries, and leading to the institutionalization of state nationalism based on group ethnicity, that the

diverse patterns of identification and difference that ultimately framed the imagined community settled on the principles of exclusion and inclusion that would
overdetermine the troubled concept of the nation. Thus, what came to be
thought of as "Frenchness," as the editors of *Writing New Identities* put it, "is
not based on ethnic origin. Rather, it is based on the individual's acceptance of
the progressive, rationalist, and universalistic values of the enlightened nation-
state. Any individual can become a citizen of the state by becoming like, that is,
by assimilating as one and the same. However, in the demotic-unitarian state a
national language is central" (Smith and Brinker-Gabler 3). Beyond ethnicity,
then, imperial European nations--and France in particular--were founded on the
principle of inalterable cultural superiority over their colonial subjects, and the
mastery of the national language became the primordial sign of the sense of division that produced colonial hierarchy and difference.

     The implicit universalism that lay at the heart of the colonial venture
was, of course, an intrinsically Eurocentric one, inscribing European culture and
history as the centrifugal force to which inferior non-European civilizations were
drawn and through which they would redefine themselves. During the apogee of
European colonialism from the eighteenth through the twentieth centuries, the
British system of "separate and unequal" found its measure in the French principle of cultural assimilation, which held out the ephemeral prospect of acceptance, of "cultural whitening," if the colonial subject could shed all visible
traces of his or her cultural background and baggage, including dress, speech
patterns, and even the tales and myths of childhood. As E. J. Hobsbawm puts
it:

The sense of superiority which thus united the western whites, rich, middle-class and
poor, did so not only because all of them enjoyed the privileges of the ruler, especially when actually in the colonies. . . . France believed in transforming its subjects
into Frenchmen, notional descendants (as school textbooks insisted, in Timbuctoo
and Martinique as in Bordeaux) of 'nos ancêtres les gaulois' (our ancestors the
Gauls), unlike the British, convinced of the essential and permanent non-
Englishness of Bengalis and Yoruba. (*The Age of Empire* 71)

It is in this way that the patterns of European belonging and exclusion were
drawn; in a vicious circle of division and dissension, the rules of "Frenchness"
were first constructed, and subsequently contested, by metropolitan perceptions
of "racial" and cultural difference.

     Although this propulsion to gallicize is central to French colonial ar-
ticulations of self and "other," the paradoxes generated by the intersection of
immigration and ethnicity are quite evident even without the added complexities
of a perceived "otherness." While France has a total immigrant population of
about 3 million, out of a national total of 55 million,[1] by and large the term
"immigrant" is not taken to refer to other Europeans such as, for example, the
Portuguese, who presently constitute the predominant immigrant group in
France. In the case of these groups, difference becomes, for all practical purposes, a non-issue because of the absence of overt racial markers. Rather, as
Winifred Woodhull succinctly points out: "it refers to the influx of non-
Europeans, some of whom are not immigrants at all. These include people from
France's overseas departments in the Caribbean (Martinique and Guadeloupe), as

well as from former French colonies such as Vietnam, Senegal, Cameroon, and the Maghreb (Algeria, Morocco, and Tunisia)" (32).

Within such an overall framework of difference and displacement, one that selectively impacts specific groups of non-French non-immigrants, I would like to concentrate on the situation of the Antillean citizens of the *DOM* (*départements d'outre-mer*), or overseas departments, and the insistent, ineluctable hybridities that inform their paradoxical socio-cultural inscription. These hybridities of the French Caribbean condition tend to center on intersecting issues of ethnic and cultural pluralism that are the corollaries of the colonial site. While, on the one hand, the complex divisions and discontinuities of Caribbean history provide the essential basis for these patterns of pluralism, such questions are also the product of both the departmentalization process begun in 1946 and the massive wave of migration to the metropole that occurred in its wake. Here, the role of the state agency Bumidom (Bureau pour le Développement des Migrations des Départements d'Outre-Mer) was a crucial one; ostensibly set up to alleviate the post-war labor shortage in France by encouraging and policing emigration from French colonies, its demographic policies allowed it to establish an emigration quota for Guadeloupe and Martinique of 5,000 persons per year, as early as 1965. When such numbers are read in conjunction with the figures for those leaving for the metropole of their own accord, we see that over 50,000 migrants from Martinique alone left for France during the decade from 1965 to 1975.[2] These subjects took their indigenous patterns of cultural *métissage* (hybridity) with them to the former colonial capitals, thus giving rise to a form of transnational affiliation that increasingly influences both the shape and performance of popular culture--particularly in the areas of music, film, television, drama, dance, and fashion. Decades of such movement have resulted in more than 400,000 people of French West Indian descent or origin residing on the French mainland, with more than three-quarters of them living in the Paris area.[3] And if, as Alain Anselin's study has shown, this population stood at over 320,000 as early as 1982--a figure more or less equal to the individual populations of Guadeloupe or Martinique, and nearly three times that of French Guiana--then his conclusion that "a third island is situated in the heart of Europe . . . one West Indian in three lives in France" (*L'émigration antillaise* 110)[4] is by no means an overstatement of contemporary realities. The socio-cultural complexities generated by the population of this "third island," circulating as it does between department and metropole, enlarge the concept of a regional diaspora, and are just as telling, perhaps, as the dislocation and doubleness that are the more obvious signs of the imagined community created by departmentalization.

These hybrid communities maintain a level of ties to their homelands that effectively problematizes traditional notions of belonging, and of the difference between "home" and "away." As a result, there is also a doubling of these sites of affiliation that blurs fixed notions of identity and erases the distinction between positionality and place: "Almost all French West Indian families have members living in France. . . . The constant crossing of the Atlantic tends to undermine the distinction between 'France' and the West Indies" (Burton 12). Such social patterns ultimately have the effect of repositioning and globalizing identity as a product of the departmental encounter itself; as Anselin points out, "French West Indians no longer migrate, they circulate," their ceaseless, circular movement suggesting a modernist nomadism where migrating metaphors of difference disrupt the hierarchic assumptions of both center and periphery (*L'émigration antillaise* 266).

These hybrid patterns of social inscription and circulation are themselves contested by the historical notion of *la plus grande France* (greater France), a principle that found perhaps its most telling expression during the Colonial Exhibition of 1931. Here, the ineluctable collision between "otherness" and *francité* (Frenchness) was to lead to the renouncing of cultural difference and the wholesale adoption of Frenchness. As Panivong Norindr cogently explains, "For this utopic idea of *la plus grande France* to take hold in the French imaginary, cultural difference would first have to be erased; French culture was to be disseminated and, in return, cultural allegiance pledged" (236). It is this principle of cultural effacement and integration which has been extended in the present and which seeks to erase all expressions of cultural specificity as un-French. Further, the belief in ethnic and cultural homogeneity that drives such divisive notions of the "essence" of Frenchness tends to ignore the realities of population exchange through migratory movements, concentrating instead on the *visible* markers of ethnic or cultural difference that allow the majority population to single out and code these subgroups as "other," and therefore implicitly undesirable.

For the population of the French Caribbean, although the departmental law of 1946 had bestowed the same rights and privileges upon them as on any other French citizens, the material realities of geographical distance, ethnic and cultural difference, and colonial history mean that these territories resemble *colonies* of France rather than constituting equal political entities (that they theoretically are). Beverley Ormerod makes this point well: "the French Caribbean islands . . . are still owned and ruled by France. Their official status as Departments of France has not greatly altered the realities of political and cultural colonialism" (3). In terms of their values, their traditions, and their language, then, the French Antilleans must continually renegotiate their place in relation to the totalizing French "nous" (we) in order to be able to assert their own complex specificity within the larger context of subjection to the metropole.

The departmentalization which paradoxically drew these territories further into the ambit of the metropole instead of expanding their capacity for self-determination created territories that are both French and West Indian, yet more than the sum of the two, thus orienting them towards a politics, ethnicity, and language of the Creole. This cultural and geopolitical duality forces Antilleans to constantly redefine their identity in the space that separates their exile within the metropolitan definition of "home" from a Caribbean creolized designation of difference. These complex considerations give rise to the creative in-betweenness that Homi Bhabha has described as "that intermittent time, and interstitial space, that emerges as a structure of undecidability at the frontiers of cultural hybridity" ("DissemiNation" 312). It is here, at the intersection of so many conflicting sites of French Caribbeanness and creoleness, that we may locate the work of the Martinican writer Suzanne Dracius-Pinalie and the Guadeloupean Gisèle Pineau. By interrogating the core criteria of alienation, exile, and doubling that undergird articulations of Caribbean identity in modern metropolitan France, these authors take a particular interest in the ways in which these elements impact the place and perspective of women. Both authors examine the double colonization to which women have historically been subjected and the array of psychological tensions that inhibit their attempts to inscribe themselves in society. Perhaps the primary issue that their protagonists confront is that of negotiating the dualities of the metropolitan and Antillean influences as they search for an adequate definition of "home."

Finding an adequate definition of "home," or locating a space that will allow the subject to mediate between the conflicting metropolitan and departmental sites, is a primary concern of Dracius-Pinalie's 1989 novel *L'autre qui danse*. Dracius-Pinalie effectively problematizes the issue in a number of ways: she presents as her protagonists two *métis* sisters, Rehvana and Matildana, who are Martinican-born but who have lived in Paris since childhood. The sisters adopt differing attitudes toward their acquisition of cultural inscription and authenticity. On the one hand, the constant sense of displacement and lack of belonging that disrupts Rehvana's metropolitan existence eventually leads to her return to Martinique. On the other hand, Matildana's relative success at the process of socio-cultural integration, first as a student at the Sorbonne, then, following her own return to her homeland, as an engaged teacher and journalist, raises critical questions concerning the divergent paths and possibilities produced by the dynamics of cultural authenticity. The opposing trajectories of the protagonists allow the author to interrogate the roles of "race" and displacement in the construction of French Caribbean cultural identity in the contemporary era. Through their ethnicity and their location in the metropole, Rehvana and Matildana embody the pervasive pluralism that forms the principal framework of the Caribbean's socio-historical heritage. The complexity of Caribbean creoleness, as a space of crossing and of exchange, is inscribed in the novel through these characters--the "racial" and cultural hybridity of Caribbeanness is figured through their complex subjectivity as well as through the sense of unease which arises from their frustrated desire to name either metropole or department as "home." It is in their disparate ways of coming to terms with these realities that the differing trajectories of Rehvana and Matildana assume their true importance.

The cultural hybridity embodied by these characters thus exemplifies "the history of postcolonial migration, the narratives of cultural and political diaspora . . . the poetics of exile" described by Bhaba (*The Location of Culture* 5). For these inhabitants of "the third island," who legitimately inhabit a space that continues to identify them as "other," the fact that their creoleness renders them both French and West Indian raises important issues of inscription. If the dualities of such double inscriptions transform the possibilities of metropole and department into a framework that is "both" and "neither," then the exploration of these boundaries will lead to the creation of alternative articulations of Caribbean modernity.

Both Edouard Glissant's theory of *antillanité*, which predicates the core of Caribbean identity structure upon the conflation of geopolitical discontinuity, ethnic admixture and cultural pluralism, and the notion of *créolité* put forward by Jean Bernabé, Patrick Chamoiseau, and Raphaël Confiant, which takes the Creole language as a metaphor for the Caribbean condition, reflect the doubling and difference that create the conditions for the emergence of new possibilities for cross-cultural communication. In practice, the innate complexities of post-colonial cultural creolization, both in the metropole and the Caribbean,

result in double-voiced narratives such as *L'autre qui danse,* whose alterity
hinges upon recognizing the impossibility of either erasing or effectively renego-
tiating the fissures that insistently link metropole and department.

The contrasts between Rehvana and Matildana interrogate the paradoxes
of exile within the "center," and reflect the unsettling geopolitical dualities that
define the French overseas departments. Rehvana's eventual death in Paris, following a brief return to Martinique--where she had sought to reintegrate herself
into an Antillean way of life--provides the basic armature of the plot. Her lack of
rootedness in Parisian society, where she has lived since early childhood, drives
her to behavioral and psychological extremes. Her persistent unease in the domain of the colonizing Other leads her to turn to her Caribbean origins, ethnicity, and culture as a path to authenticity. She confronts her metropolitan alienation through a search for integration in a variety of ways, which include terrorism and submission to physical battery. Rehvana aligns herself with the
"Ebonis-Fils-d'Agar," a terrorist group which plans to blow up the Centre Pom-
pidou. As a rite of passage, she must undergo beatings, tattooing, being locked
in a trunk for days, and fasting; ultimately she ends up in the hospital. This
self-imposed violence is intended to help her find a "racially" pure identity. In
contrast, Matildana appears at ease with her multi-ethnic heritage as well as with
her ability to read and write both French and Creole; she first uses her pluralism
to integrate herself into student life at the Sorbonne, where she studies Classics,
and then engages in cultural activism upon her return to Martinique. She simply
accepts her ethnic and cultural pluralism as a means of inhabiting many contem-
poraneous worlds of being.

It is precisely Rehvana's dual heritage as a displaced *métisse* that lies at
the heart of the various disjunctures she unsuccessfully attempts to confront and
correct throughout the course of the novel. What sets Rehvana apart from her
fellow Caribbean exiles, like her boyfriend Jérémie, who was born in Paris of
Guadeloupean parents and for whom "Guadeloupe and Martinique . . . remain
fantasies of folklore" (30),[5] or the terrorist group the Fils d'Agar, which is made
up of Antillean-African "wannabes" (displaced [non]Africans), is the fact that
she, like her sister Matildana, was born in the Antilles. Although she lives in
the metropole, she still sees "her native but still foreign Fort-de-France" (18)[6] as
a privileged space for the construction of her identity. Matildana, on the other
hand, is "comfortable in her strangely polychromatic skin . . . an unbelievable
beauty positioned at the intersection of countless centuries, a sumptuous, con-
trasting harmony of converging races" (39).[7] Importantly, then, her identity is
characterized by her recognition and valorization of her ethnic and cultural pluralism. The contrast between the sisters' differing trajectories reflects the multiple patterns of exile experienced by those of Guadeloupean and Martinican descent, in particular the impasse encountered by those like Rehvana who engage
in a doomed but insistent search for a redemptive racial authenticity through the
rediscovery of her creole culture.

For both sisters, then, the main factor that defines their identity is that
of difference. For Rehvana, this difference--from both metropole and
department--is intrinsically negative and oppositional, and leads to the fragmentation of her identity which is represented through the tensions of a narrative of
displacement. For Matildana, on the other hand, this same condition is presented as ordinary and unsurprising; it positions her within a framework of lib-

eratory pluralism that survives the move from one geocultural site to another, and even thrives on it. After Rehvana moves to Martinique in search of authenticity, she attempts to live without modern conveniences. Indeed, her deliberate plunge into a traditional, mythicized past--one upon which Antilleans themselves have turned their backs as the country became modernized--becomes irrevocably entwined with her tacit submission to Eric, the young Martinican with whom she undertakes this voyage of self-discovery. It is this dual subjugation to both gender and culture that leads to the dissolution of Rehvana's identity. The commentary implicit in the tone of the narrative is finally made explicit in a single, succinct phrase which summarizes her double bind: "She does all this for Eric, and because it is the Caribbean way" (122).[8] The deep irony expressed in this sentence demonstrates the extent to which the complexities of exile and authenticity remain problematic for the female Caribbean subject. This constant sense of displacement that disrupts Rehvana's life sets in motion the tragic trajectory that ultimately ends in pregnancy, poverty, disgrace, and death. Systematically beaten by her boyfriend, she escapes and later finds a teaching job. She loses this job, however, and ends up borrowing money to return to Paris. There, she and her daughter starve to death.

In Matildana's case, it is perhaps the unproblematic nature of her polysemic cultural identity that inscribes her as a positive emblem of cultural complexity. Already demonstrably at home in the metropole, Matildana moves back to Fort-de-France after completing her studies at the Sorbonne, and immediately continues to study and work with linguistic and cultural aspects of Creole: "she studies linguistics and Creole, while collaborating, in her spare time, on a local paper that works to highlight . . . the cultural, political and social activity of the Caribbean" (323).[9] Through her use of the Creole language and the plural Caribbean perspective of the new journal, Matildana inscribes herself as an icon of her own culture's multiple possibilities As such, Matildana simultaneously symbolizes and extends the potentialities of her Caribbean heritage into positive creole patterns, and her triumph stands in contrast to her sister's defeat.

In her novel *L'exil selon Julia*, Gisèle Pineau takes an alternative approach to interrogating the complex issues attached to patterns of migration to and exile within the metropole. Pineau's first-person narrator recounts a series of key moments in the life of her Guadeloupean family, drawing a parallel, as Dracius-Pinalie does, between the story of the family and the alienation and displacement that have been the corollaries of the "national" history of Guadeloupe and Martinique in the modern period. However, whereas Dracius-Pinalie subverts the hierarchies and oppositions that ground the hybridities born of the colonial encounter, Pineau adopts an approach that concentrates on the pitfalls of assimilation and the continuing sense of homelessness that is the lot of migrants from the DOM. To do so, Pineau focuses on the experiences of her narrator's paternal grandmother, Julia; Man Ya, as she is known, the matriarch of Pineau's displaced Guadeloupean family, encounters the unchanging nature of the metropolitan vision of the Other and the attendant forms of racism this entails in the post-colonial period; this encounter serves to illuminate the themes of exclusion, marginality, and difference that derive from her move from the periphery to the center. The feeling of being Other shapes the experience and the life stories of both the narrator and her grandmother.

The family had migrated to France in the great waves that sent both Antillais and others to that country--initially as part of a post-war labor force--in the 1950s and 1960s. The novel opens with the imminent return of the narrator's family to their native Guadeloupe after an 11-year period spent in France. For Maréchal, Daisy, and their five children, the most pressing question is one of authenticity and belonging, immediately formulated in a rhetorical fashion by the narrator: "Are they still Guadeloupeans?" ("Eux-mêmes sont-ils encore gens de Guadeloupe?") (25). By framing this theme of exile in spatial and temporal terms, Pineau immediately raises the question of whether the family's stay in France has made them less Caribbean and more French.

The opposition between "home" and "away" recurs repeatedly in the narrative, which is structured around the major themes of assimilation and difference as they relate to the family's life in the metropole. Thus, the question the narrator asks of Daisy and Maréchal, "Why did they leave their country?" (36),[10] is reinforced by repeated references to the metropole as "Là-Bas" (Over There) and "Pays-France" (Country-France), and the latter is implicitly opposed to Guadeloupe, "Le Pays" (The Country). Prior to the family's departure, the advantages of displacement are presented as myriad: "Profit from France! Profit from your opportunity to grow up there! Here, all the young brats speak Creole. You can learn how to speak French French" (36).[11] This binary framework effectively establishes the socio-cultural displacement that characterizes the departmental-metropolitan axis of the text.

The parallel trajectories of metropolitan unease traced by the narrative encompass the narrator's traumatic experience of French school, and the grandmother's painful attempts to integrate into a "foreign" culture. Called "Bamboula," among other names, by her white classmates, and encouraged to "Go back home" ("Retourner dans ton pays") (110), the narrator is singled out as different by the teacher as well: "Children! The Black Girl has already finished her work! You can do the same!" (80).[12] Perennially out of place, the narrator is quintessentially double--French yet not French, "racially" other in the center of her geopolitical "home." For Man Ya, who functions as the family's bulwark against adversity, there are similar moments of disjuncture, which culminate in her arrest for wearing her son's French military uniform in the street: "Man Ya had no desire to create a scandal, she only wanted to stop the rain. She hadn't realized the problems that could arise from wearing a military greatcoat in the streets of Aubigné" (98).[13] This confrontation between the norms of the metropole and those of Guadeloupe is further exacerbated by the fact that Man Ya speaks only Creole and is therefore not understood by the French police officers. Throughout the novel, the family constantly suffers the isolation caused by ignorance and is stigmatized by a society that refuses to recognize their Frenchness.

What is perhaps the ultimate confirmation of their difference comes in the most banal of ways, on television: "RACISM becomes the only possible subtitle of our favorite serials. . . . It is painfully clear that their world ignores us" (144).[14] Shows like "Zorro," "Le Sergent Garcia," and "Thierry La Fronde" suddenly become suspect when the narrator reaches the age of twelve or so. Their manifest social difference brings home to them the fact that TV is not in fact an ideal, escapist world, but reflects the real conditions of everyday existence. Thus, blacks are absent, segregated from television, just as they are on the street.

When the moment of Man Ya's return to Guadeloupe finally arrives, it is described in terms of abandonment and alterity: "She is leaving us to ourselves . . . abandoning us to France" (191).[15] Her existence in the domain of the Other leads to a questioning of where she belongs: "Of course I'd like to go back to my own country. But which country?" (194).[16] Here, Pineau forcefully expresses Man Ya's fear of finding herself homeless because of time spent away from Guadeloupe and suggests that the *neither/nor* binary is an inescapable consequence of the peregrinations of the French/West Indian migrant subject.

Eventually, when the rest of the family returns to the Caribbean (Martinique), their immediate recognition of people and places tells them that they have, indeed, come home: "The faces express the same suffering and the same dreams. The Creole that Man Ya spoke to us is here, in the street, in the market, at school, completely free" (244).[17] By claiming their creoleness, the family valorizes a culture which rejects the total adherence demanded by metropolitan *francité*. The non-hierarchical character of the region makes it a rich meeting place of diverse cultures: "Small countries that have a little of everything . . . the good Lord threw together color, language, religion, and nationality in this spot, to see how they would all get along" (61).[18] From the narrator's perspective, Man Ya is the emblem of this Caribbean pluralism, and at the end of the novel her cultural legacy is recognized as being the "Pathways opened up by her Creole speech" ("Sentes défrichées de son parler créole") (303). In this fashion, the pluralism and resistance intrinsic to Creole are made the principal symbols of a cultural identity defined by its difference from the metropole.

Hybridity, then, is presented in radically different guises in these two texts, but from its earliest inscription as a form of monstrosity in nineteenth-century texts to these recent post-colonial incarnations, it reflects changing notions of "home" and "away" and the ways in which these concepts are continually transformed. As such, it illustrates Bhabha's assertion that "hybridity . . . reverses the effects of the colonialist disavowal, so that other 'denied' knowledges enter upon the dominant discourse and estrange the basis of its authority" (*The Location of Culture* 114). In the face of these metropolitan discourses of exclusion, French Caribbean patterns of post-colonial hybridity constitute a new framework for nationalism and modernity, undermining and rewriting traditional definitions of pluralism and *francité*. It is perhaps in such subversions of the metropolitan concept of unicity that the true value of such hybridity lies.

NOTES

1. See Sidonie Smith and Gisela Brinker-Gabler's "Introduction" (7).

2. See Alain Anselin's "West Indians in France" (113).

3. See Richard D. E. Burton's "Introduction: The French West Indies à *l'heure de l'Europe*" (12).

4. My translation.

5. "Guadeloupe et Martinique ne représentent . . . qu'un aimable folklore." All translations from the novels are my own.

6. "sa Fort-de-France natale et cependant étrangère."

7. "bien dans sa peau étrangement polychrome ... cette incroyable beauté neuve au confluent de tant de siècles, cette fastueuse harmonie contrastée de toutes races convergentes."

8. "Elle fait tout cela pour Eric, et parce que c'est antillais."

9. "elle étudie la linguistique et le créole, tout en collaborant, à ses moments perdus, à un jeune hebdomadaire caribéen qui s'applique à rendre compte ... des activités culturelles, politiques et sociales du monde antillais."

10. "Pourquoi ont-ils quitté leur terre?"

11. "Profitez de la France! Profitez de votre chance de grandir ici-là! Au pays, la marmaille parle patois. Profitez pour apprendre le français de France."

12. "Les enfants! La Noire a déjà fini sa copie! Alors, vous pouvez le faire aussi!"

13. "Man Ya n'a pas voulu outrager la France, seulement barrer la pluie. Elle n'a pas vu le mal qu'il y avait à marcher en manteau militaire dans les rues d'Aubigné."

14. "RACISME devient le mot unique qui sous-titre nos feuilletons favoris. . . . Leur monde nous ignore d'une évidence nouvelle."

15. "Elle nous laisse à nous-mêmes . . . Elle nous abandonne à la France."

16. "Je veux bien retourner dans mon pays. Mais quel pays?"

17. "Les visages expriment mêmes souffrances et mêmes rêves. Le créole que Man Ya nous causait est ici, dans les rues, au marché, à l'école, en liberté."

18. "Des petits pays où on a déposé de tout un peu. ... Le Seigneur a assemblé là toutes couleurs, langues, religions, nations, pour voir comment les gens allaient se comporter."

WORKS CITED

Anselin, Alain. *L'émigration antillaise en France: la troisième île.* Paris: Karthala, 1990.

---. "West Indians in France." *French and West Indian: Martinique, Guadeloupe and French Guiana Today.* Eds. Richard D.E. Burton and Fred Reno. London: Macmillan Caribbean, 1995, 112-118.

Benítez-Rojo, Antonio. *The Repeating Island: The Caribbean and the Postmodern Perspective.* Trans. James E. Maraniss. Durham: Duke University Press, 1992.

Bernabé, Jean, Patrick Chamoiseau, and Raphaël Confiant. *Eloge de la créolité.* Paris: Gallimard, 1989.

Bhabha, Homi K. "DissemiNation." *Nation and Narration.* Ed. Homi K. Bhabha. New York: Routledge, 1990, 291-322.

---. *The Location of Culture.* New York: Routledge, 1994.

Braudel, Fernand. *The Identity of France.* Trans. Sian Reynolds. New York: Perennial Library, 1988.

Burton, Richard D.E. "Introduction: The French West Indies *à l'heure de l'Europe.*" *French and West Indian: Martinique, Guadeloupe and French Guiana Today.* Eds. Richard D.E. Burton and Fred Reno. London: Macmillan Caribbean, 1995, 1-19.

Dracius-Pinalie, Suzanne. *L'autre qui danse.* Paris: Seghers, 1989.

Glissant, Edouard. *Caribbean Discourse: Selected Essays.* Trans. J. Michael Dash. Charlottesville: University Press of Virginia, 1989.

Hobsbawm, Eric. *The Age of Empire 1875-1914.* New York: Vintage, 1989.

---. *Nations and Nationalism since 1780.* New York: Cambridge University Press, 1990.

Norindr, Panivong. "*La Plus Grande France:* French Cultural Identity and Nation Building under Mitterand." *Identity Papers: Contested Nationhood in*

  Twentieth-Century France. Eds. Steven Ungar and Tom Conley. Minneapo-
    lis: University of Minnesota Press, 1996, 233-258.
Ormerod, Beverley. *An Introduction to the French Caribbean Novel.* London:
    Heinemann, 1985.
Pineau, Gisèle. *L'exil selon Julia.* Paris: Stock, 1996.
Renan, Ernest. "What Is a Nation?" *Nation and Narration.* Ed. Homi K. Bhabha. New
    York: Routledge, 1990, 8-22.
Smith, Sidonie, and Gisela Brinker-Gabler. "Introduction. Gender, Nation and Immi-
    gration in the New Europe." *Writing New Identities: Gender, Nation, and
    Immigration in Contemporary Europe.* Ed. Gisela Brinker-Gabler and Sido-
    nie Smith. Minneapolis: University of Minnesota Press, 1997, 1-30.
Woodhull, Winifred. "Ethnicity on the French Frontier." *Writing New Identities:
    Gender, Nation, and Immigration in Contemporary Europe.* Ed. Gisela
    Brinker-Gabler and Sidonie Smith. Minneapolis: University of Minnesota
    Press, 1997, 31-61.

Textualizing the Immigrant Community: Françoise Ega's *Lettres à une Noire*

Patrice J. Proulx

> For me, Fort-de-France was like a dream. . . . Wasn't it the point of departure for other lands? "Other lands," for Martinicans, are those places created by God for them to visit one day: Guyana, Venezuela, Caracas, North America, and, above all, France.[1] (*Le temps des madras* 24)

> This brutal revelation overwhelmed me. I was the grand-daughter of a slave? First of all, what are slaves?[2] (*Le temps des madras* 50)

Françoise Ega, born in Martinique in 1920, joined the French Air Force in 1946, living and working in Indochina and Madagascar before moving to Marseille with her husband, where she spent most of the rest of her life. Ega, who died of a heart attack in 1976, published only one work during her lifetime--*Le temps des madras* (1966). This text, which could be classified as a fictionalized autobiography, is recounted from a child's point of view and portrays life in Martinique in the 1920s and 1930s. Dedicated to three women--her mother, an aunt, and a French benefactor--and focusing in particular on the fortitude demonstrated by women in raising their families, the text clearly bears witness to Ega's gynocentric perspective. *Le temps des madras*, while not overly tied to tradition, has little in common with the contestatory stance to be found in her second work.[3] *Lettres à une Noire*, published posthumously in 1978, evokes the world of the Antillean immigrant in Marseille in the early 1960s, a period during which a high rate of unemployment on the islands forced record numbers of Antilleans to relocate to France. Ega's text centers on issues relating to the exploitation of Antilleans in the workforce, especially women, looking specifically at the way in which their ethnic and cultural identities are either effaced or reshaped by the French in order to better fit their own stereotyped conceptualizations. The text also traces out the relationship of the immigrant heroine to writing, exploring the complex question of her access to writing and her search for legitimization, and ultimately situating the protagonist, in Mireille Rosello's terms, as a "femme de ménage de lettres" (working woman of letters) (213).[4]

As the title implies, the text takes the form of a series of letters, covering the period from May 1962 to June 1964. In this epistolary work,[5] the protagonist's chosen addressee is a Brazilian woman named Carolina Maria de Jesus who has devoted herself to working with the disadvantaged in the shantytown of São Paulo. Maméga[6] launches directly into her subject matter without a lengthy preamble--this directness will characterize her style throughout the narrative, as she brings to light the ways in which the immigrant poor have been disempowered. The first letter, which situates Maméga in relation to her addressee, makes manifest the constructed nature of the relationship between the two women; the protagonist reveals that she knows of Carolina only through an article she read in *Paris Match*, underscoring the fact that the two women will never meet, nor will they ever read each other's writing. The connection between them lies mainly in their shared interest in ameliorating the conditions facing those who are oppressed. While the relationship is "imaginary," that does not make it any less important in terms of the way it structures the text or in terms of its function as a springboard for Maméga's narrative. As Porter Abbott asserts in *Diary Fiction*: "The crucial issue is not the existence or non-existence of an addressee but the degree to which the addressee is given an independent life and an active textual role in the work" (10).[7] Maméga herself refers to the necessity of invoking a symbolic interlocutor, implying that Carolina's existence serves to ground her text and to provide her with the "authorization" she requires in order to write. She derives strength from her solidarity with this woman who lives half-way across the world: "If you hadn't become my oracle, I would have thrown my project out the window, telling myself, 'what's the sense of writing about this?' " (12).[8] Instead, she will persist in her efforts to inscribe the stories of those who too often find themselves silenced.

The crucial importance of this soul mate figure becomes all the more clear when the protagonist evinces the physical and psychological realities of her writing, including the attempts by her family members to discourage her from her enterprise. First of all, Maméga has great difficulty securing the materials with which to write--she uses notebooks and pencils which often disappear if they are not carefully hidden away. Finding the time and the space to write is an ongoing problem; most often, she must snatch bits of time while riding to work on the bus or while the children are studying, conditions hardly propitious to the development of her writing. Her children and her husband--peripheral characters who are not fully realized in the text--openly ridicule her literary pretensions, unable to see any possible value in what the protagonist herself terms her "gribouillage" (scribbling) (126). Even more importantly, her subject matter is brought into question by her husband in a manner which highlights the way in which texts written by ethnic minorities are likely to be read: "Qui veux-tu que ça intéresse, des histoires de nègres?" (Who do you think will be interested in niggers' stories?) (36).

This lack of support from her family, however, especially during the early stages of her writing venture, certainly reinforces the doubts in Maméga's mind about the validity and the aesthetic value of her writing. Indeed, as a writer of Antillean origin whose maternal language is Creole,[9] she questions the legitimacy of her attempts to write in the language of the "other": "avais-je le droit d'ainsi malmener la langue de Molière? Moi, une pauvre négresse?" (Did I have the right to abuse the language of Molière like this? A poor Negress like me?) (84). It is evident that her position as a lower-class working woman conflicts with her vision of an authentic woman writer. In her study of Ega's text, Rosello demonstrates how the divergent cultural codes ascribed to the *femme de lettres* (woman of letters) and to the *femme de ménage* (housemaid) have traditionally established and maintained barriers between the two: "Writing when seen as a luxury, a superfluous activity, contributes to the construction of the woman of letters as an artist, claimed by the intelligentsia (considered a masculine universe), and cut off from the working world" (214).[10] Rosello later affirms that, for Ega's protagonist, the decision to work and the decision to write are inextricably linked, the one having served as impetus for the other. The protagonist exhibits great strength by continuing to write even when confronted with overwhelming odds--the cathartic nature of the writing process provides her with the motivation to persevere, despite the fact that she questions her language skills: "Carolina, knowing how to bring words together, to make phrases and be able to read them, even if what one writes is in pidgin French or Javanese, leaves one feeling incredibly relieved" (17).[11]

Thus, through her letters to Carolina, Maméga becomes the voice of a heavily exploited and practically disenfranchised population of immigrant workers in Marseille. The protagonist undertakes a series of menial jobs in a sort of anthropological quest to document the conditions in which others in the Antillean immigrant community find themselves. As she informs Carolina, "C'est bien simple: je ne pourrai jamais en parler en connaissance de cause si je ne sais pas ce que cela est" (It's very simple: I could never discuss this knowledgeably if I don't know what it's about) (13). Her objective, then, will be to observe and to collect the stories of others who are suffering from their lives as immigrants, focusing in particular on women who find their only option is to work as *femmes de ménage*. In fact, as she emphasizes later in the text, "we are categorized by the government and by the French in general as being housemaids first and foremost, just as the Polish are considered to be agricultural workers and the Algerians unskilled road workers" (137).[12] While she herself feels privileged, in the sense that she has the freedom to "refuser la condition d'esclave" (refuse to be treated like a slave) (14), she attempts to help those who are being mistreated--underpaid and overworked. She strives to defend the rights of poor immigrant workers, despite her own precarious position in the workforce, challenging the employers' recalcitrance to give benefits to their workers through her knowledge of employees' rights. In one episode, for example, she insists that a young woman being forced to work while ill take time off to see a doctor, informing the indignant employer that her maid would not be coming back to work after all.

Indeed, Maméga's letters contain numerous anecdotes recounting the harshness and the forced aspects of the working conditions to which she and her compatriots are routinely subjected. She equates the disenfranchised state of these workers to slavery: "Est-ce la traite qui recommence?" (Is the slave trade beginning again?) (35). Indeed, many of the workers she meets have had their passage to France paid by their future employers, leaving them to reimburse the seemingly insurmountable debt after their arrival in Marseille.[13] There is no "transition" time during which the new arrivals can adapt to the new socio-cultural realities of life in France. For the most part, they must begin work immediately, and they quickly become isolated from others in the immigrant community. Maméga clearly articulates this problematic situation in an early letter to Carolina which also makes reference to the mixed racial heritage of Antilleans: "The employers pay the cost of the trip for young women who want to see other lands, and off they go! Mulattos, *chabines*, Negresses, and *capresses* leave the island and latch on to vacuum cleaners during the flight, the better to begin their work upon arrival" (34).[14] The alienation of the women who serve as housemaids is obviously to the employers' advantage, as it keeps them from establishing ties of solidarity which could lead to a more effective questioning of the system and their rights within it. They live in close contact with people with whom they can never have an authentic relationship--paradoxically, while their place is on the margins of these families, they become increasingly implicated in their lives, and may come to know them better than their own families: "Le plus pénible, je crois, pour une femme de ménage, c'est l'odeur de la vie des autres" (I think what is most difficult for a housemaid is the odor of others' lives) (17).

Thus, in order to better identify the abominable conditions in which these women work, Maméga finds herself toiling as a housemaid, encountering discriminatory practices from the very beginning. One of the issues which rises to the forefront is the erasure of identity to which Antillean workers are subjected. The protagonist describes the absurdities and the inherent racism of the situation in a passage illustrating the way in which her employers gloss over her own name in order to "simplify" things and to increase their own comfort level, either through the bestowal of a French first name, such as Marie or Julie, or an insistence on calling her by a name they had used with a previous maid: "For the first time since entering into the profession of housemaid, I have a first name--my employer gave it to me. She doesn't want to change her habits, so it is I who will change my first name; I'll be called Renée until the real Renée comes back" (128).[15] It seems clear that the strategic naming of the Antillean housemaids stems from the desire to deny their individual identity and their alterity, and to reduce them to one in an interchangeable series of immigrant workers who become assimilated when they are forced to conform to the expectations of their French employers by suppressing their unique socio-cultural differences and by assuming prescribed identities. Maméga realizes that within this invisible and seemingly infinite chain of workers, the existence of which relegates all of them to an inferior status, her efforts to enact any real change in the racist attitudes displayed by the majority of her employers will be continually thwarted. In a passage which cogently illustrates this idea of "interchangeability" among the maids, the protagonist relates an episode in which one of her employers asks her if she likes oysters--before Maméga can reply, the wife interjects: "Peut-être qu'elle ne les aime pas! l'autre Noire n'en a jamais mangé quand elle était là!" (Maybe she doesn't like them! The other black woman never ate them when she was here!) (93). Maméga is not alone among her family members, of course, in suffering the nefarious consequences of French racism. She must also comfort her children, who are "traités de chinois, de négros, de pieds-noirs ou de gitans" (called Chinese, niggers, Algerian-born Frenchmen, or gypsies) (47). Once again, where racism is concerned, the blurring of boundaries between different ethnicities is evident--a single stereotypical image becomes all-encompassing in its attempt to efface individual identities.

The protagonist, then, as a member of a minority ethnic group, must deal on a daily basis with the hostility of her employers--a hostility reflected in the reality that she is required to carry out tasks she realizes that no white woman would be asked to do, spending long hours needlessly scrubbing the recently cleaned stairs and carrying out long-neglected household repairs, for example. Rather than refuse to perform these tasks, however, she instead hopes to impress her employers by doing the job as well and with as much dignity as possible, in order to improve conditions for those who will follow; certainly, one could question the ultimate sagacity of such a strategy, given that her acquiescence counteracts the transgressive objectives of her original enterprise. While she does eventually quit jobs which become overly demanding or demeaning, Maméga tries to suppress her anger and rarely confronts her own employers, "par égard envers mes soeurs qui viennent par pleins bateaux se placer en France" (out of consideration for my sisters who come by the boatload to find jobs in France) (34).

In addition to the isolation she suffers while in the homes of her French employers, Maméga often feels estranged from the Antillean community at large. She testifies to her disillusionment at the reluctance of some of her fellow immigrants to concern themselves with the fate of others, claiming, for example, that even the members of the association founded by Antilleans themselves to assist those who have recently emigrated to France refuse to help the worst-off among them, displaying an elitist attitude designed to refute those they consider inferior. In this regard, as Annabelle Rea observes, "ces hommes, selon Maméga, font preuve de la même cruauté que les patronnes blanches" (these men, according to Maméga, show the same cruelty as do the white women employers) (300). Due to this repudiation by certain groups of Antilleans, she feels her own displacement all the more keenly: "I am and will remain a foreigner, because of my skin color, and here, among other blacks, I'm told that it isn't my place, because I'm a maid!" (134).[16] In describing a dinner held in honor of people from the different *départements*, Maméga underscores the fact that, while Corsicans from all different strata of society--students, lawyers, fishermen, and musicians--mingle freely together, Antilleans display a remarkable lack of solidarity, stemming in large part from class differences: "They only whisper it, my dear Carolina, they would never admit it to themselves . . . and yet it's true, Antilleans have more difficulty living together, in Europe or elsewhere, than those belonging to any other immigrant community" (51).[17] Maméga envisages a more inclusive movement which would engage Antilleans as a group in the recovery and validation of their history. In her eyes, a salutary transformation can only occur with a more profound understanding of the past: "But why, then, are there certain blacks who draw the curtains on what constitutes our blackness? It's not by hiding a wound that one heals it, to the contrary" (135).[18]

It is only by means of her textual self-inscription that the protagonist will be able to invoke the specificity of her Antillean origins. At the same time, as shown in the previous example, she displays an awareness that there is more at stake here than the destabilizing of individual identities--she must confront the erasure of the past in a broader sense. In this regard, a statue of the Black Virgin in a local abbey functions as an important figure in the recuperation of her history. To celebrate Candlemas, she goes to St. Victor's Abbey to pray before the statue; the Virgin's skin color, similar to Maméga's own, puts her at ease. She visits the crypt, and the presence of the martyrs' tombs causes her to reflect upon the gaps and blanks in Antillean history: "I start to envy those peoples who only need look to discover their history and deep inside I cry out: 'Where is my past? Is it nothingness?' Then the smile of the Black Virgin reassures and calms me" (71).[19] Rea underscores the way in which the statue of the Black Virgin in Ega's text not only functions as "the symbol of working Antillean women" but also "serves as a link with her Antillean past, totally absent from the surrounding European context, as it reminds Maméga of her mother back home and the storytellers she listened to as a child" (300).[20]

Her visit to the abbey, though, while providing a brief respite from the punishing demands of her job, cannot sustain her on a daily basis. The protagonist, who feels constantly fatigued by her attempts to negotiate the differences in her life as a housemaid and in her capacity as wife and mother in her own large family, reveals that her husband has always been completely against her taking jobs as a maid. He voices his misgivings on several occasions, insisting that after a certain point she will no longer be able to separate herself from her "role" as housemaid, a prospect which concerns and frightens both of them: "The one time you have the chance to leave behind your saucepans and your role as guinea pig! . . . You'll have soaked up this life to such an extent that you'll never get out of it!" (145).[21] While she manages to keep up her writing, transcribing numerous descriptions of the back-breaking, mind-numbing tasks she must carry out at the whim of her employers, the protagonist recognizes the veracity of her husband's words, as her body itself comes to emblematize her untenable position. Arthur Flannigan-Saint-Aubin analyzes the inscription of the black body in *Lettres à une Noire*, insisting on the ways in which relentless exploitation by French employers will indelibly mark the immigrant worker--in this case, the protagonist: "Even when she is no longer a domestic, the narrator expects to be treated like one because she has the body of one. Her body is permanently altered and acquires an entire language of its own. . . . The sadism of her *dames* is imprinted indelibly on her body" ("Reading and Writing" 54). Another example will serve to point out the way in which the colonized body serves as commodity. In one of the final jobs she undertakes, Maméga works at a booth at the International Fair selling products from the French Antilles. Her employer, also of Antillean origin, immediately "corrects" her when she begins her sales pitch by announcing the range of "colonial" products available: " 'Don't say colonial goods! say: goods from Overseas.' It was a subtle difference, and it only concerned cinnamon: across from me, however, a living colonial product [Renée] unhappily followed her uncompromising employers" (191).[22] She thus calls attention to the colonialist tendencies which continue to underlie the relationship between France and her former colonies.

The protagonist, like her husband, realizes that, at some point in the near future, despite her undaunted courage in the daily struggle to overcome a variety of tribulations, her contestation will of necessity take on a new form. She is exhausted from raising her own five children, suffers from numerous ailments brought on by the arduous conditions of her work, and is both physically and psychologically unable to continue in her role as housemaid. Concomitantly, in one of her final letters, she suggests that it will soon be time to terminate her epistolary venture, an observation which reinforces the idea of the link between working and writing posited earlier. In this letter, Maméga reveals the disillusionment underlying her decision: "It's true, Carolina, that there is nothing to tell you that you don't already know. The days and the years are all alike, the *dames* will stay the same, anonymous and sad" (213).[23] Nevertheless, she instinctively understands that she will remain actively engaged in the struggle to effect change in the Antillean immigrant community by other means, most likely through the publication of her work. While she initially feels "immobilisée" (paralyzed) (217) after the completion of her manuscript, Maméga senses the revolutionary potential of her project and feels reinvigorated at the thought of her words appearing in print: "Hope is born again in spite of everything, for my manuscript is being read" (217).[24] Thus, she remains optimistic that, however slowly, change will take place, and that those who have been discriminated against because of their origins outside of the Hexagon will be able to more fully assume their identity and reclaim their history within the parameters of French society.

Two brief texts contained in an appendix bear witness to the autobiographical aspect and the documentary value of *Lettres à une Noire*--one is a collective message by the inhabitants of the immigrant Marseillais neighborhood (La Busserine) in which Ega herself had lived and worked. A short passage from this text, written to honor the author after her death, testifies to the recognition of Ega's actual contributions to that community: "She was truly the soul of our neighborhood. Her initiatives and her social activities were numerous" (225).[25] Ega's significance as an immigrant writer lies primarily, then, in the intersections of her work, her writing, and her activism. The testimonial value of her text does not in any way negate its aesthetic value, but rather serves to illustrate the liberatory possibilities which arise from this kind of life/writing. Through her textualizing of the immigrant community in *Lettres à une Noire*, Ega plays an important role in giving voice to those who have been silenced.

NOTES

1. "Fort-de-France, pour moi, était un rêve. . . . N'était-ce pas l'endroit où l'on venait pour atteindre d'autres pays? Les 'autres pays,' pour les Martiniquais, sont des endroits que Dieu a créés pour qu'ils y aillent un jour: la Guyane, le Venezuela, Caracas, l'Amérique du Nord et surtout la France." All translations are my own.

2. "Cette brutale révélation me bouleversa. Comment, moi, j'étais petite-fille d'esclave? Tout d'abord, qu'est-ce que c'était que les esclaves?"

3. Arthur Flannigan-Saint-Aubin notes that both of Ega's works have "remained in the periphery of the literary canon" ("Reading Below the Belt" 300) and are little known outside of the French Antilles.

4. See Rosello's "*Lettres à une Noire* de Françoise Ega: la femme de mé-

nage de lettres" for a complete analysis of this term.

5. See Annabelle Rea for a discussion relating to the generic classification of Ega's text. Rea postulates that the work can be situated as "un roman épistolaire, une autobiographie épistolaire, un récit d'esclave, une lettre ou un journal" (an epistolary novel, an epistolary autobiography, a slave narrative, a letter, or a diary) (302).

6. The name of the protagonist in this text is also that used by Ega's friends in referring to her (see Emile Monnerot's preface to *Lettres à une Noire*, 5).

7. Cited in Pascale De Souza, 65.

8. "Si tu n'étais pas devenue mon égérie, j'aurai tout flanqué par la fenêtre en me disant 'à quoi bon écrire des choses?' " The epistolary nature of the text also serves to implicate the reader more directly in the subject matter. Diane Cousineau speaks to this issue, positing that "the letter sustains our belief in the immediacy of truth and the communicability of lived experience, the subtle movement and intensity of emotion" (28).

9. See De Souza's "Ces femmes qui s'écrivent: *Une si longue lettre* de Mariama Bâ et *Lettres à une Noire* de Françoise Ega," and Christiane Makward and Odile Cazenave's "The Others' Others: 'Francophone' Women and Writing" for insightful analyses of the alienation which often affects native speakers of Creole who feel forced to repress their language in favor of French.

10. "Envisager l'écriture comme un luxe, une activité gratuite, contribue à faire de la 'femme de lettres' une artiste, récupérée par l'intelligentsia (pensée comme l'univers masculin), et coupée du monde du travail."

11. "Carolina, savoir réunir des mots, en faire des phrases et pouvoir les lire, même si ce que l'on écrit est en petit nègre ou en javanais! Cela donne une impression incroyable de soulagement."

12. "nous sommes classées par le gouvernement et la France entière comme devant être avant tout femmes de ménage, comme les Polonais sont ouvriers agricoles, les Algériens terrassiers." As Jean Goosen comments in relation to the actual working conditions of French Antillean women, "Both sexes are restless in their jobs, but the women especially tend to leave work as housemaids to take temporary positions in hospitals which offer no security at all but seem less demeaning to them" (49).

13. Clarisse Zimra discusses government-sponsored emigration practices during this time of massive unemployment in the French Antilles in which Bumidom (Bureau pour le Développement des Migrations des Départements d'Outre-Mer) would pay for a one-way ticket to France. Zimra echoes Ega's framing of the immigrants' plight: "The system has been called a new slave trade" (58).

14. "Elles [les dames] paient le voyage aux filles qui veulent voir du pays, et hop! Mûlatresses, chabines, négresses et capresses laissent l'île et attrapent l'aspirateur au vol pour commencer à se faire les pieds en arrivant."

15. "Pour la première fois depuis que je me suis lancée dans la profession de femme de ménage, j'ai un prénom, la dame me l'a donné. Elle ne veut pas changer ses habitudes, c'est moi qui changerai de prénom, je m'appellerai Renée en attendant que la vraie Renée revienne."

16. "Je suis et resterai l'étrangère, à cause de ma peau, et ici, parmi les nègres, on me dit que c'est pas ma place, parce que je suis bonne!"

17. "Ils se le disent bien bas, ma pauvre Carolina, ils ne voudront jamais se l'avouer . . . et pourtant c'est vrai, les Antillais vivent beaucoup plus difficilement entre eux, en Europe ou ailleurs, que n'importe quelle autre communauté étrangère."

18. "Mais pourquoi donc y a-t-il des nègres qui tirent le rideau sur ce qui est notre négritude? Ce n'est pas en cachant une plaie qu'on la guérit, au contraire."

19. "Je me prends à envier tous les peuples qui n'ont qu'à regarder pour lire l'histoire de leur passé et je crie en mon for intérieur: 'Où est-il mon passé? est-ce un néant?' Alors le sourire de la Vierge Noire me rassure, me calme."

20. "le symbole des Antillaises travailleuses [qui] sert de lien avec son passé antillais, totalement absent du context européen environnant car elle rappelle à Maméga sa mère au pays ou les conteuses qu'elle écoutait en tant qu'enfant."

21. "Pour une fois que tu as la possibilité de laisser les casseroles et de servir de cobaye . . .! Tu seras tellement imprégnée de cette vie que tu ne pourras plus en sortir!"

22. " 'Ne dites pas tous les produits coloniaux! dites: tous les produits d'Outre-mer.' C'était une nuance et il ne s'agissait que de cannelle: pourtant, en face de moi, un vivant produit colonial [Renée] suivait sans rire des patrons intransigeants."

23. "Il est vrai, Carolina, qu'il n'y a plus rien à te dire que tu ne saches déjà. Les jours ressembleront aux jours, les années aux années, les dames seront toujours les mêmes, anonymes et tristes."

24. "L'espoir renaît malgré cela, car on lit mon manuscrit."

25. "Elle fut véritablement l'âme de nos quartiers. Ses initiatives, ses activités sociales étaient multiples."

WORKS CITED

Cousineau, Diane. *Letters and Labyrinths: Women Writing/Cultural Codes.* Newark: University of Delaware Press, 1997.

De Souza, Pascale. "Ces femmes qui s'écrivent: *Une si longue lettre* de Mariama Bâ et *Lettres à une Noire* de Françoise Ega." *Etudes francophones* 13.2 (1998): 63-78.

Ega, Françoise. *Lettres à une Noire: récit antillais.* Paris: L'Harmattan, 1978.

---. *Le temps des madras: récit de la Martinique.* 1966. Paris: L'Harmattan, 1989.

Flannigan-Saint-Aubin, Arthur. "Reading Below the Belt: Sex and Sexuality in Françoise Ega and Maryse Condé." *The French Review* 62.2 (December 1988): 300-312.

---. "Reading and Writing the Body of the *Négresse* in Françoise Ega's *Lettres à une Noire.*" *Callaloo* 15.1 (1992): 49-65.

Goosen, Jean. "The Migration of French West Indian Women to Metropolitan France." *Anthropological Quarterly* 49.1 (1976): 45-52.

Johnson, Ilona, and Christiane Makward. "La longue marche des femmes Franco-Antillaises: fictions autobiographiques de Mayotte Capécia et Françoise Ega." *Elles écrivent des Antilles (Haïti, Guadeloupe, Martinique).* Ed. Suzanne Rinne and Joëlle Vitiello. Paris: L'Harmattan, 1997, 309-321.

Makward, Christiane, and Odile Cazenave. "The Others' Others: 'Francophone' Women and Writing." *Yale French Studies* 75 (1988): 190-207.

Rea, Annabelle. "Les femmes au travail dans *Lettres à une Noire.*" *Elles écrivent des Antilles (Haïti, Guadeloupe, Martinique).* Ed. Suzanne Rinne and Joëlle Vitiello. Paris: L'Harmattan, 1997, 297-306.

Rosello, Mireille. "*Lettres à une Noire* de Françoise Ega: la femme de ménage de lettres." *L'héritage de Caliban.* Dir. Maryse Condé. Pointe-à-Pitre: Éditions Jasor, 1992, 213-32.

Zimra, Clarisse. "Négritude in the Feminine Mode: The Case of Martinique and Guadeloupe." *Journal of Ethnic Studies* 12.1 (1984): 53-77.

THE AFRICAN DIASPORA
IN FRANCE

Writing New Identities:
The African Diaspora in Paris

Odile Cazenave

The most recent developments in francophone African literature include ground-breaking novels produced by young first-generation African authors living in France.[1] Most of these authors, originally from countries in sub-Saharan Africa such as Senegal, Cameroon, Guinea, the Ivory Coast, Zaïre (now the Congo), and the Republic of Congo, are in their twenties and thirties. With the exception of well-established writer Calixthe Beyala, most of them are authors on the rise. As they abandon the mainstream African novel[2] to explore more personal avenues, these authors are creating a new type of literature. In their systematic de-centering of both novelistic forms and themes, they raise new questions about post-colonial identities and cultures, and thereby participate in the shaping of the African diaspora in France. Rather than focusing on Africa, a significant number of their works show a common interest in African immigrants and questions of displacement.

This thematics is not new. Indeed, the question of displacement and identity was one of the predominant themes of the African *roman de formation* of the 1960s and 1970s, as seen in Bernard Dadié's *Un nègre à Paris* (1959) and Cheikh Hamidou Kane's *L'aventure ambiguë* (1961). In these novels, however, the protagonist is generally a student living in France for a limited period of time, and the narrative is rarely framed in terms of immigration.[3] In contrast, most of today's new diasporic texts not only portray Africans in France as individuals having difficulty adjusting and integrating into French society, but they also--and perhaps primarily--examine a larger picture, that of community and place viewed in terms of multi-culturalism and transculturation. By so doing, they point to such questions as how immigrants are defined and perceived in contemporary French society.

This corpus displays three main characteristics. First, it can be described as a literature of detachment. As such, it shows little interest in Africa and Africans and rejects the automatic association of African writers with engaged literature.[4] Secondly, it is a literature of displacement which raises questions about identity with regard to space, gender, class, and race.[5] Finally, it constitutes a literature of immigration, which focuses on the dynamics that migration entails for both men and women.[6]

Generally speaking, the literature of immigration in France has for the most part been associated with immigrants of Maghrebi origin and, by extension, with what has been called the *Beur* novel (written by those born in France to Maghrebi parents), which emerged in the early to mid-1980s. Why, then, is *Beur* literature automatically identified as belonging to the category "literature of immigration" when texts from the African diaspora are often not included in it? Furthermore, the ways in which the category is used to include or exclude certain groups raises questions about how the center and borders of a literary corpus are defined and how immigrant communities are perceived. In this chapter, I will examine new representations of the African diaspora in France in a series of texts written primarily by Congolese and Cameroonian authors[7] in order to suggest a rethinking and a redefinition of the general concept of the literature of immigration.

Like *Beur* literature, the writing of what has at times been called "Black Babel," "Black Beurs," or "the New Black generation,"[8] appeared in the mid-1980s. Texts such as *A la recherche du cannibale amour* (1988) by Cameroonian Yodi Karone, and his compatriot Simon Njami's *Cercueil et Cie* (1985) and *African Gigolo* (1989), set the tone for this type of writing. These first novels reject all ties with Africa, as the characters distance themselves from anything that has to do with Africans or Africa. In the same way, the authors refuse to be labeled African writers, in the sense that they do not see themselves as engaged in a socio-realist mission. *African Gigolo* is a perfect example of such a plea for individualism.[9] Moïse, the narrator of this text, makes a point of showing a total lack of interest in the cause of Africa. A Cameroonian, he leaves his country to study in France, but soon afterwards stops attending his courses without his family's knowledge. As the title of Njami's novel suggests, Moïse uses his charms, if not as a commodity, then at least as a vehicle which enables him to blend into French society and pass for a Parisian; he dresses with great care, surrounds himself with white friends, frequents the Parisian bourgeoisie, and ignores anything remotely connected with blacks or the black milieu in Paris. Using the third-person pronoun "they" to refer to his fellow Africans, he makes it clear that he wants to separate himself from them, and he criticizes Africans in France who dream of a monolithic, utopian Africa and think they can make a difference while in France. At first sight, he shows no particular interest in race or questions of identity and hybridization, and acts as if Africa has been erased from his background. It resurfaces abruptly, however, through a letter from his mother announcing that his father is not well, and that he should come and visit them. The possibility of a trip back to Cameroon after a ten-year absence forces him to confront the lies that envelop his entire life: he has used his pursuit of university degrees as a pretext to prolong his stay in France, claiming to be studying hard, while in reality never taking any exams. Indeed, a closer look at the text reveals a pervasive anxiety which permeates the novel, forcing the reader to reflect on the consequences of the narrator's behavior. In this sense, the novel tells a story of procrastination, each episode enabling the protagonist to put off confronting questions about his identity. Viewed in this light, sex and love are devoid of any meaning for Moïse and serve only to help him avoid dealing with difficult questions. At the climactic point when he redeems himself by killing a man who had inflicted sexual violence and humiliation upon him, he paradoxically sees his act as a sacrificial gesture that saves him and finally enables him to face a possible return to his country.[10] This episode, which serves as a catalyst, reveals the suffering behind the mask of interracial harmony and hybridity he had put on. At this point, he is at last able to confront the central issue in his life: his deculturation and what he now perceives as a lack of authenticity.

In *African Gigolo* and other texts in the same vein, the main character's denial of any identity crisis, of any problematic adjustment to French geographical and socio-cultural space becomes the central focus of the narrative. These novels all portray the protagonists' fierce resistance to being identified as immigrants because of the often negative connotations of the term. Their primary preoccupation is therefore that their blending into French society be taken as a given. Philippe Camara's *Discopolis* (1993) is perhaps the most telling example. Here, the fact that the protagonist is African is barely mentioned, and the novel never addresses any questions related to displacement, integration, or multi-culturalism, focusing instead on the world of music, nightclubs, and drugs. How, then, do we determine whether such works qualify as examples of the literature of immigration? At what point do we, as readers or as critics, start looking at a text as part of this body of literature: when it discusses the experience of immigration or when it refuses to do so? when the writer's origins are taken into account, regardless of the topics addressed in the text, or when, regardless of the writer's origins, the protagonist is an immigrant? when the protagonist's status as an immigrant contributes only peripherally to the development of the plot, or, on the contrary, when it is central to the narrative?

Unlike *African Gigolo,* Biyaoula's *L'impasse* (1996) raises questions of identity and authenticity from the outset. Here, the text centers on Joseph, whose increasing alienation derives from his double displacement within French society and within his own community. Joseph's alienation can be viewed as a three-step process: it first manifests itself through his shock and difficulty readjusting to African ways of life when he goes to the Congo for a brief vacation after being away for eleven years. Although we do not know what caused him to leave, we can surmise that it was due to financial difficulties and to the hopes his family placed in him. Upon his return, some of the tension between Joseph and his family results from his failure to project the image they expect: because he is dressed casually, does not own a suit, has not earned a degree from a French university, and does not have a car, he is unable to pass for a successful Parisian, thus shattering the myth that his family and friends continue to entertain about France and about Africans living in France. Secondly, he paradoxically finds it hard to return to his life in France after this trip: in addition to anxieties related to unemployment, he experiences feelings of tension toward the African community, especially its women, and he sharply criticizes such acts as their lightening their complexion, which he interprets as an act of mimicry indicative of their attempts to imitate white women.[11] Joseph's description of these women, with its images of imprisonment and enslavement, suggests the transposition of his own feelings onto the female body: instead of addressing the question of his own identity, he evades it by transferring it onto women and what he views as their alienated bodies. The first two stages of his evolution, then, the visit home and subsequent confrontation with his life in France, make him aware of both his fragmentation and his inability to reconstruct a satisfying world to live in, causing him to give up.

Joseph's transformation in the third phase shows that he is unable to combine diverse cultural codes as he attempts to construct and define his own self. Instead, he ends up creating an artificial identity that is the negation of his initial principles. At this point, part of his refusal to face his own alienation leads him to place all the blame on the white community. His growing resentment toward this community even includes his girlfriend, whom he considers a representative of her race, an attitude which finally leads to their breaking up and causes his initial mask of interracial harmony to progressively disappear, like Moïse's, thus revealing doubts about the possibility of interracial relationships. Finally, Joseph's alienation takes the form of hysteria, leading to his institutionalization and treatment in a psychiatric unit. In particular, his therapy with a French psychiatrist renowned for his supposed knowledge of old Africa convinces Joseph to mimic his compatriots' extravagant life style and skin bleaching. He puts on weight in order to project an image of success and only wears suits, even when he is cleaning bathrooms at his new job. This ultimate form of Joseph's alienation suggests that he has adopted the very same behavior he originally despised and now seeks to conform to the expectations that those back home have for immigrants.

In *L'impasse*, Biyaoula focuses on Africans in both France and Africa. The narrator's sharp attack on his fellow Africans' relentless urge to copy and adopt an appearance that seems to connote success raises a number of important questions about the forms mimicry takes, from the use of bleaching creams to the social pressures surrounding interracial relationships. These issues all point to a central concern: for Africans who have settled in France, what does it mean to have an "authentic" identity in the context of immigration? Indeed, Joseph repeatedly raises the question of what it means to be a "real" African when living away from his primary culture. This question, which recurs in other texts such as Njami's *African Gigolo* and Kesso Barry's *Kesso, princesse peuhle*, is left unanswered. Unlike the protagonists of many Antillean novels, for example, Joseph does not embark on a search for origins or collective history that would give him a sense of being anchored, and he never shows any longing for his homeland. At the same time, however, he feels at a loss as he comes to realize that his experience in France is empty and meaningless, thus putting into question the role of the African community in France.

Biyaoula's second novel, *Agonies* (1998), again explores the themes of appearance and belonging, within both French society and the African immigrant community. It does so in particular by describing the excessive importance given to "la sape."[12] The world depicted here, the suburban environment and housing projects of Château Rouge, is even more somber than that portrayed in *L'impasse*, and the novel creates a sense of fragmentation, suffocation, and despair. Unlike the earlier novel, *Agonies* focuses on the community of Congolese immigrants rather than on a single character. Through the stories and parallel destinies of two couples--a Congolese teenager and a young white Frenchman, and the teenager's aunt and a compatriot from a rival ethnic group--Biyaoula highlights underlying ethnic tensions affecting the community. In this work, collective disapproval of interracial and inter-ethnic relationships results in dramatic consequences. Because he fears becoming a laughing stock, the teenager's father locks her up, beats her, and eventually sends her back to the Congo without letting her finish school, rather than allowing her to continue her relationship with the white Frenchman. Similarly, the other couple breaks up because of rumors circulated among the group which lead to the death of two people. Besides portraying such ethnic tensions, *Agonies*, like *L'impasse*, also denounces the excessive importance attached to appearance, an obsession which leads to fraud and other forms of illegal activity in the immigrant community.

Alain Mabanckou's[13] *Bleu-Blanc-Rouge* (1998) again focuses on the Congolese immigrant community in Paris. In this novel, the phenomenon of "la sape" criticized by Biyaoula becomes a central concern, as do the illegal activities which are a direct consequence of it--reselling metro tickets, stealing checkbooks, and fabricating false identity papers. At the same time, *Bleu-Blanc-Rouge* addresses issues similar to those found in Cameroonian J. R. Essomba's *Le paradis du Nord* (1996), which centers on such consequences of illegal immigration as the exploitation of African immigrants (from Cameroon, in Essomba's case) by the French as well as by some of their compatriots. Both novels have dramatic endings. In *Le paradis du Nord*, an escalating series of petty crimes and misunderstandings culminates in the death of one of the two main characters, who is being chased by the police, while the other (Jojo) is arrested on charges of rape, attempted homicide, and drug trafficking. Innocent of the first two charges, and completely unaware that he is carrying drugs, Jojo is constantly manipulated by others--a prostitute finds him a newspaper delivery job through her protector, for example, but unbeknown to him, there are drugs hidden in the papers. Similarly, in *Bleu-Blanc-Rouge*, the protagonist ends up in jail for his role in illegally reselling metro tickets and assuming a false identity. Throughout his stay in Paris, he, like Jojo, is at the mercy of a group of shady characters--all Africans--who involve him in illegal activities. At the end of the novel, after serving his jail sentence, he awaits his imminent deportation to Brazzaville, fearfully contemplating the humiliation of becoming "la risée du quartier" (the laughing stock of the neighborhood) (215).

Bleu-Blanc-Rouge portrays a well-established and well-organized network operating in Paris into which new arrivals are integrated and through which they are initiated into the life of crime that will finance their "sapes" (clothes). By tracing the evolution of three characters who move between Paris and Brazzaville--Massala-Massala the narrator; Moki "the Parisian" who serves as go-between and is responsible for Massala-Massala's coming to Paris; and Préfet, the person pulling the strings behind the shady dealings--the novel gives a detailed account of how the network functions and explores some of its consequences. In particular, it describes how some Congolese youths, lured by the myth of Paris as the land of opportunity and success, come to France on a tourist visa, then try to work their way into French society by circumventing the system. By foregrounding Massala-Massala's perspective, Mabanckou reveals what are often the harsh realities behind the myth: the expectation that new arrivals participate in criminal activities which, in Massala-Massala's case, means ending up in jail and being deported.

The narrative form of *Bleu-Blanc-Rouge*, a diary written from jail, recalls *Ici s'achève le voyage* (1989) by Cameroonian Léandre-Alain Baker. Both novels consist of a long flash-back that explains the events leading to the narrator's imprisonment--in the case of *Ici s'achève le voyage*, these include an altercation during which the narrator stabs and kills the former lover of his French girlfriend, who subsequently accuses him of intended homicide. By adopting this narrative structure and by exploring the interconnected trajectories of exploiters and victims, both authors highlight the risks and potential dangers involved in the experience of immigration. This emphasis on the tragic consequences of immigration leads Mabanckou to look at "la sape" from the perspective of both Brazzaville and Paris. Besides criticizing the importance attached to appearances, he stresses the responsibility of those who, like Moki, live in France, yet promote themselves in Africa as the embodiment of problem-free immigration and financial success, thereby perpetuating the mythical image of Paris as a kind of paradise that corresponds to the Brazzaville characters' dreams. The juxtaposition of the two locations brings out the sharp contrast between the myth and the reality Massala-Massala encounters in Paris--crime as the solution to unemployment, the dimly lit maid's room on the seventh floor shared by many of Moki's transient acquaintances, false identities (Massala-Massala is given two French names), and the stock letter sent to the girlfriend back home depicting France as a land of plenty and describing the narrator's new-found wealth. Whether portrayed in Paris or Brazzaville, the immigrants in *Bleu-Blanc-Rouge* are reproached for creating unattainable dreams that encourage their compatriots to embark upon a hazardous enterprise which frequently leads to disillusionment. In Biyaoula's and Mabanckou's representations of the recent Congolese diaspora in France, then, two main points stand out: their debunking of the myth of France as a land of opportunity and their critical analysis of Africans' attitudes in both France and Africa.

Calixthe Beyala's *Le petit prince de Belleville* (1992) and its sequel, *Maman a un amant* (1993), which both focus on the daily life of Malian immigrants in Belleville, add a gender component to the portrayal of the immigrant community.[14] Indeed, all Beyala's "Parisian" novels, including the recent *Amours sauvages* (1999), examine the ways in which gender modifies the experience of sub-Saharan African immigrants. Unlike her male characters, who, like

Abdou in *Le petit prince de Belleville*, look toward the past, long for their home in Africa, and worry about losing their status and authority, her female characters look to the benefits of immigration and welcome the opportunity to change and to assume a new identity. In these texts, Beyala explores the question of immigration in terms of its potential for African women.[15] In particular, she considers the renegotiation of identity as central to women's experience of migration: all her works demonstrate how identity is closely bound to a geographic location and how displacement and a change of place entail a transformation of gender roles and a redefinition of power relationships.

In *Le petit prince de Belleville*, Beyala uses the alternating voices of a seven-year-old child, Loukoum, and his father, Abdou Traoré, to underscore the contrast between Abdou's great disillusionment and his problems adjusting to a new environment and his wives' and child's transformation as they discover a new way of thinking and behaving. Abdou's marginalization is portrayed as closely related to his being labeled an immigrant and experiencing the negative connotations associated with the term: "At immigration, you registered my body and wrapped it in contempt, in hatred. In your wide-open eyes I was already suspected of rape or murder. Obsessed with sex. A pile of mud whose role is to obstruct people's memories and spread AIDS" (*Le petit prince de Belleville* 37). Vulnerable and alienated because of his status as an immigrant, he feels even more powerless at home where the women and children in his family no longer listen to him. In contrast, the female characters, especially in *Maman a un amant*, take initiatives and look toward the future, even though the extent of their authority remains limited.[16] Viewed as a whole, Beyala's representation of women shows a progression from the earlier novels (*Le petit prince de Belleville* and *Maman a un amant*), in which women form part of a family and belong to the Malian immigrant community, to her more recent texts (*Assèze l'Africaine* [1994] and *Les honneurs perdus* [1996]), which depict single women without a family who come to Paris in order to change and reinvent themselves.

Most of the works written by members of the new diaspora in France share a common thematics in their protagonists' lack of direction, their difficulty setting goals in life; the impossibility of their blending into French society and, most crucially, their resistance to being part of a displaced African community in France. These protagonists must therefore find a balance between France and Africa and must individually resolve problems related to biculturalism and bilingualism. While most of them acknowledge the risks associated with immigration and assimilation into a different culture, they also see an Africa they no longer understand or identify with. For these characters, the presence of an African community in France, with its displaced or modified cultural practices, is no longer perceived in terms of the comfort and stability it can provide, but rather in terms of its potentially negative impact on the individual. Consequently, fragmented identities and the resulting transformation of power dynamics within the family and the community become the central issue in the corpus.

These works powerfully portray the problematic relationship of the characters to the concept of immigration. To a large extent, the varying perspectives on the immigrant community--feeling part of it or refusing to be involved in it--reflect common negative perceptions of non-European immigrants, par-

ticularly the view of immigration as a static situation rather than a transforma-
tive process, as a source of economic hardship rather than of opportunity. Refusing to see immigration as a single, uniform experience, however, writers such
as Njami, Beyala, and Mabanckou undermine the usual profile of the immigrant.
In particular, their subversion of stereotypical racial images and their use of language serves to create a plural, more positive image of immigrants.[17] In this
sense, they contribute to what Michel Laronde calls the "decentering" of the
notion of the literature of immigration by emphasizing both its plurality and its
post-colonial nature.[18]

     With their emphasis on racial stereotypes, conflictual family relation-
ships, and dilemmas related to migration, belonging, and integration, the most
recent novels of the African diaspora (mid-1990s on) have many affinities with
Beur fiction.[19] Both literary corpuses develop the thematics of delinquency and
of getting around the system, and both frequently use figures such as teachers,
welfare workers, or police officers to embody the locus of institutional power.
Unlike *Beur* novels, though, which often emphasize the marginalization of both
the individual and the community as a whole, the novels of the African diaspora
do not demand the right to be different or to create a new collective identity, but
rather put into question the very idea of a homogeneous African community and
its role in the construction of a stable identity.

     At the same time, the emergence of a new category of African writers
in France calls for a redefinition of the term "literature of immigration." By using the expression in the plural--"littératures des immigrations"--Laronde highlights the diverse nature of the writers and texts the term designates. This plurality raises the question of terminology: should the new corpus of African fiction
be described as "afro-française" (as opposed to "franco-française" and "arabo-
française"), as Laronde suggests (34-35), or, using Benatta Jules-Rosette's so-
cio-literary definition, should it rather be categorized as part of the genre she
calls Parisianism?[20] Certainly, the texts discussed in this chapter seem to fit the
category "afro-française," but with the caveat that the two geographical markers
contained in the term suggest cultural and national affiliations which may not
accurately reflect some of the writers' profiles. Although they may feel attracted to the multi-cultural, cosmopolitan nature of Paris, they do not necessarily identify with the French. On the other hand, while some of the authors see
themselves as Parisians, others do not identify solely with Paris, as Jules-
Rosette's term suggests, and they portray other places in their novels. For these
reasons, I have chosen instead to use the expression "Afro-Parisian writers" in
my work, since it combines the two main components of this new literature: the
cultural influence of both a continent and a metropolitan space, Africa and Paris,
in the writing of new identities.

     In a broader context, these recent voices from the African diaspora
contribute to the creation of new identities in Europe, as well as in France.[21] As
such, they form part of a global phenomenon, that of new literatures in the
making that attest to the renegotiation of collective identities, both national and
transnational. The new generation of African writers in France should, then, be
understood not only in terms of post-colonial immigration and literature within
France, but also in light of the redistribution of non-European populations within

Europe. Such migrations blur cultural and literary borders as well as geographical ones, thereby revealing the inadequacy of preconceived notions relating to immigration, and highlighting the need to reassess the way in which the new bodies of literature are classified. The writers discussed in this chapter all seek to bring about such a remapping, and the diversity of their voices testifies to the plural nature of their immigrant identities. Their appearance on the literary scene thus contributes to the reconfiguration of geographical and cultural borders, and reenvisions the experience of immigration in France.

NOTES

1. This chapter uses elements of my forthcoming book on the new African diaspora in France (*Nouvelle Afrique sur Seine: le roman afro-parisien dans la France d'aujourd'hui*).

2. The mainstream African novel written in French typically contains realistic depictions of the author's culture and society and generally addresses socio-political issues such as the evils and aftermath of colonization and of the new neo-colonial elite. When the writer is a woman, the novel also deals with women's triple role in society as daughter, spouse, and mother.

3. Ousmane Sembène's *Le docker noir* (1956) and *Voltaïque* (1962) were exceptions at the time.

4. *Cercueil et Cie* (1985) and *African Gigolo* (1989) by Simon Njami, *Le nègre Potemkine* (1988) by Blaise N'Djehoya, and *Discopolis* (1993) by Philippe Camara are good examples of this literature of detachment.

5. Kesso Barry's *Kesso, princesse peuhle* (1989) and Daniel Biyaoula's *L'impasse* (1996) illustrate this emphasis on displacement.

6. Novels that fall into this category include Calixthe Beyala's "Parisian" novels, *Le petit prince de Belleville* (1992), its sequel *Maman a un amant* (1993), *Assèze l'Africaine* (1994), *Les honneurs perdus* (1996), and *Amours sauvages* (1999); J. R. Essomba's *Le paradis du Nord* (1996); and Alain Mabanckou's *Bleu-Blanc-Rouge* (1998).

7. The texts selected for this analysis are: Simon Njami's *African Gigolo*, Daniel Biyaoula's *L'impasse* (1996) and *Agonies* (1998), Alain Mabanckou's *Bleu-Blanc-Rouge*, J. R. Essomba's *Le paradis du Nord,* and Calixthe Beyala's *Le petit prince de Belleville* and its sequel, *Maman a un amant.*

8. See Bernard Magnier's "Beurs noirs à Black Babel."

9. This paragraph on *African Gigolo* as well as the section on *L'impasse* use elements from my forthcoming article, "African Diaspora in France: Questions of Identity and Culture."

10. This humiliation suddenly makes Moïse realize he is living in a vacuum, and the violence of his act serves as a catharsis by making him aware of his own alienation.

11. See Homi Bhabha's analysis of mimicry in *The Location of Culture* (1994): this concept can be applied to a post-colonial context . In the eyes of the protagonist, African women's acts of mimicry reproduce "the problematic of *post*-colonial subjection" (90). See also Françoise Lionnet's *Postcolonial Representations: Women, Literature, Identity* (1995) and her analysis of the female body as "a privileged code for a range of messages which, in the end, serve only to enslave this body to the ambiguous images that the cultural code carries, translates or creates" (98).

12. This term refers to a trend affecting Congolese youths (especially in the 1980s) who spend all their money on clothes and who try to raise funds for a ticket to

France in order to become "Parisians," which for them and their family and friends back home represents the ultimate form of success.

13. Alain Mabanckou is best known as a Congolese poet and author of the recent *Les arbres aussi versent des larmes* (1997). *Bleu-Blanc-Rouge* is his first novel.

14. Beyala was in fact the first to introduce the new focus on immigrants living in France (as opposed to Africans on the continent) and to deal with the community as a whole, rather than with a single immigrant.

15. See also Odile Cazenave, "Calixthe Beyala's 'Parisian Novels': An Example of Globalization and Transculturation in French Society" and "Roman africain au féminin et immigration: dynamisme du devenir."

16. Beyala often uses two antithetical but complementary female characters to illustrate the opportunities and risks immigration represents. See Odile Cazenave, *Femmes rebelles: naissance d'un nouveau roman au féminin* (1996) for an analysis of this point.

17. See Mireille Rosello's concept of "declining" stereotypes in *Declining the Stereotype: Ethnicity and Representation in French Cultures*.

18. See Michel Laronde, *L'écriture décentrée* and "Les littératures des immigrations en France: questions de nomenclature et directions de recherche."

19. See Azouz Begag and Abdellatif Chaouite's *Ecarts d'identité* for an analysis of these issues as they affect the Maghrebi immigrant community.

20. See Jules-Rosette's "Parisianism: The African Writers' Reality" in *Black Paris: The African Writers' Landscape*.

21. For a detailed analysis of literature portraying these new identities (Black British literature and "Gast-Arbeiter literatur," for example) in the new Europe, see Gisela Brinker-Gabler and Sidonie Smith's *Writing New Identities: Gender, Nation and Immigration in Contemporary Europe* (1997), especially the chapter entitled "Gender, Nation, and Immigration in the New Europe."

WORKS CITED

Baker, Léandre-Alain. *Ici s'achève le voyage*. Paris: L'Harmattan, 1989.

Barry, Kesso. *Kesso, princesse peuhle*. Paris: Seghers, 1989.

Begag, Azouz, and Abdellatif Chaouite. *Ecarts d'identité*. Paris: Seuil, 1990.

Beyala, Calixthe. *Le petit prince de Belleville*. Paris: Albin Michel, 1992.

---. *Maman a un amant*. Paris: Albin Michel, 1993.

---. *Assèze l'Africaine*. Paris: Albin Michel, 1994.

---. *Les honneurs perdus*. Paris: Albin Michel, 1996.

---. *Amours sauvages*. Paris: Albin Michel, 1999.

Bhabha, Homi K. *The Location of Culture*. London: Routledge, 1994.

Biyaoula, Daniel. *L'impasse*. Paris: Présence Africaine, 1996.

---. *Agonies*. Paris: Présence Africaine, 1998.

Brinker-Gabler, Gisela, and Sidonie Smith, eds. *Writing New Identities: Gender, Nation and Immigration in Contemporary Europe*. Minneapolis: University of Minnesota Press, 1997.

Camara, Philippe. *Discopolis*. Paris: L'Harmattan, 1993.

Cazenave, Odile. *Femmes rebelles: naissance d'un nouveau roman africain au féminin*. Paris: L'Harmattan, 1996.

---. "Calixthe Beyala: l'exemple d'une écriture décentrée dans le roman africain au féminin." *L'écriture décentrée*. Ed. Michel Laronde. Paris: L'Harmattan, 1996, 122-148.

---. "Roman africain au féminin et immigration: dynamisme du devenir." *Changements au féminin en Afrique noire: anthropologie et littérature*. Vol. 2. Ed. Danielle de Lame and Chantal Zabus. Paris: L'Harmattan, 1999, 49-69.

---. "Calixthe Beyala's 'Parisian Novels': An Example of Globalization and Transculturation in French Society." *Sites* 4.1 (Spring 2000): 119-127.

---. *Rebellious Women: The New Generation of Female African Novelists*. Boulder: Lynne Rienner Publishers, 2000.

Dadié, Bernard. *Un nègre à Paris*. Paris: Présence Africaine, 1959.

Essomba, J. R. *Le paradis du Nord*. Paris: Présence Africaine, 1996.

Hargreaves, Alec G. *Immigration and Identity in Beur Fiction: Voices from the North African Community in France*. Oxford: Berg, 1997.

Jules-Rosette, Bennetta. *Black Paris: The African Writers' Landscape*. Urbana: University of Illinois Press, 1998.

Kane, Cheikh Hamidou. *L'aventure ambiguë*. Paris: Julliard, 1961.

Karone, Yodi. *A la recherche du cannibale amour*. Paris: Nathan, 1988.

Laronde, Michel. *Autour du roman beur*. Paris: L'Harmattan, 1993.

---. *L'écriture décentrée*. Paris: L'Harmattan, 1996.

---. "Les littératures des immigrations en France: questions de nomenclature et directions de recherche." *Le Maghreb Littéraire* 1.2 (1997): 25-44.

Lionnet, Françoise. *Postcolonial Representations: Woman, Literature, Identity*. Ithaca: Cornell University Press, 1995.

Mabanckou, Alain. *Les arbres aussi versent des larmes*. Paris: L'Harmattan, 1997.

---. *Bleu-Blanc-Rouge*. Paris: Présence Africaine, 1998.

Magnier, Bernard. "Beurs noirs à Black Babel." *Notre Librairie* 103 (October-December 1990): 103-107.

N'Djehoya, Blaise. *Le nègre Potemkine*. Paris: Lieu Commun, 1988.

Njami, Simon. *Cercueil et Cie*. Paris: Lieu Commun, 1985.

---. *African Gigolo*. Paris: Seghers, 1989.

Rosello, Mireille. *Declining the Stereotype: Ethnicity and Representation in French Cultures*. Hanover: University Press of New England, 1998.

Sembène, Ousmane. *Voltaïque*. Paris: Présence Africaine, 1962.

---. *Le docker noir*. 1956. Paris: Présence Africaine, 1973.

Daniel Biyaoula: Exile, Immigration, and Transnational Cultural Productions

Dominic Thomas

> Impasse: A predicament affording no obvious escape.
> Constriction: The act of compressing an organ in order to cause it to falter.
> Metamorphosis: An abrupt physical change occurring in certain anthropoids in order to allow their development. (*Trésor de la langue française*)[1]

LES FRANCOPHONIES A PARIS

The *New York Times* published a telling article on October 8, 1996, entitled "Neocolonialists Seize the *French* Language." The italicization of the word "French" in the heading seemed to suggest that various intercultural dynamics were altering the French language in such a manner as to render it unrecognizable, and that these influences were perhaps closer to contaminating rather than enriching the language, particularly since the article evoked a "crisis." However, the author nevertheless did acknowledge that France, while continuing to serve as the publishing capital of the francophone world, is almost exclusively being recognized for works published in French by francophone authors (that is, essentially, authors writing in French from within France's post-colonial communities or from beyond the Hexagon). This is confirmed by a cursory glance at recent winners of what is arguably France's most prestigious literary award, namely the Prix Goncourt: Tahar Ben Jelloun from Morocco, Patrick Chamoiseau from Martinique, and Amin Maalouf from Lebanon.

Significantly, similar phenomena are to be evidenced in the anglophone world, although the discourse this has generated is strikingly different in the absence of an "anglophone" movement attempting to maintain London as the center for cultural productions in English. Indeed, the majority of the most critically acclaimed writers in Britain today are from the so-called Commonwealth or ex-British colonial territories, authors such as Salman Rushdie, Caryl Phillips, J. M. Coetzee, Nadine Gordimer, Wole Soyinka, and Derek Walcott. Of course, as with Daniel Biyaoula and Alain Mabanckou, who provide the focus of this chapter, this situation is further problematized by writers whose roots are located *outside* the metropole, but who are living *within* the metropole. This chapter will examine Biyaoula's 1996 novel *L'impasse* and will also discuss his second novel, *Agonies* (1998), and the 1998 novel by his Congolese compatriot, Mabanckou, *Bleu-Blanc-Rouge*.

EXILE AND DISPLACEMENT

I would like to begin by briefly exploring the term "Afro-Parisian" that is increasingly being used to describe the literary productions of francophone sub-Saharan authors residing in France (most notably, Biyaoula, Mabanckou, and Calixthe Beyala, who are arguably the most well-known in this relatively select group of writers). What interests me is what such labels in fact designate-- what they seek to include and simultaneously exclude. Similar questions have been raised by Alec Hargreaves and Michel Laronde in their ground-breaking studies of *Beur* writers.[2] At what point do the works of these authors cease to belong to the corpus of Maghrebi literature, and why, for example, is Tahar Ben Jelloun considered to be a Moroccan novelist and not a *Beur* author? Indeed, similar processes are at work when one employs the term *Afro-Parisian* to describe this relatively new corpus of literary works. Why was a Congolese author such as Tchicaya U Tam'si, for example, who resided in Paris most of his productive life, never systematically referred to as an *Afro-Parisian* writer, and why are Biyaoula and Mabanckou considered *Afro-Parisian* while their compatriot Henri Lopès, who also lives and writes in France, is known as a Congolese author? Rather than attempting to answer these questions, I will simply insist on the need to explore the usefulness of these categories, and focus instead on more productive ways of looking at this literary corpus. A transnational approach, perhaps, could afford readers a better contextual framework, one that would take into account questions of labor mobility, immigration laws, and youth culture in an attempt to uncover some of the intercultural dynamics evidenced in the literary productions of francophone sub-Saharan authors in general. For, as Mabanckou asks: "What is the role of the writer in the face of rising racism, in the face of immigration, the deliquescence of French society? Why is it that with the end of the century only a few weeks away, Africans continue to be mesmerized by Europe, and by France in particular?"[3]

TRANSNATIONAL COMMUNITIES

In his 1989 essay, *La question des littératures nationales en Afrique noire*, Adrien Huannou argued that inclusion in a national literary corpus should be premised upon the following criteria: "Since all that belongs to a nation is national, and since a literature is made up of all the literary works of a country or region, then all the oral and written works produced by the nationals of an

African state constitute a national literature. There are therefore as many national literatures as there are states in Africa" (34).[4] According to this definition, both Biyaoula and Mabanckou would clearly be considered Congolese authors. Indeed, other factors seem to support this view, since both authors were awarded the *Grand Prix Littéraire de l'Afrique Noire* for their first novels, published in 1996 and 1998 respectively.[5] What is particularly striking in both Biyaoula's and Mabanckou's narratives, and in other texts produced by francophone sub-Saharan African authors who have chosen to situate their narratives in both Africa and France (most significantly the works of the Cameroonian novelist Calixthe Beyala), is the variety of ways in which transnational communities are organized outside the homeland, how cultural practices are maintained, challenged, and transformed as they are subjected to multiple influences, and how ethnic, national, and regional rivalries are exacerbated and replicated in the transnational setting.

Some of the most important explorations of these notions have taken place recently in Beyala's *Les honneurs perdus* (1996) and in Biyaoula's *L'impasse*. What is so fascinating about these novels is the manner in which the narratives shift between Cameroon and Paris in the case of the former, and Paris and the Congo in the latter, establishing on-going associations between the two spaces. At what point, then, does Beyala stop being a Cameroonian novelist and become an Afro-Parisian one? Is she, for example, Afro-Parisian when she writes about immigration in France (*Maman a un amant*) and Cameroonian when the focus is Africa (*Assèze l'Africaine*)? In *Les honneurs perdus*, the epigraph explores the tenuous relationship between *francité* (Frenchness) and *francophonie* (francophony), *français* (French) and *francophone*: "Le Français est francophone mais la francophonie n'est pas française." This sentence may at first seem relatively straightforward and could be translated as: "The French language is francophone but francophony is not French." This interpretation would emphasize, or perhaps reject, the attempts that have been made to gather francophone countries under the aegis of the Hexagon's control, thus maintaining Paris as the ex-colonial "center." However, the capitalization of the word "Français" problematizes and destabilizes that meaning, and the translation then becomes: "French people are francophone but francophony is not French." Whichever translation one uses, the fact remains that "francophony" is *not* French, and Beyala, along with other francophone authors, underlines the plurality of francophone cultural productions.

RECUPERATION

With this problematics in mind, and given that Beyala has put into question the hierarchical status of *francité*, what are we to infer from the fact that she was awarded the *Prix François Mauriac* for her 1994 novel *Assèze l'Africaine* and the *Grand Prix du Roman* in 1996 for *Les honneurs perdus*, both given by the most conservative of French institutions, the *Académie Française* (French Academy)? In what way has her residency in France (and in Paris in particular) enabled or rendered acceptable such attempts to bring the margins into the mainstream?

What Beyala's works in fact create is a framework that now makes it impossible, or at least irresponsible, to study France as a monolithic entity. A more useful approach would be to examine the contradictions inherent in contemporary society in order to better understand the ways in which the very notion of "otherness" continues to be complicated. While immigrants struggle to achieve integration, the monocultural perspective has been displaced, and, as Homi Bhabha has argued, the need "to think beyond narratives of originary and initial subjectivities and to focus on those moments or processes that are produced in the articulation of cultural differences" (1) would seem all the more essential, as we attempt to "locate" culture in spaces that are not easily identifiable. As far as this particular context is concerned, one which addresses issues of transnational and intercultural dynamics between several areas of the francophone world, memory, too, is located elsewhere, somewhere perhaps--to borrow Paul Gilroy's idea of the "Black Atlantic"--on the "Black Mediterranean" that separates France from its former North and sub-Saharan African colonial territories.[6]

In *Les honneurs perdus*, the first 200 pages are set in what Beyala calls Couscousville, on the outskirts of Douala, while the topography of the second half of the book shifts to Belleville's immigrant population in Paris.[7] Here, the Belleville community is described as a "tribu immigrée" (tribe of immigrants) (247), thus underlining their displaced status, as well as their former links with their respective countries of origin. The novel is thus situated in a transnational setting, one that further problematizes the connections between France and the former colonial territory. The transnational dimension is highlighted, as memories are shared by protagonists living in Africa and those who have established residence in France. The experiences narrated in the text echo the epigraph, and the sense of universal sameness suggested by the singular noun francophony no longer sufficiently expresses the plurality and multiplicity of perspectives contained in the experiences of the protagonists. Instead, the monolithic, hegemonic discourse of the former colonial center is transformed through the inscription of a transnational dimension that continues to define the inextricable links between French and francophone cultural politics and productions.

The movement between these transnational spaces is perhaps one of the most interesting aspects of Biyaoula's novel *L'impasse*. Indeed, one could argue that the notion of "*retour*" (return) is one that has always characterized francophone literature, whether in the form of Aimé Césaire's *Cahier d'un retour au pays natal* and Aminata Sow Fall's *Le revenant*, or in the experiences of exile or travel recounted in the works of Cheikh Hamidou Kane, Camara Laye, Bernard Dadié, and others.[8] For these reasons, I will explore the notion of return as it plays out between the two symbiotically linked transnational spaces of France (mostly Paris) and the Congo (Brazzaville and Pointe Noire) by examining the structural framework of *L'impasse*. The novel is divided into three sections: "*Première constriction*" (first constriction), which comprises the main protagonist's (Joseph Gakatuka) departure for Brazzaville from France; the "*Deuxième constriction*" (second constriction), which includes his return to Paris; and finally, the third section entitled "*La mue*" (the transformation).

DESCENT ON THE CONGO

Significantly, the novel begins in a transnational space, namely Paris's largest airport, Roissy-Charles-de-Gaulle, as Joseph prepares to board a flight for Brazzaville. For Joseph, this journey represents a return to his native land after an absence of fifteen years. For other passengers, this journey is not simply a return, but rather a "descente" (descent) to the Congo, that is, "the vacation one spends back home (in Congo-Brazzaville) after putting together one's collection," namely "the essential, even obligatory set of clothes the adventurer must procure for himself before carrying out a 'descent' " (Gandoulou 209).[9]

This cultural and social practice, which is particular to the community of Congolese immigrants, is a central focus of the novel. As Joseph gets off the plane in Brazzaville and is reunited with his family and friends, he comes to realize that there is a significant discrepancy between the image he offers and that which his people expect of him: "It doesn't take me long to figure out that they expected something of me, that I didn't bring it from France, that I do not embody an ideal, that I am shattering people's dreams" (30).[10] This distance is in part due to his fifteen-year absence, to the experience of exile, and to the significant societal changes the Congo has undergone during Marxist-Leninist rule, but is more specifically linked to his failure to correspond to the image that is expected of young men returning from exile in Paris. In a socio-anthropological study of young Congolese men in the metropole, *Au cœur de la sape: mœurs et aventures de Congolais à Paris*, Justin-Daniel Gandoulou outlines the fundamental tenets of this phenomenon: "For these young people, *la sape* is the symbol of the West that is conveyed by a certain social class of Congolese. . . . *Sapeurs* strive to imitate the outward appearance of those who have reached the upper social echelons in Brazzaville" (18-19).[11]

The term "sape" originates in slang and designates clothing and the art of dressing, while the verb "saper" means "to wear beautiful, trendy clothes in an elegant fashion, to be dressed up to the nines," and a "sapeur" is "a person who is very interested in *la sape* and who practices it" (Gandoulou 210).[12] When these young men leave the Congo for Paris, they are welcomed by a network of compatriots who provide them with housing and with working papers, thus enabling them to adjust rapidly to the transformations caused by exile. Because the socio-economic circumstances of residing in France are extremely challenging, and have little to do with the mythic images of life in France the young immigrants had internalized, these *aventuriers* (adventurers) will draw upon their tremendous resourcefulness in order to achieve their primary objective of eventually making a glorious descent on Brazzaville. This is often a lengthy process, one that begins at a young age in the Congo, and that is sustained over the years through a transnational dialogue with young men who have already undertaken the quest. Indeed, these young men are so well-prepared when they arrive in Paris that they are already acquainted with its topography, in particular, its monuments and the metro. Moki, a protagonist in Mabanckou's *Bleu-Blanc-Rouge*, for example, explains the importance of clothing to an attentive crowd of listeners: "Clothes are our passport. Our religion. France is the country of fashion because it's the only place on earth where you can still judge people by appearances" (78).[13] Moki's words contain an adaptation of the French saying "l'habit ne fait pas le moine," according to which one should *not* judge people by appearances. Here, Mabanckou has subverted this proverb, changing it to "l'habit fait le moine" in order to underscore the importance given to appearances in the world of the *sapeur*. This emphasis on appearances also manifests itself in changes in hair color, efforts to gain weight, and attempts to lighten the skin, all of which are linked with the interiorization of prejudicial constructs that have their origins in colonial times.[14] Attaining the status of "Parisien" therefore brings the young adventurer increased respect, social mobility, and appeal to women.

In *L'impasse,* Joseph has established residence in France for the purpose of finding employment, and does not participate in the socio-cultural practice of *la sape*. However, he chooses to ignore it at his own peril, since when he returns to the Congo, he effectively fails to fulfill his family's expectations, and his brother Samuel informs him of his shortcomings: "He cleared his throat and then told me that there were rules to follow, that I might not like wearing suits, but that I was a Parisian, that a Parisian has an image to uphold, and that the members of my family would be permanently disgraced if there were a Parisian among them who did not resemble one" (39).[15]

The transnational experience, the hybridity of the subject, and the question of belonging and not-belonging to either space become increasingly problematic. Indeed, Joseph's relationships with people at "home" are increasingly characterized by notions such as separation, distance, and barriers. While his national status as a citizen of the Congo has not changed, he is viewed by his compatriots as an outsider: "Listen Joseph, you must understand that you're almost a foreigner here in Brazza" (81).[16] However, there is no room for his French life within his Congolese one. His relationship with Sabine, a white French woman, for example, is perceived as unacceptable, and Biyaoula's second novel, *Agonies*, explores the complex nature of exogamous unions, particularly when they take place between an African woman and a French man. Furthermore, Joseph is informed that the values he has acquired as an immigrant living in Paris have no currency in the Congo: "forget about how things take place in France" (93).[17] He soon learns that the identity he claims for himself is irrelevant, and that he must accept instead the identity of *Parisien* which has been constructed for him, and act accordingly. In addition, his own image of Africa, his perception of his homeland born of his exile, does not correspond to reality, thus further displacing him: "When I'm in Poury . . . I dream of Brazza, of the warmth in which one lives there. But once I'm back there, I realize that things aren't any better" (96).[18] By the time Joseph finally returns to Paris, he has compromised his identity, relinquished his autonomy, and given in to the demands of his family and friends.

THE HEXAGONAL QUEST

> Friends tell stories, friends wonder
> The younger ones cry, the older ones wonder
> Who is this Cevos Ceniakos? Listen,
> Cevos Ceniakos is that handsome fellow lost in Paris
> But, he's, he's, he's the most sought after man on earth.
> -- Papa Wemba, *Matuba*[19]

Whether through the images available in literature and popular discourse, on television, or in the music of Congo-Zaire's most celebrated performer, Papa Wemba, Paris remains a mythic construct: "one word was all it took for us to find ourselves as if by magic in front of the Eiffel Tower or the Arc de Triomphe or on the Avenue des Champs-Elysées" (Mabanckou 36),[20] and "everyone thought of Paris as the center of the modern world, as well as the world center for *la sape*" (Gandoulou 19).[21] For Joseph, however, displacement to France is initially conceived as a quest to solve the following mathematical equation: "x + African man + African woman + cosmetic products = skin decolorization + hair straightening" (86).[22] He is finally able to solve the equation by recognizing that the enigmatic "x" refers to the constructed superiority of whites over blacks. However, the process through which Joseph reaches this conclusion has much to reveal about France itself and about the situatedness of the African immigrant in France, and it ultimately contributes to the complex process of uncovering the mythic constructs that undergird the continued positive representation of Paris in the African imagination. Indeed, this is also Mabanckou's project in *Bleu-Blanc-Rouge*, in which he charts Moki's itinerary: "Throughout the novel, he will be the victim of this 'Blue-White-Red' dream. He will be the one who will inform his compatriots at home, the one who will remained trapped in the mirage. But he will have pursued his goal to the end" (Herzberger-Fofana).[23]

Moki's proximity to France and French culture allows him to distinguish between illusion and reality, to expose the delusionary qualities of the imaginary construct and to challenge the assimilationist dream contained in the invocation of the blue, white, and red of the French flag. Indeed, the cover of the novel created by Saliou Démanguy Diouf combines a multitude of ethnic features and a variety of colors (blue, white, red, black, and orange) in what can only remind one of what Françoise Lionnet has described in her analysis of anti-racist posters in France as the "indeterminate, inclusionary identity" in which "the other and the self clearly share a space and an intersubjective realm in which hair, eye and skin color are secondary to the ability to engage in another form of identification: that which is mediated by the geographical space of France" (103). As an immigrant, Joseph is an outsider in France and is unambiguously made to feel that way through his repeated experiences of racism. Some of the more striking occurrences take place during a dinner at his girlfriend's parents' home. Sabine's father provides an example of the type of ignorance and prejudice to which Joseph is constantly exposed. When Joseph politely comments upon the nice home in which his family lives, for example, Mr. Rosa takes it upon himself to discuss the fact that Joseph lives in public housing:

>   - For you it must be a nice change from home! Apparently it's even worse there!
>   - It's not the same thing.
>   - Yes it is, because Alain told us that people in your countries live in appalling, inhumane conditions. He was quite overwhelmed, very shocked even. . . . It must be quite pleasant for you to live in a civilized country even if you're in public housing! . . . And how do you see yourself? Because after all this time, you can't feel much like a real African anymore![24] (154-155)

The way in which these comments are phrased, along with the statement, "I hope that I have not upset you in any way" (155), force Joseph to remain silent and to "decline" the invitation to respond through fear of offending the host who has extended hospitality to him.[25] Furthermore, Mr. Rosa's conclusion underlines the inescapability of Joseph's African origins, since invoking them

simultaneously reconfirms them, thus emphasizing the impossibility of
Joseph's becoming integrated.

While opposition to racism in France may be widespread, the manner
in which immigrants continue to be perceived remains problematic. The images
of himself that Joseph has internalized reflect the prejudicial representations of
immigrants generated by institutionalized racism. Although racial injustice is
intellectualized and rationalized in order to objectify those subjected to it and to
deny them their humanity, rather than addressing the issue of racism, society
focuses instead on sensational topics such as problem areas (HLMs and ZUPs),
crime, single parenthood, drugs, and poverty.

In *L'Impasse*, for example, Joseph's relationship with Sabine
undergoes a gradual disintegration due to racial tension, when Joseph
experiences increasing pressure as a result of his position as immigrant--
unemployment, social ostracism, and racism. At the same time, his compatriots
condemn his exogamous union, viewing it as a form of betrayal and as a refusal
to accept other Africans. Somewhat paradoxically, when Sabine tells him that
his mistake lies in seeing himself through the eyes of others, she actually
anticipates the manner in which Joseph will recover his self-esteem. However,
her comments also reveal her faith in the ability of their relationship to survive
outside of societal expectations. While Sabine is able to overcome social
prejudice in her pursuit of a relationship with Joseph, the pressures on her are
radically different in nature from those confronting Joseph. Indeed, Joseph
begins to manifest physical symptoms in the form of severe headaches, acute
depression, and anxiety that culminate in his subsequent mental breakdown. The
point of no return occurs when his friend Dieudonné is murdered, and this event
marks, symbolically, the end of his union with Sabine and the end of the
second "constriction."

METAMORPHOSIS AND TRANSFORMATION
The final section of the novel, called *"La mue"*--a term which can
signify molting, sloughing, shedding, metamorphosis, and transformation--
explores Joseph's attempts to recover from his breakdown. *La mue* is an
important notion to the extent that it underlines the reciprocal nature of
transnational influences: on the one hand, the transformational imperative that
immigrants must respond to if they are to be integrated, and on the other, the
cultural and social changes that the presence of immigrants brings about in the
receiving territory--a dynamic that anti-immigrant rhetoric characterizes as a form
of contamination. In Joseph's case, these transformations are mediated through a
number of factors which include fashion, race, and broader identitarian concerns.
Indeed, as Edouard Glissant observes in *Caribbean Discourse*:

There is a difference between the transplanting (by exile or dispersion) of a people
who continue to survive elsewhere and the transfer (by the slave trade) of a
population to another place where they change into something different, into a new
set of possibilities. It is in this metamorphosis that we must try to detect one of the
best kept secrets of creolization. Through it one can see that the mingling of
experience is at work, there for us to know and producing the process of being. We
abandon the idea of fixed being. (14)

A number of interesting expressions in French are pertinent to this investigation. One such expression, *changer de peau* (to shed one's skin), for example, takes on particular significance because of the racial identity of the narrator. The similar idiomatic expressions *mal dans sa peau* (ill-at-ease) and *se mettre dans la peau de quelqu'un* (to put oneself in somebody's place), when used in the context of immigration, evoke the assimilationist ideal of blending in by assuming a French identity. Joseph relinquishes his struggle with racial identity and finds salvation through the assistance of the ironically named Dr. Malfoi, a psychotherapist. The therapy leads to the recovery of his self-esteem through his acquisition of the status of *adventurer* and *sapeur* which his family had demanded: "I've got to conform completely to the image I present to others, to the image they expect" (268).[26] His psychotherapist also finds him a job, which allows Joseph to plan a successful *descent* on Brazzaville in two years time. After this transformation, Joseph gradually begins to command the respect of his immigrant peers and to attend social gatherings. However, as Mabanckou demonstrates through his protagonist Moki, "this duplicity and this ambivalence lead to a personality change" (Herzberger-Fofana),[27] and this new-found social life often produces only superficial relationships, making Joseph and Moki poor role models for a new generation of disenfranchised immigrant African youths.

When Joseph discovers a few months later that Sabine has a child, his refusal to entertain the possibility that the child is most likely his underscores his relinquishing of the idea of parenthood and the potential for reconciliation that the hybrid child would offer. Here, Biyaoula seems to be suggesting the impossibility of forming human relations across racial divides, given the current sociological make-up of contemporary France. A second, somewhat symbolic moment leads to more liberating possibilities. At a party, Joseph meets a young man called Justin, whose nickname, *"le Goudron"* (tar), echoes Joseph's own childhood name *Kala* (coal) and circles back to the opening sequence of the novel in which he is referred to as being dark like "tar" (15). This circular structure suggests that Justin's and Joseph's stories are interchangeable, and Joseph himself recognizes the similarities between their respective itineraries in Justin's account of his exile and immigration. The latter's death in a car accident later that evening may ultimately lead to Joseph's salvation, since it gives him new energy with which to engage in psychotherapy sessions and forces him to recognize the superficiality of his new image. The ending of *L'impasse*, then, suggests that other "adventurers" may one day have different lives in which their origins become clearer and their journeys less painful.

In many ways, the notion of "descent" as it is employed by Biyaoula functions as a symbol for transnationalism, one that is not fully encompassed by the concept of "return" discussed earlier or contained in Glissant's use of the term "detour."[28] Unlike "return" and "detour," the term "descent" evokes the many communities and populations that are transformed by their belonging to complex transnational communities outside of their homeland; foremost among the communities and populations affected, one would include the community of origin, the receiving territory, and of course those whose identities as immigrants are transfigured through the experience of transplantation or displacement.[29]

NOTES

1. "Impasse: Être dans une position ou situation qui ne présente pas d'issue favorable.

Constriction: Action d'opérer une compression sur un organe pour provoquer un arrêt de son fonctionnement.

Mue: Renouvellement en une seule fois du tégument de certains anthropodes afin de permettre leur croissance."

2. See Alec G. Hargreaves's *Voices from the North African Immigrant Community in France: Immigration and Identity in Beur Fiction* and Michel Laronde's *Autour du roman beur: immigration et identité*.

3. See Pierrette Herzberger-Fofana's "Un entretien avec Alain Mabanckou, poète et romancier du Congo": "Quelle est la place de l'écrivain face à la montée du racisme, face à l'immigration, à la déliquescence de la société française? Pourquoi dans ce siècle qui s'achève dans quelques semaines, les Africains continuent-ils de vouer une fascination à l'Europe, et en particulier la France?" All translations are my own unless otherwise cited.

4. "Puisque est national ce qui appartient à la nation et puisqu'une littérature est l'ensemble des oeuvres littéraires d'un pays ou d'une région, l'ensemble des oeuvres littéraires orales et écrites produites par les ressortissants d'un Etat africain constitue une littérature nationale. Il y a donc autant de littératures nationales que d'états en Afrique."

5. I have expressed my reservations as to the usefulness of the national approach to francophone sub-Saharan African literatures elsewhere. See, for example, my "Constructing National and Cultural Identities in Sub-Saharan Francophone Africa."

6. See Gilroy's *The Black Atlantic: Modernity and Double Consciousness*.

7. Interesting parallels can be made between her work and that of her *beurette* counterparts, most notably Farida Belghoul, Ferrudja Kessas, and Soraya Nini, in whose novels the various challenges associated with assimilation, exile, and integration are foregrounded.

8. See Césaire's *Cahier d'un retour au pays natal*, Fall's *Le revenant*, Kane's *L'aventure ambiguë*, Dadié's *Un nègre à Paris*, and Laye's *L'enfant noir*.

9. "les vacances qu'on va passer au pays (Congo-Brazzaville), après avoir constitué sa gamme"; "ensemble de vêtements nécessaires voire obligatoires que l'Aventurier doit se procurer avant d'effectuer une 'descente.' "

10. "Je ne mets pas longtemps pour comprendre qu'on attendait quelque chose de moi, que je ne l'ai pas apporté de France, que je ne donne pas vie à un idéal, que je brise des rêves."

11. "La Sape c'est, pour ces jeunes, le symbole de l'Occident véhiculé par une certaine classe sociale congolaise . . . les Sapeurs s'évertuent à imiter l'aspect extérieur des gens arrivés au sommet de l'échelle sociale à Brazzaville."

12. "porter avec élégance de beaux vêtements (à la mode); être tiré à quatre épingles"; "personne qui s'intéresse beaucoup à la Sape et qui la pratique."

13. "Le vêtement est notre passeport. Notre religion. La France est le pays de la mode parce que c'est le seul endroit au monde où l'habit fait encore le moine" (78).

14. See Gandoulou 144-146.

15. "Il s'éclaircit la gorge puis il me dit qu'il y a des règles à respecter, que je ne les aime peut-être pas, les costumes, mais que je suis un Parisien, que le Parisien a une image à défendre, que pour eux, les gens de ma famille, ce sera la honte insoluble qu'il y ait un Parisien parmi eux qui ne ressemble pas à un Parisien."

16. "Ecoute, Joseph, faut comprendre que tu es presqu'un étranger à Brazza."

17. "oublie comment ça se passe en France."

18. "Quand je suis à Poury . . . je rêve de Brazza, de la chaleur dans laquelle on y vit. Mais sur place, je m'aperçois que ce n'est pas mieux."

19. Quoted in Gandoulou, 199.

"Les amis racontent, les amis se demandent
Les cadets pleurent, les aînés se demandent
Qui est Cevos Ceniakos? Écoute,
Cevos Ceniakos c'est le beau gars perdu dans Paris quoi
Mais, c'est, c'est, c'est l'homme le plus demandé de la terre quoi."

20. "Un seul mot, Paris, suffisait pour que nous nous retrouvions comme par enchantement devant la Tour Eiffel, l'Arc de Triomphe ou l'avenue des Champs-Elysées."

21. "Les uns et les autres considèrent Paris comme le centre du monde moderne, et aussi le centre mondial de la Sape."

22. "x + Africain + Africaine + produits cosmétiques = décoloration de la peau + défrisage des cheveux."

23. "Il sera tout au long du roman la victime de ce rêve 'Bleu-Blanc-Rouge.' Il sera celui qui va alerter les compatriotes restés au pays, celui qui va être pris dans le traquenard d'un mirage. Mais il aura poursuivi son objectif jusqu'au bout."

24. "- Mais vous, ça doit quand même vous changer de chez vous! Il paraît que c'est encore pis!
- Ce n'est pas la même chose.
-Oui, parce qu'Alain nous a raconté que les gens dans vos pays vivent dans des conditions épouvantables, inhumaines. Il a été très bouleversé, très choqué. . . . Ça doit tout de même être agréable pour vous de vivre dans un pays civilisé même si vous êtes dans un H.L.M.!. . . Et vous vous considérez comment? Parce que, après tout ce temps, vous ne devez plus vous sentir comme un vrai Africain!"

The terms ZUP and HLM stand for a "zone à urbaniser en priorité" and "habitation à loyer modéré." ZUP designates a zone that is scheduled for priority housing development and HLM refers to rent-controlled government housing. Mr. Rosa seems to use these terms interchangeably to signify government housing, and for want of a better term, I have used "public housing" for the purpose of the translation.

25. See Mireille Rosello's *Declining the Stereotype: Ethnicity and Representation in French Cultures.*

26. "Et faut que je me conforme totalement à l'image que je dois donner aux gens, celle qu'ils attendent."

27. "cette duplicité, cette ambivalence aboutissent à un changement de sa personnalité."

28. See Glissant's discussion of "diversion" and "reversion" in *Caribbean Discourse.*

29. I would like to thank Mireille Rosello for reading and commenting on an earlier version of this chapter, and in particular for her suggestion that I incorporate Glissant's work in my discussion of transnationalism.

WORKS CITED

Beyala, Calixthe. *Le petit prince de Belleville.* Paris: Albin Michel, 1992.
---. *Maman a un amant.* Paris: Albin Michel, 1993.
---. *Assèze l'Africaine.* Paris: Albin Michel, 1994.
---. *Les honneurs perdus.* Paris: Albin Michel, 1996.
Bhabha, Homi K. *The Location of Culture.* London: Routledge, 1994.
Biyaoula, Daniel. *L'impasse.* Paris: Présence Africaine, 1996.
---. *Agonies.* Paris: Présence Africaine, 1998.

Césaire, Aimé. *Cahier d'un retour au pays natal.* Paris: Présence Africaine, 1939.
Dadié, Bernard. *Un nègre à Paris.* Paris: Présence Africaine, 1959.
Fall, Aminata Sow. *Le revenant.* Dakar: NEA, 1976.
Gandoulou, Justin-Daniel. *Au cœur de la sape: mœurs et aventures de Congolais à Paris.* Paris: L'Harmattan, 1989.
Gilroy, Paul. *The Black Atlantic: Modernity and Double Consciousness.* Cambridge, MA: Harvard University Press, 1993.
Glissant, Edouard. *Caribbean Discourse: Selected Essays.* Trans. J. Michael Dash. Charlottesville: University Press of Virginia, 1989.
Hargreaves, Alec G. *Voices from the North African Immigrant Community in France: Immigration and Identity in Beur Fiction.* New York: Berg, 1991.
Herzberger-Fofana, Pierrette. "Un entretien avec Alain Mabanckou, poète et romancier du Congo." <www.arts.uwa.edu.au/MotsPluriels/MP1299mabanckou>
Huannou, Adrien. *La question des littératures nationales en Afrique noire.* Abidjan: Editions CEDA, 1989.
Kane, Cheikh Hamidou. *L'aventure ambiguë.* Paris: Julliard, 1961.
Laronde, Michel. *Autour du roman beur: immigration et identité.* Paris: L'Harmattan, 1993.
Laye, Camera. *L'enfant noir.* Paris: Plon, 1954.
Lionnet, Françoise. "Immigration, Poster Art, and Transgressive Citizenship: France 1968-1988." *Substance* 76/77 (1995): 93-108.
Mabanckou, Alain. *Bleu-Blanc-Rouge.* Paris: Présence Africaine, 1998.
Rosello, Mireille. *Declining the Stereotype: Ethnicity and Representation in French Cultures.* Hanover: University Press of New England, 1998.
Thomas, Dominic. "Constructing National and Cultural Identities in Sub-Saharan Francophone Africa." *Not on Any Map: Essays on Postcoloniality and Cultural Nationalism.* Ed. Stuart Murray. Exeter: University of Exeter Press, 1997, 115-134.

Migrating Genders in Calixthe Beyala's Fiction

Nicki Hitchcott

A post-colonial traveller herself, Calixthe Beyala has produced four novels that consider the cultural and psychological effects of migration from sub-Saharan Africa to France. Whereas Beyala's early novels limit the geographical space of the narrative to the African continent,[1] Paris becomes a centripetal force in much of her more recent writing: the action of the two Loukoum novels[2] (*Le petit prince de Belleville* [1992] and *Maman a un amant* [1993]) centers on the Parisian "arrondissement" of Belleville; and in both *Assèze l'Africaine* (1994) and *Les honneurs perdus* (1996), the female protagonist retraces Beyala's own itinerary, leaving Cameroon for the capital of France.[3] In each novel, the experience of migration leads male and, in particular, female characters to renegotiate their gender identities across the constantly shifting border space between France and Africa. This chapter will discuss the ways in which "femininity" and "masculinity" are reconfigured in Beyala's fiction through the trajectories of black African immigrants in France.

In *Assèze l'Africaine*, the first stage in the eponymous heroine's migration takes place on African soil when she moves from rural Eton country to Douala to live with Awono and his daughter, Sorraya. On arrival in the Cameroonian city, Assèze is struck by the "cultural transsexuals" she observes sitting outside the Ramsec Hotel: "On the right, opposite Monoprix and Prisunic is the Ramsec Hotel where whitified blacks imitate their white colleagues. They are what they are, neither whites nor blacks, sort of cultural transsexuals, vaguely businessmen, slightly loutish, and basically undesirable" (66).[4] Immediately, the text begins to draw a parallel between acculturation and gender identity. Lactification here goes hand in hand with demasculinization, pointing to the ways in which cultural migration can have a destablizing effect on normative gender roles.[5] Later in the novel, a similar point is made about women and education by Sotteria who, when the now educated Assèze returns to her village, declares that "these bookish women are like women who become men through playing sport" (134).[6] As an educated woman, Assèze defies her biological destiny and therefore represents a challenge to predetermined gender roles. Furthermore, as a cultural emigrant she is viewed, like the hotel's customers, as an "unnatural" being, whose "Westernization" has impacted on her gender identity, even before she leaves for France.[7]

In Douala, the most important channel for the cultural values of the West appears in the figure of Sorraya, the girl whom her father believes to be so "whitified" (61) that he brings Assèze into their home to act as role model for his daughter. Sorraya, too headstrong and self-confident to be influenced by "la cambroussarde" (the country bumpkin), becomes pregnant and undergoes an illegal abortion. Awono is so disappointed that he holds Assèze responsible for Sorraya's lost virginity, identifying the two women as "la femme adultère et . . . sa complice" (the adulterous woman and . . . her accomplice) (189). His solution is to send Sorraya to France and to arrange sewing lessons for Assèze, pushing the latter back into an acceptably "feminine" mold and resigning himself to the former's acculturation. Assèze, however, resists Awono's attempt to control her gender identity. Having seduced Sorraya's lover, Océan, Assèze begins to feel in control of her own destiny.[8] When Awono dies, leaving her nothing in his will, Assèze decides to leave for France.

Before she arrives there, Paris, for Assèze, is the quintessence of the "feminine": "For blacks, Paris has always rhymed with silk, lace, jewels, shopping malls--not to mention dresses, gowns, coats, and gadgets which make girls look like Giant Rose" (231).[9] However, the multiplicity of images of femininity which confront Assèze in exile lead her ultimately to lose sight of her own gender identity. She recalls: "What bothered me most of all was my own state of womanliness. I was no longer sure, in fact, that I was a woman!" (343).[10] Having been bombarded with other people's notions of what a woman should be, Assèze's femininity becomes destabilized, thus leading to an identity crisis. While she does not see herself as the kind of cultural transsexual she observed in Douala at the Ramsec Hotel, she nevertheless becomes unable to identify herself as a woman.

Similarly, in *Les honneurs perdus*, Saïda finds that migration disrupts the conventional femininity she had adopted in Cameroon. Although she arrives in Paris with a wedding dress and a medical certificate proving her virginity, her traditional Muslim sexual morality is soon called into question when she describes her own feelings of arousal on hearing her unmarried Senegalese landlady, Ngaremba, making love. This scene is followed by one in which Saïda attempts to lecture Ngaremba on the immorality of her behavior while simultaneously flattering her on her desirability to men. In a fit of laughter, Ngaremba remarks, "But Saïda, you're talking like a man!" ("Mais tu me parles comme un homme, Saïda!") (237). The fact that she can "talk like a man" and experience sexual excitement exposes the fragility of Saïda's identity of "jeune fille" (virgin) to which she so rigidly clings. It also suggests that for Saïda, like Assèze, the experience of migration is one of gender dislocation, in which familiar codes are reconfigured.

The loss of a locatable identity is a common thread in Beyala's migrant fiction, and is symptomatic of what Gloria Anzaldúa defines as living in a "borderland":[11]

Chicanos and other people of colour suffer economically for not acculturating. This voluntary (yet forced) alienation makes for psychological conflict, a kind of dual identity--we don't identify with the Anglo-American cultural values and we don't totally identify with the Mexican cultural values. We are a synergy of two cultures with various degrees of Mexicanness or Angloness. I have so internalized the borderland conflict that sometimes I feel like one cancels out the other and we are zero, nothing, no one. (63)

Indeed, Beyala's novels provide an interesting perspective on Anzaldúa's analysis in that it is specifically the gender identities of African people which become dislocated through their experience of the border zone. Normative notions of femininity and masculinity become destabilized and threatened by the expectations of the majority ethnic culture of France. *Les honneurs perdus* depicts the ambivalent figure of a Moroccan immigrant, Ibrahim, who, while apparently happy to sleep with Blandine in exchange for a plane ticket to Paris, refuses to have sex with his fiancée, Saïda, leading Ngaremba to accuse him of impotence: " 'That bloke is impotent,' she [Ngaremba] said. 'It's perfectly normal. What sort of life do immigrant men have? Some of them spend so long without touching a woman that, as soon as one appears, they forget how to do it' " (350).[12] Indeed, the narrative implies that Ibrahim cannot cope with the fact that, at fifty, Saïda is still a virgin. While Ngaremba is right to suggest that his "impotence" is a result of his migration to France, it is more specifically the transformation of his moral and sexual codes which are at the root of his rejection of Saïda. For this Moroccan immigrant male, Saïda embodies the gender clash between the cultural spaces of Islam and France, since she is a Muslim woman who is both a virgin and prepared to have sex with him outside marriage.[13]

Migration from Africa to Europe often forces men to reconsider the traditional gender roles which are not questioned in their countries of origin. As Alec Hargreaves writes:

In recent decades, legislation has been adopted in many industrialized countries aimed at establishing at least formal equality between men and women, though in practice many inequalities persist. Most immigrants of Third World origin come from countries where even formal equality does not exist: power is vested primarily in the father, whose authority extends over most decision-making areas and who generally serves as the breadwinner while the mother attends primarily to domestic tasks. (108)

This is certainly the kind of family model that Abdou Traoré exports from Mali to Paris in *Le petit prince de Belleville*: M'am and her co-wife, Soumana, perform all the household chores while Abdou works as a refuse collector. Furthermore, it is the French state's failure to acknowledge traditional African--in this case, polygamous--family structures that ultimately strips Abdou of his patriarchal authority and prompts M'am to reevaluate her own gender role.[14] When French feminist Madame Saddock reports Abdou to the authorities for defrauding the social security system, M'am takes his place as head of the household, running her own jewelry company and becoming her husband's boss when he is eventually released from prison. Thus, it is predominantly in relation to his wife's personal transformation that Abdou is forced to reconsider the gender constructs he imported from sub-Saharan Africa.

Reading Ama Ata Aidoo's play, *Anowa*, Carole Boyce Davies concludes that, "Aidoo seems to say that being a woman is a position often defined in relation to serving the male. Woman, then, comes to occupy the position in society against which male identity is installed" (68). This related position of woman explains the way in which, in *Le petit prince de Belleville*, Abdou's gender identity begins to collapse when his two wives, M'am and Soumana, come into contact with feminist ideology, represented in the text by the ambivalent figure of Madame Saddock: "Since the women in my house have been serving themselves large measures of independence, since they've been drinking from that sap, I've been learning how not to be a man. Who am I then? An immigrant. One mouth too many. A passing breath of air. I've lost my point of reference" (162).[15] Here, the text demonstrates the extent to which alternative gender roles for African women have implications for African men. M'am and her co-wife Soumana's exposure to alternative femininities causes Abdou's masculinity to fall into crisis because it relies on the maintenance of patriarchal definitions of gender identities. Once femininity is no longer fixed, then masculinity is destabilized. Thus, Abdou has to learn how not to be a man, because if woman is no longer defined in relation to man, then the reverse is also true. Unable to locate himself in this unfamiliar landscape, Abdou can only identify himself through the eyes of the other: as an immigrant, as insignificant and transient as a passing breath of air and, as racist rhetoric insists, a burden on the French state.

Whereas, before his incarceration, Abdou very much conforms to the French racist stereotype of the black African immigrant male (dishonest, sexually voracious, polygamous, and physically violent), on his release from prison, he is described as totally transformed. Having lost his job as a refuse collector, Abdou claims he is happy to be working for his wife. Moreover, he helps M'am in the kitchen and constantly showers her with flowers and gifts. According to Loukoum, "he is no longer quite the same" ("il n'est plus vraiment le même") (245). The reader thus infers that the exile of prison has provided a second experience of migration which allows Abdou to reinvent himself outside the polarized set of cultural oppositions presented by Africa and France.[16]

Abdou is a rare example in Beyala's fiction of a three-dimensional African male. The only other complex figure of African masculinity is drawn through the character of Abdou's son, Loukoum, the child narrator-protagonist of *Le petit prince de Belleville* and *Maman a un amant*. Although born in Mali, Loukoum was brought to France at a young age and, for this reason, his own gender identity is, to a certain extent, constructed around media images of western masculinity. According to Abdou, "He [Loukoum] is reluctant to put on a djellaba. He wants to wear suits like Sylvester Stallone, exactly the same ones so that he does not feel lost" (*Le petit prince* 198).[17] The reference to Stallone is an apposite one, not only highlighting the influence of Hollywood cinema on second-generation immigrant youth culture, but also emphasizing the way in which males of immigrant origin--like Loukoum and Stallone--are forced to consciously construct images of socially acceptable masculinity.[18]

On the other hand, Loukoum has inherited cultural codes from his parents and, as a Muslim eldest son, from his father in particular. Although Abdou claims that Loukoum is reluctant to put on a djellaba, when they go to the mosque, Loukoum seems proud to be wearing it and even emphasizes the fact that it is the same as his father's (80). For Loukoum, the opposing masculinities represented by the Stallone-style suit and the traditional djellaba do not appear to generate conflict for his own gender identity. However, they do affect the way in which he relates to women of immigrant origin, especially his mother, M'am.

In *Maman a un amant*, M'am's affair with Etienne Tichit forces Loukoum to reevaluate his mother's gender role. When he sees her dancing with Tichit in a strappy dress, he comments that, "to see her, you couldn't imagine she's got family responsibilities" ("à la voir, on ne pouvait pas imaginer qu'elle a des responsabilités familiales") (70). While Loukoum can admire his mother's beauty, he cannot reconcile her new image with the one he has created for her. Suddenly M'am has become a sexualized being for Loukoum, no longer containable within his preconceived notion of "mother." Later, when Loukoum becomes convinced that M'am, again dressed seductively, is using the pretence of attending her adult literacy class in order to continue seeing Tichit, he tells her in anger that she is not his mother (183). It thus appears that although Loukoum can place himself fairly easily in the Franco-Malian borderland, he finds his mother much more difficult to locate.

As translator of his mother's private musings in *Maman a un amant*, Loukoum also functions as a site of mediation between the normative gender roles he has inherited from his father and the alternative femininities explored by M'am in France. Moreover, Loukoum's role as linguistic translator mirrors the cultural translation of M'am's gender identity in France. According to Homi Bhabha, "in order to objectify cultural meaning, there always has to be a process of alienation and of secondariness *in relation to itself*. In that sense there is no 'in itself' and 'for itself' within cultures because they are always subject to intrinsic forms of translation" (210).[19] In each of the four migrant novels under discussion, Beyala exposes the ways in which immigrant women's femininities are translated as the women travel through the seemingly opposing cultural spaces of Africa and France.

This notion of translation also explains the fact that all three of Beyala's migrant heroines--M'am, Saïda, and Assèze--renegotiate their femininity through a sexual encounter with a majority ethnic male in France. These metaphorical migrations empower the women to rethink the traditional gender roles they had previously accepted without question, and to reassert themselves as women on their own terms. After her affair with Tichit, M'am describes herself as "plus tout à fait la même ni tout à fait une autre" (no longer completely the same, nor completely another) (*Maman* 187). Whereas before meeting Tichit she had internalized the traditional premise that "woman is born kneeling at man's feet" (21, 240),[20] at the end of the novel she sees Abdou not as her master but as her "soleil déchu" (fallen sun) (240). Thus, the affair empowers M'am to make informed and conscious choices about her own gender role and to evaluate more critically that of her husband. Her love, she claims, reinvents her (208).

Similarly, in *Les honneurs perdus*, when Saïda Bénérafa finally loses her virginity, it is again with a white Frenchman, Marcel Pignon Marcel.[21] This experience is presented as a rebirth: "I felt like a new woman" ("Je me sentais une femme neuve") (396). No longer identified as a fifty-year-old virgin, Saïda is able to redefine herself: "I was strong. No children. No husband yet. But indestructible" (397).[22]

For Assèze, the black-white sexual relationship is more complicated. She meets Monsieur Alexandre, a rich French record producer, while she is trying to secure a record deal for her exploitative lover, Océan. Although she knows that Alexandre is married, Assèze's relationship with him reads as a love affair between equals. The complication lies in the fact that, unbeknown to Assèze, Alexandre's wife is Sorraya, the girl she lived with in Douala. Initially, Alexandre fulfills a similar narrative function to Tichit and Marcel in that, through her relationship with him, Assèze begins to question her future with Océan whom she eventually leaves. Ultimately, though, the majority ethnic lover in *Assèze l'Africaine* has a more complex role in that, when Sorraya commits suicide because she is unable to live as a hybrid (339), Alexandre decides to marry Assèze. The book, a retrospective narrative, opens with Assèze living a self-effacing lifestyle, going to church every day, her husband threatening to divorce her for her inertia. Like M'am and Saïda, she uses the knowledge she gains from a migrant sexual relationship to make a choice, albeit to adopt a more conventionally "feminine" role.

All of this is not to say that Beyala is suggesting that immigrant women need to undergo some kind of cross-cultural sexual initiation in order to assert agency; rather, the white lovers, like Loukoum's narration, act as mediators who help the women to translate their own gender identities. In other words, Tichit, Marcel, and Alexandre function as "objects of otherness" (Bhabha 211) with and through which the female subjects identify. As such, cross-cultural sexual intercourse crystallizes the process of hybridity which, as Homi Bhabha explains, generates new cultural meanings and new subjectivities:

If . . . the act of cultural translation (both as representation and as reproduction) denies the essentialism of a prior given original or originary culture, then we see that all forms of culture are continually in a process of hybridity. But for me the importance of hybridity is not to be able to trace two original moments from which the third emerges, rather hybridity to me is the "third space" which enables other positions to emerge. (211)

Indeed, the polarized hybridity which Bhabha rejects is also problematized through Beyala's migrant women, in particular Sorraya in *Assèze l'Africaine*, who describes her own frustrated attempts to acculturate: "All my life I've lived with my ass between two stools. I tried to ape the whites. It's not my fault! In Africa they made us believe we were backward. I believed it. I wanted to

Frenchify myself, dig out every trace of black in me. Because black is dirt. Black is destitution. Black is a curse. I hated myself for being African. I wanted to be like Dupond, Durand. It was absurd" (331).[23] It is the recognition of her impossible hybridity which motivates Sorraya's suicide. She tells Assèze: "I'll never be seen as a white woman. I don't belong anywhere. I'm a hybrid" (339).[24] This negative hybridity resulting from an attempt to bridge a gap between two apparently discrete cultural spaces also generates the "cultural transsexuals" Assèze witnessed at the Douala hotel. What Sorraya represents is not Bhabha's "third space," but the alienation that ensues when a migrant attempts to privilege one set of cultural meanings over another.

Metaphorically, Sorraya's death is inevitable since she attempts to fix her identity through acculturation rather than accepting, as Renato Rosaldo suggests, that the concept of an "authentic" culture is tenable only as a "useful fiction" (217). In *Le petit prince de Belleville*, M'am's co-wife, Soumana, also dies once she is brainwashed by the ideology of Madame Saddock. Soumana's realization that, as an illegal immigrant woman in France, she literally has nowhere to go is demonstrated in the scene where, having recalled Madame Saddock's views on domestic violence, she collapses in tears in the kitchen (93-94). Soumana wants to acculturate but, unlike Sorraya, lacks the economic means to gain entry to the cultural space of France. However, what the two women have in common is the mistranslation of both their own gender identities and those of French women as essential and given.[25]

The individuals in Beyala's fiction who do survive migration are those who, like the symbolically nicknamed "Débrouillardes" (Resourceful Women) in *Assèze l'Africaine*, undergo a process of "transculturation" rather than attempt acculturation into the majority ethnic culture of France. Françoise Lionnet writes that: "[Transculturation's] specifically spatial connotations demarcate a pattern of movement, across cultural arenas and physical topographies, that corresponds more accurately to the notion of 'appropriation,' a concept more promising than those of acculturation and assimilation, and one that implies active intervention rather than passive victimization" (326). Transculturation thus implies movement through the "third space" from which, as Bhabha has suggested, new positions will emerge. Gender identity, like cultural identity, is not fixed, and the experiences of migration and exile force women and men to renegotiate their gender identities across a wide range of often contradictory sites. More importantly, for immigrant women of African origin, transculturation connotes agency. Through transculturation, women like M'am and Saïda become "migrating subjects" (Boyce Davies 37) whose physical migrations give them the space to constantly reposition themselves as "women."

NOTES

1. The narratives of *C'est le soleil qui m'a brûlée* (1987) and *Tu t'appelleras Tanga* (1988) both unfold in fictional African cities. In Beyala's third novel, *Seul le diable le savait* (1990), Mégri, the protagonist, makes a brief, fantastical trip to Paris. However, although the novel ends with Mégri's departure for France, the text is located

in Africa. Interestingly, Beyala's recent novel, *La petite fille du réverbère* (1998), returns to Cameroon.

2. Loukoum is one of the main characters in both these novels.

3. Calixthe Beyala was born in New Bell, Douala, in 1961. She now lives in Paris.

4. "A droite, en face de Monoprix et de Prisunic, il y a le *Ramsec Hôtel* où des Nègres blanchisés imitent leurs confrères blancs. Ils sont ce qu'ils sont, ni Blancs, ni Nègres, des espèces de transsexuels culturels, vaguement hommes d'affaires, voyous sur les bords, et tout au fond pouilleux." All translations in this article are my own.

5. This is, in a way, the reverse of the myth exposed by Fanon whereby sex with a white woman was viewed by black men as a means of achieving "authentic" virility (58).

6. "ces femmes des livres, c'est comme des femmes qui deviennent des hommes à force de faire du sport."

7. This view is reversed when Assèze finds herself expelled from school by the new teacher. Dismayed, Awono asks the Countess what Assèze will now become. The Countess replies, "une femme" (a woman) (*Assèze* 169). Here, the text suggests that once it is decided that she will no longer be educated at school, Assèze is temporarily reincorporated into normative femininity. However, when Assèze decides to travel to France as an illegal immigrant, the only form of identification she is carrying is her school identity card.

8. Here she consciously performs her femininity, striking what she believes to be a "feminine" pose (*Assèze* 191).

9. "Pour un Nègre, Paris a toujours rimé avec soie, dentelles, bijoux, galeries-- et encore des robes, des tuniques, des manteaux, des gadgets qui donnent aux filles l'allure Rose Géante."

10. "Et ce qui me perturbait par-dessus tout, c'était mon propre état de femme. Je n'étais plus sûre, en réalité, d'en être une!"

11. Anzaldúa defines a borderland as "a vague and undetermined place created by the emotional residue of an unnatural boundary. It is in a constant state of transition. The prohibited and forbidden are its inhabitants" (3).

12. " 'Ce type est impuissant,' dit-elle [Ngaremba]. 'C'est normal. Quelle vie ont les immigrés? Certains restent si longtemps sans toucher à une femme qu'ils en perdent les moyens dès qu'il s'en présente une.' "

13. In spite of her decision to sleep with Ibrahim, Saïda still demonstrates the extent to which she has internalized patriarchally defined gender roles when she insists that Ibrahim cannot be impotent since only women have sexual problems (350).

14. For a discussion of the legal maze facing polygamous immigrant families in France, see Hargreaves 114-116.

15. "Depuis que les femmes servent de longues rasades d'indépendance dans ma maison, depuis qu'elles boivent de cette sève, j'apprends à ne plus être un homme. Qui suis-je? Un immigré. Une bouche encombrante. Un courant d'air qui passe. Je n'ai plus de repère" (162).

16. The transformation is, however, not a permanent one as Abdou's infidelity continues even after M'am has left and subsequently returned in *Maman a un amant*.

17. "il [Loukoum] répugne à mettre la djellaba. Il veut des costumes comme ceux de Stallone, exactement les mêmes, de crainte de se sentir perdu."

18. Yvonne Tasker analyzes the way in which Stallone's star image has consciously shifted in his attempt to be taken seriously (83-87).

19. Emphasis in the text.

20. "la femme est née à genoux aux pieds de l'homme."

21. Although M'am, of course, is not a virgin when she has sex with Tichit, he tells her that since she has never had an orgasm, she is still a virgin (*Maman* 78).

22. "J'étais forte. Pas d'enfants. Pas encore de mari. Mais indestructible."

23. "Toute ma vie, j'ai vécu le cul entre deux chaises. J'ai essayé de singer le Blanc. C'est pas de ma faute! En Afrique, on nous faisait croire que nous étions des arriérés et moi, j'y ai cru. Je voulais me franciser, désincruster toute trace de noir en moi. Parce que le noir c'est la saleté. Le noir c'est la misère. Le noir c'est la malédiction. Je m'en voulais d'être africaine. Je voulais ressembler à Dupond, à Durand. C'était ridicule."

24. "Jamais je ne serai considérée comme une Blanche. Je n'appartiens à rien. Une hybride."

25. Abdou also refuses to recognize the fictional nature of normative gender roles in both Mali and France. This failure leads him to experience his exile as a "poison" which eats away at his flesh (*Le petit prince* 7).

WORKS CITED

Aidoo, Ama Ata. *Anowa*. London: Longman, 1970.

Anzaldúa, Gloria. *Borderlands/La Frontera: The New Mestiza*. San Francisco: Aunt Lute, 1987.

Beyala, Calixthe. *C'est le soleil qui m'a brûlée*. Paris: Stock, 1987.

---. *Tu t'appelleras Tanga*. Paris: Stock, 1988.

---. *Seul le diable le savait*. Paris: Le Pré aux clercs, 1990.

---. *Le petit prince de Belleville*. 1992. Paris: J'ai Lu, 1993.

---. *Maman a un amant*. 1993. Paris: J'ai Lu, 1995.

---. *Assèze l'Africaine*. Paris: Albin Michel, 1994.

---. *Lettre d'une Africaine à ses soeurs occidentales*. Paris: Spengler, 1995.

---. *Les honneurs perdus*. Paris: Albin Michel, 1996.

---. *La petite fille du réverbère*. Paris: Albin Michel, 1998.

Bhabha, Homi. "The Third Space." *Identity, Community, Culture, Difference*. Ed. Jonathon Rutherford. London: Lawrence and Wishart, 1990, 207-221.

Boyce Davies, Carole. *Black Women, Writing and Identity: Migrations of the Subject*. London: Routledge, 1994.

Fanon, Frantz. *Peau noire, masques blancs*. Paris: Seuil, 1952.

Hargreaves, Alec G. *Immigration, "Race" and Ethnicity in Contemporary France*. London: Routledge, 1995.

Lionnet, Françoise. "*Logiques Métisses*: Cultural Appropriation and Postcolonial Representations." *Postcolonial Subjects: Francophone Women Writers*. Ed. Mary Jean Green et al. Minneapolis: University of Minnesota Press, 1996, 321-343.

Rosaldo, Renato. *Culture and Truth: The Remaking of Social Analysis*. London: Routledge, 1993.

Tasker, Yvonne. *Spectacular Bodies: Gender, Genre and the Action Cinema*. London: Routledge, 1993.

New *Sans-papiers* Rhetorics in Contemporary France

Mireille Rosello

Since the 1990s, new cultural images have been added to the range of recognizable representations of the immigrant. Over time, the French government has come to privilege the concept of *clandestins* (illegal immigrants), insisting that the integration of legal immigrants would be jeopardized if new population flows were not strictly controlled. Soon, literature and cinema began to reflect this new trend, often in order to criticize the government's anti-immigration policies and the cultural myths that developed in such a tense atmosphere. The distinction between so-called *clandestins* and legal immigrants was already culturally well-established when it was further complicated by the "affair" of the undocumented Africans of Saint-Bernard Church in the summer of 1996. Choosing to relinquish the illusory protection provided by invisibility, undocumented immigrants decided to mobilize and, after months of patient struggle, 300 African families occupied Saint-Bernard Church and managed to secure the media's undivided attention. In this chapter, I propose to listen to the voices that have spoken since 1996, and to ascertain what is new in the fictional and non-fictional discourses that have emerged from the affair. This widely publicized event, which legitimized the coinage of the term *sans-papiers* (undocumented immigrants) constitutes a linguistic and political watershed.

The *sans-papiers* wanted the French public to know that their alleged "illegality" was not due to the fact that they had entered the country illegally, but was often the result of incoherent legislation: according to their critics, the

Pasqua immigration laws were less effective in controlling the arrival of new immigrants than they were in creating a situation where undocumented immigrants found themselves caught in vicious administrative circles. Partly because the *sans-papiers* movement is only a few years old, and partly because the mobilization of these immigrants had urgent political and practical goals, the type of discourse generated by the Saint-Bernard affair did not at first take the form of fictional works. Nonetheless, this event may represent the beginning of a new movement, the emergence of literature by undocumented immigrants. Popular novels and films such as Didier Van Cauwelaert's 1994 Goncourt prize-winner *Un aller simple* and Jean-Luc and Pierre Dardennes' film *La promesse* had already clearly demonstrated that the mixture of fiction and illegal immigration could constitute an explosive cultural and ethical, comic or tragic, cocktail. I would suggest, however, that when the *sans-papiers* started speaking for themselves, a new rhetoric of demands suddenly replaced earlier appeals for tolerance and benevolence.

At first, a proliferation of political speeches, media coverage, activists' slogans, and public declarations constituted almost all the commentary on the confrontation between the 300 families and the government. Besides the television images and newspaper articles that often defined the parameters of this national debate, theoretical essays began to propose analyses of the movement. Finally, two of the *sans-papiers'* spokespersons wrote autobiographies that came out soon after the end of the summer of 1996: Ababacar Diop's *Dans la peau d'un sans-papiers* and Mamady Sané's *Sorti de l'ombre: journal d'un sans-papiers*. A few years later, Madjiguène Cissé added a woman's voice to the chorus with the publication of *Parole de sans-papiers* in which an entire chapter is devoted to the "sans-papières" (131-146).

In their autobiographies and essays, Cissé, Diop, and Sané underscore one of the most important aspects of their struggle: their desire to convince their audience that illegal immigrants have been arbitrarily portrayed as intruders. For these authors, the *sans-papiers* are not delinquents, but rather the victims of injustice. Cissé reminds her readers that "refugees" are defined in existing international agreements that delimit the definition of persecution. International organizations such as L'Office Français de Protection des Réfugiés et Apatrides (OFPRA), for example, exclude women who are the victims of "rape, excision, forced marriages, and the criminalization of adulterous sexual relationships in certain countries" (Cissé 114).[1] Diop also emphasizes that undocumented immigrants must not be confused with unemployed homeless people. For the former, choosing visibility in 1996 meant having the chance to show that they had been active participants in the economic and social life of the nation and that they were not criminals but had been criminalized. In this regard, Diop writes:

At the time, nobody talked about "sans-papiers"; the term had not been coined yet. One of the first articles devoted to our cause was entitled: "The SOS sent by the Illegal Immigrants from Saint-Ambroise."

We had opted for a new form of struggle and decided to come out into broad daylight in order to point to tragic situations created by the laws themselves. We wanted to force the French to see, to open their eyes. We really wanted to show that we were not afraid of repression. We no longer wanted to live in the shadow of the law.[2] (76)

Diop's autobiography thus records a moment of linguistic change and theorizes the choice made by the group. Like the word *Beur*, the expression *sans-papiers* was coined by the minority group who chose to add to the range of available cultural concepts rather than reappropriating a preexisting but pejorative description of themselves.[3] Just as the generalization of the use of the *Beur* label soon led to criticism and rejection even within the community that created it, the designation *sans-papiers* will never be innocent: even if it is perceived by immigrants themselves as an improvement over the notion of *clandestin,* which implicitly justified repressive policies, it cannot serve as a euphemism. Calling someone an undocumented immigrant does not suggest lawlessness, but the prefix connoting lack ("sans") clearly reminds us that the goal of the *sans-papiers* is not to reconcile themselves to the situation or to reclaim a preexisting identity. As Jacques Derrida, who has taken a public stance in favor of providing them with documents, points out:

We assume that those we describe as undocumented [*sans-papiers*] are lacking something. He is "un-," she is "un-." What exactly is missing? They lack what the document in question represents, rights and the right to rights. We assume that anyone who does not have documents ultimately does not have rights and is virtually an outlaw. When we deny them normality and civic identity, we come close to stripping them of identity altogether.[4] ("Quand j'ai entendu" 4)

In other words, the new designation reflects a new set of problems rather than a general improvement of the migrants' situation: like most linguistic changes, the adoption of the word *sans-papiers* is a double-edged sword whose implications need to be contextualized. Politically, there is no doubt that the move from *clandestin* to *sans-papiers*, initiated by the migrants themselves, was considered a desirable alternative. The term *clandestin* portrayed the illegal immigrant as having deliberately broken immigration laws whereas *sans-papiers* suggests that human beings have been relegated to the margins of society because of a lack of documentation, which is treated as an inalienable fact and not considered to be a result of their actions. Consequently, the word *clandestin* implicitly suggests that returning to the country of origin would restore the individual's legitimacy; *sans-papiers*, on the other hand, implies that the situation would be solved if the state provided the immigrants with the appropriate documents. Nevertheless, some of the implications of the new designation could prove to be more problematic than the status quo because of two related consequences of the paradigm change: *sans-papiers*, emphasizing as it does the result of a situation rather than its causes, downplays the migrant's trajectory. And while it may be necessary to deemphasize the past when it is wrongly construed as a series of illegal acts, this erasure of the past also elides much of the migrant's agency. This is an ironic reversal given that the whole *sans-papiers* movement started when a group of African families mobilized and organized themselves. Perhaps more importantly, the stress on absence and lack ("sans") raises the issue of how to obtain documents, thus giving rise to questions of strategies and tactics. If it were clear that the *sans-papiers* had rights, their request for legalization (*régularisation*) would ultimately be straightforward, even if complicated by labyrinthine administrative procedures. The most important claim of the *sans-papiers*, however, is that they are excluded from access to rights: they seek to convince the public and the government that their individual stories should be examined precisely because the blanket application of immigration laws leads to contradictions and injustices. They thus find themselves in the position of having to demonstrate that such legal texts cannot take into account the complexity of some migrants' situations.

Two tactics are likely to prevail when an individual finds himself or herself in such a situation. The first type of rhetoric available can be called a discourse of supplication, in which migrants emphasize their own misfortune and invoke the host nation's sense of hospitality. The definition of political asylum tends to encourage such a discourse: persecuted individuals appeal to the state's generosity and beg to be protected from their own government. The whole dialogue is framed by a request, and the language used in the negotiation puts the government official in the position of powerful host who is capable of giving back what has been lost. This necessarily establishes a problematic gray area between rights and pity, between eliciting compassion and demanding the application of international regulations. At the center of the debate on asylum seekers, there remains the issue of what narratives must be produced in order for the status of refugee to be recognized. In *Réfugiés et sans papiers: la République face au droit d'asile XIXe-XXe siècles*, Gérard Noiriel points out that nineteenth-century asylum seekers often felt compelled to implore the mercy of the administration in writing and to adopt a consistently self-deprecating attitude: "refugees often believe that it is by devaluing themselves that they have the best chance of moving their judges. One of the most important functions of these letters is to elicit the authorities' pity, and, as everyone knows, one only feels pity for the weak" (279).[5]

In Noiriel's text, there is an interesting and almost imperceptible slippage between the beginning and the end of the sentence: at first, the author seems be stating that the refugees' choice was a conscious tactic which may or may not have been internalized ("refugees often believe..."). By the end of the sentence, though, the audience is implicitly asked to approve the immigrant's choice as an almost unavoidable consequence of the way the system operates-- "as everyone knows," the potential refugee cannot appear strong for fear of being denied the status of refugee. Because of the solipsistic logic, which the ironic tone of the passage criticizes, a strong refugee can never become a refugee: all refugees are weak. What is even more shocking to Noiriel is that international recognition of the right to asylum does not seem to have altered the refugee's rhetoric.

At a time when arbitrariness is the rule, it is no wonder that refugees have recourse to a rhetoric intended to generate pity in those who have power over them. On the other hand, it is highly surprising to discover that, in spite of the complete institutionalization of the right to asylum after World War II, self-deprecation is still such a common way of ob-

taining satisfaction. For in theory, asylum-seekers are no longer invoking pity but demanding justice.[6] (280)

The *sans-papiers*, on the other hand, clearly had no intention of resort-
ing to a rhetoric of generosity, and their positioning often represents a radical
departure from the paradigm of the refugee: because they have often been in
France for as long as ten years, because they often have proper accommodations
and stable jobs, and feel that they have been wrongly construed as newcomers
who are in the process of being integrated, their self-presentation frequently
reverses the traditional request for generosity on the part of the state. Sané, for
example, returns repeatedly to the idea that his past gives him rights because of
his ancestors' role in liberating France during World War II: "I have thought
long and hard about my ancestors' itinerary and I have concluded that a French
person would never be treated like that in Africa. And above all, I think that we,
the descendants of France's liberators, do not deserve such treatment in France"
(17).[7] Not only does Sané present himself as an individual involved in a social
struggle, but he also insists that the debt to be repaid is not on his side. Far from
pleading, far from even referring to the notions of generosity and open-
mindedness, he requests what he perceives as his due, the payment of a moral
debt owed to his ancestors. At the risk of seeming repetitive, his text comes back
to the same point every few pages, and it is difficult for the reader to decide
whether his litany is a tactic or an obsessive reformulation of a devastating sense
of injustice. Nor is it clear whether this type of discourse will become a new
cultural model which will slowly make its way into the mindset of his readers
(will the French realize that the *sans-papiers* issue is linked to post-colonial
debts?) or if it is the only way of expressing a deep-seated sense of historic injustice (in which case the *sans-papiers* have inherited the injustice done to their
forefathers and it is difficult to see why the children would be better treated than
the Senegalese Riflemen of World War II depicted by Ousmane Sembène in his
1988 film *Camp Thiaroye*).

Cissé's autobiographical *Parole de sans-papiers* goes even further
partly because it was published after the new Socialist government had passed
legislation which was intended to counter the nefarious effects of the Pasqua
laws. According to Cissé, the "Chevènement law" voted in on May 11, 1998,
"shows that the relationship between France and Africa remains 'utilitarian' "
(156). Cissé claims that the state continues to treat Africa as a reservoir of cheap
labor, thus depleting the continent of the most talented individuals who could
contribute to its development.

The assertive tone of the *sans-papiers*, their determination to demand
what they perceive as their rights, and their desire to put an end to injustice are
worth noting because they are bound to affect related discourses, in particular
the language used by others to respond to pleas for generosity and benevolence.
This raises the question whether their new positioning will be more or less effective at eliciting sympathy and feelings of solidarity in the French public at
large and whether organizations will find it hard to adopt this new stance without radically modifying their role as facilitators. This is not to say that the traditional rhetoric of supplication is about to disappear altogether: this is why it is

crucial to ascertain where new distinctions and boundaries are currently being drawn in order to differentiate between all the "sans-" (have-nots) of contemporary society.

Indeed, cultural categories are difficult to change. *Notre Dame de Paris*, the highly successful musical that continues to draw crowds and functions as a shared cultural reference, contains direct allusions to the *sans-papiers* affair. The third song in Act I is entitled "Les sans-papiers," and the original "cour des miracles" (den of thieves) portrayed in Victor Hugo's novel has been modernized and includes dancers who represent undocumented immigrants. It can certainly be argued that these songs have contributed to making the *sans-papiers'* cause more widely known--perhaps demonstrating that it does not take radical artists to elicit a generally positive reaction from the French public. However, the musical version of *Notre Dame de Paris* has also inherited from Hugo a tendency to view the oppressed as a monolithic group to be pitied. The song which contains the direct reference to the *sans-papiers* plays on the resemblance between the terms "sans-papiers" and "sans-abri" (homeless), and alludes to crowds massed behind the walls of the city, seeking refuge. In particular, it highlights the increasing numbers of these asylum seekers, suggesting that thousands will soon become millions. However, it is not clear whether the audience is expected to make a distinction between foreigners, s*ans-papiers*, homeless people, and asylum seekers. It is admittedly very difficult to make such distinctions effectively since a variety of marginalized groups share some of the problems experienced by the *sans-papiers*. In *Adieu to Emmanuel Lévinas*, Derrida notes that there are similarities between "the foreigner, the immigrant (with or without papers), the exile, the refugee, those without a country or a state, the displaced person or population" (64), but he then goes on in the same sentence to observe that his list refers to categories that must be carefully distinguished from each other.[8] Nonetheless, after warning us about the dangers of confusion, Derrida moves on, sidestepping his own recommendation, as if the task of making distinctions is a second step that other urgent tasks always force lower down the list of priorities. To a certain extent, even the very desire to differentiate is problematic, since each border drawn between categories runs the risk of introducing new hierarchical levels of exclusion, such as good and bad migrants, and acceptable and unacceptable *sans-papiers*.[9]

When an author chooses laughter and derision as a strategy, the dilemma experienced by Derrida--who is forced to privilege one level of argument over another even if this means delaying the search for more accurate definitions--can be solved by using self-consciously excessive satire and ironic reversals. Humor and irony, when used in a provocative fashion, may thus provide an alternative discourse, particularly in fictional works. An author's deliberate blurring of categories can then be used as a source of biting humor rather than as a weapon against those who have been marginalized. Sandrine Bessora's recent novel is a remarkably uncompromising example of this new aggressive stance. Cryptically entitled *53 CM*,[10] this first novel is written by an author whose potentially vulnerable identity is both hidden and revealed in her irreverent fictional autobiography. Bessora's tactics of self-representation can be seen as the opposite of the message contained in the songs of *Notre Dame de Paris*. Zara, the first-person narrator, wants no compassion, and her assertiveness knows no bounds. There is no such thing as going too far in this farcical parody of the immigrant's trials and tribulations: not only does this *sans-papiers* choose to anger rather than to plead or please, but she also does not hesitate to experiment with the master's tools at the risk of destroying much more than the master's house. One of her weapons of predilection is precisely the blurring of categories.

The first rhetorical gesture that destabilizes any attempt at eliciting stereotypical compassion is the author's portrayal of herself as a potentially privileged individual: she comes from an educated, upper-middle-class family, and she does not hesitate to make fun of her sheltered childhood in her biracial family. The father, born in Lambaréné in Gabon, is a "Noir teint en noir pour cacher ses cheveux blancs" (black who dyes his hair black to hide his white hair) (56). In similar fashion, the mother from Lausanne is presented as a "Blanche, teinte en blonde pour cacher ses cheveux chatains" (white who dyes her hair blonde to hide her dark hair) (55). These two initial portraits of the parents tenderly accuse both of them of sharing the same kind of harmless vanity, a common denominator that humorously relegates their different skin colors to the level of secondary importance. Even more importantly, the autobiographical flashbacks stand in sharp contrast to the stereotypical image of a poor, uneducated African: the daughter of a diplomat, the narrator is a jet-setter who follows her parents from one prestigious post to the next. Moving between Brussels, Geneva, Washington, DC, Florida, and France, she perceives the world through the filter of what she knows to be a privileged perspective: "One day, we leave for Florida in Daddy the Ambassador's gray Cadillac. . . . The French school is private, our nest always very classy."[11] Her privileged background--and this will come as a surprise to those who think they have understood the rhetoric of the *sans-papiers* of Saint-Bernard--does not shield her from ubuesque administrative problems. Her endless quest for the elusive "cat' de séjour" (residence permit) makes her life an endless misery. As for her daughter, stuck between her mother's two (Swiss and Gabonese) passports and a plethora of dissenting administrators' opinions, she has no legal existence: "*Your* daughter is a figment of *your* imagination for she is not qualified to have been born: you don't fit into the framework of the law" (86).[12]

Bessora's guilt-free recognition of some of her privileges may well send contradictory signals to readers who are used to less complex figures of undocumented immigrants. Even if the father's image as a successful diplomat is qualified by stories about his childhood under colonial rule, some will probably think that she needs no help and that there is no reason to feel sorry for her-- and this may well be one of the messages of the novel. Indeed, the sudden realization that (upper-middle-class) undocumented immigrants both exist and want no pity may be a salutary shock to our cultural system which has more or less forgotten that its portrayal of the "sans-" (have-nots) already has implicit consequences.

Bessora is no subaltern. And she can speak. When she chooses to parody popular culture, she becomes extremely polemical. Her tactic is not to teach us a forgotten past: rather, she prefers to parody the use of confusing categories and to launch a barrage of provocative associations, brandishing analogies as powerful if unsubtle rhetorical weapons. Unlike Derrida and his cautious desire to make distinctions, she does not hesitate to practice a violent form of confusion between different historical events with the intention of disturbing, angering, and perhaps rudely awakening readers who, like historians or philosophers, may still be in search of better-defined categories. In the following passage, for example, the absence of distinctions is used to provoke readers and to denounce liberal guilt and compassion.

Like our dear blond-haired children, I love cartoons: I am still very childlike. I adored Walt Disney's *Pocahontas*. It is the story of a sun-tanned Indian girl who falls in love with John Smith, a pedophile hunter of Red-Skins. Because there were lots of Red-Skin hunters, one day, Pocahontas, whose real name was Matoaka, was kidnapped by a nice settler and put on a ship. But because hunter-settlers are nice, they freed her in exchange for a ransom and an arranged marriage with a nice white farmer, John Rolfe. They called her Rebecca, destroyed her village, and took her to England where, together with a dozen Indians, she worked as a circus performer. She was 22 years old when she died. Some day, Disney will perhaps contribute to the history of Judaism with a cartoon similar to *Pocahontas:* Anne Frank, the story of a white Jewish girl who falls in love with a mustached Nazi called Hitler. There will be lots of nice Jewish-Skin hunters [chasseurs de Peaux-Juives], and one day, Anne will be deported to a concentration camp where she will think a lot while reading *Pol Pot and Milosevic in Hutuland,* a comic strip from Rwanda.[13] (25)

Here, analogy is both the enemy and the weapon, as Bessora uses a series of absurd comparisons in order to show just how nonsensical comparisons can be; by so doing, she both mirrors and denounces the impasse of discourses whose effectiveness depends on their ability to legitimize their own comparisons. At the same time, the question of what is like what, of whose situation is similar to or different from whose, becomes the precondition to any discussion of the *sans-papiers* and the quagmire where all attempts to find solutions fail.

If the novel best exemplifies what I have called "new *sans-papiers* rhetorics," it is because it suggests that some issues may have become obsolete and that it may be desirable to focus on new, more pressing problems. The refusal to ask for compassion is directly linked to Bessora's reformulation of related issues. Identity--in particular the question of hybridity, which post-colonial critics and artists have looked at from many different angles--seems to leave Bessora relatively indifferent. The anxieties expressed by *Beur* novelists about their integration, identity, origins, and religion do not appear in *53 CM*. Like the *sans-papiers* of Saint-Bernard, who displaced the issue of borders by creating a political crisis right in the middle of the French capital, Bessora knows that the question of being on the inside or the outside is not the crux of the problem. Like the undocumented immigrants whose illegality can coexist with their integration, she is always both an insider and an outsider. She knows, however, that the real issue is that of determining the modalities of that co-existence; in Bessora's case, this means co-existing with her own internal differences and with others' perceptions of her difference. In today's increasingly globalized postcolonial world, it is no longer enough to demonstrate the omnipresence of hybridity; instead, the new question is what type of *métissage* people will accept or reject. While satirizing supposedly rational desires for forms of mixing (that could be a metaphor for problem-free integration), Bessora has one of Zara's enemies explain: "Hybridization in you is even more pernicious, because it is dissimulated in a cowardly way under the apparent fusion of features: your hair is wavy although Reason demands that half of its length should be straight and the other half frizzy. Your skin is light brown although Reason requires that it be black in the sexual areas and white on the chaste parts" (187).[14]

For Bessora, the question can no longer be a choice between *métissage* and homogeneity: the narrator does not make fun of people who do not recognize the prevalence of hybridity; rather, she mocks the intolerance of those who imagine that certain types of fusion are more legitimate than others. In the passage cited above, she provocatively uses confusing terminology that would normally be the hallmark of racist thinking and thus camouflages her denunciation of racism by pairing it with a comic and seemingly harmless analogy. In this fashion, the ludicrous image of the co-existence of straight and curly hair on the same head is suddenly complicated by the supposedly equivalent vision of a patchwork of skin colors on the same body. The second image plays off the comic ideas created by the first, but the ghost of scientific racism that judges skin color in moral terms suddenly contaminates our laughter.

From a biological standpoint, Zara understands *métissage*. As the daughter of a black African man and of a white European woman, she knows that being conscious of one's mixed heritage also means being aware that one can never interpret the resulting identity as simply an addition or a subtraction. She is neither the sum of her mother and father's cultural identities, nor is she the smallest common denominator. As an author, Bessora rewrites existing narratives about multiple roots and creolized identities. Once again, the issue she raises is not whether or not a single origin can be conceptualized (for the *sans-papiers'* trajectory is clearly nomadic), nor is it about memory versus the erasure of origins since both co-exist. Indeed, she forcefully and poetically states that her own roots guarantee she will have no stability. It makes no sense, then, to ask Bessora where she is from: she is from Brussels, but also from Geneva, Washington, Gabon, and France. However, if the idea of roots does not disappear in *53CM*, it is reimagined as what Bessora calls "winged roots" (racines ailées) (57). If the *sans-papiers* of Saint-Bernard questioned the implicitly hegemonic genre of the letter of supplication by introducing the discourse of claims and justice, Bessora's fictional autobiography adopts their strategy as a starting point and provides us with an imaginative vision of what type of identity is thus created: wherever she goes, her winged roots are temporarily buried and then dug up again when the time comes to move on. In this sense, her winged roots may provide the *sans-papiers* and those around them with a powerful image that will enable them to better understand their situation: every act of burial means one thing, while every exhumation means something else, just as each *sans-papier's* identity is an incommensurable sum of losses and gains.

NOTES

1. "viol, excision, mariages forcés, criminalisation de l'adultère dans certains pays."

2. "On ne parlait pas à l'époque de 'sans-papiers'; l'expression n'avait pas encore cours. L'un des premiers articles qui nous a été consacré portait en titre: 'Le SOS des clandestins de Saint-Ambroise.'

Nous avions choisi une nouvelle forme de lutte et décidé de sortir au grand jour pour pointer le doigt sur des situations dramatiques générées par les lois elles-mêmes. Nous voulions obliger les Français à voir, à ouvrir les yeux. Nous tenions à montrer que nous n'avions aucunement peur de la répression. Nous ne voulions plus vivre dans l'ombre projetée par les lois." After being forced to leave Saint-Ambroise Church, the 300 Africans occupied Saint-Bernard Church. During the summer of 1996, the media generally referred to the movement "of the *sans-papiers* of Saint-Bernard," but the name "Saint-Ambroise" was retained on the website that the immigrants maintain.

3. Compare with Aimé Césaire's reappropriation of the term *nègre* in the Negritude movement.

4. "Ce qu'on appelle, en un mot, un sans-papiers, on suppose qu'il manque de quelque chose. Il est 'sans.' Elle est 'sans.' Il lui manque quoi, au juste? Lui ferait défaut ce que ledit papier représente. Le droit, le droit au droit. On suppose que le sans-papiers est finalement 'sans-droit' et virtuellement hors-la-loi. En lui contestant la normalité et l'identité civique, on n'est pas loin de lui contester l'identité tout court."

5. "les réfugiés estiment bien souvent que c'est en dévalorisant leur propre personne qu'ils ont le plus de chances d'amadouer leurs juges. L'une des fonctions essentielles de ces lettres consiste en effet à susciter la pitié des hommes au pouvoir, et comme chacun sait, l'on ne s'apitoie que sur les faibles."

6. "A l'époque où l'arbitraire domine, il n'est pas étonnant que les réfugiés mobilisent des arguments visant à apitoyer ceux qui les tiennent en leur pouvoir personnel. En revanche, on ne peut qu'être surpris de constater qu'en dépit de l'institutionnalisation totale du droit d'asile, après la Seconde Guerre mondiale, la dévalorisation de soi soit encore aussi fréquemment utilisée comme moyen d'obtenir satisfaction. En effet, en théorie, ce n'est plus la pitié que les demandeurs sont tenus d'invoquer, mais la justice."

7. "J'ai beaucoup réfléchi au parcours de mes ancêtres et surtout je me disais qu'un Français ne serait jamais traité de la sorte en Afrique. Et surtout je me disais que nous, les descendants des libérateurs de la France, nous ne méritons pas un tel traitement en France."

8. "l'étranger, l'immigré--avec ou sans papiers--l'exilé, le réfugié, le sans-patrie, le sans-Etat, la personne ou la population déplacée" (Derrida, *Adieu à Emmanuel Lévinas* 117-118). The 300 *sans-papiers* who occupied Saint-Bernard Church clearly constitute the tip of the iceberg. When reading Diop's autobiography, one realizes that the group was forced to draw the line somewhere, and to urge other undocumented Africans to create their own movement in a different location because the original group had to stop accepting new recruits. The perverse logic of media visibility makes the 300 Africans the legitimate representatives of all *sans-papiers* precisely because the discourse that ultimately survived the original "affair" could not have developed properly unless the crowds, whose large numbers would have turned the movement into a disorderly mass, were excluded.

10. The reader soon finds out that this title supposedly refers to the size of the narrator's backside: in a reversal of traditional Western concepts of beauty, the heroine laments her thinness, especially in the area of her behind. The title that reduces her iden-

tity to an apparently unflattering number of centimeters may also be a reference to the way in which nineteenth-century scientists treated the bodies of Africans, placing their remains in museums as examples of unusual biological curiosities.

      11. "Un jour, on part en Floride dans la Cadillac gris métal de Papa l'ambassadeur. . . . L'école française est privée; notre nid, chic, toujours."

      12. "*Votre* fille est un produit de *votre* imagination car elle est inapte à naître: vous n'entrez pas dans le cadre strict des lois."

      13. "Comme nos *chères têtes blondes* j'aime beaucoup les dessins animés: je suis restée très enfant. J'ai adoré *Pocahontas*, de Walt Disney, l'histoire de cette Indienne bronzée amoureuse de John Smith, ce chasseur de Peaux-Rouges pédophile. Comme il y avait beaucoup de chasseurs de Peaux-Rouges, un jour, Pocahontas, de son vrai nom Matoaka, fut kidnappée par un gentil colon et chargée sur un navire. Mais comme les chasseurs-colons sont gentils, ils la libérèrent en échange d'une rançon et d'un mariage arrangé avec un gentil planteur blanc, John Rolfe. Ils la baptisèrent Rebecca, détruisirent son village et l'emmenèrent en Angleterre, où avec une douzaine d'Indiens, elle exerça la profession de bête de foire. Quand elle est morte, elle avait vingt-deux ans. Un jour peut-être, Disney fera oeuvre d'historien du judaïsme avec un dessin animé du même genre que Pocahontas: Anne Frank, l'histoire d'une Juive de couleur blanche amoureuse d'un nazi de couleur moustachue, Hitler. Il y aura beaucoup de gentils chasseurs de Peaux-Juives et un jour, Anne sera razziée et déportée dans un camp de concentration où elle réfléchira beaucoup en lisant *Pol Pot et Milosevic à Hutuland*, une bande dessinée rwandaise."

      14. "Chez toi, Zara, l'hybridation est encore plus pernicieuse, car elle se dissimule lâchement sous l'apparente fusion des traits: tu as le cheveu ondulé alors que la Raison commanderait qu'il soit raide sur la première moitié et crépu sur le reste de sa longueur. Tu as la peau café crème alors que la Raison exigerait qu'elle soit noire sur les parties sexuelles et blanches sur les parties chastes."

WORKS CITED

Bessora, Sandrine. *53CM*. Paris: Le Serpent à Plumes, 1999.

Césaire, Aimé. *Cahier d'un retour au pays natal*. Paris: Présence Africaine, 1939.

Cissé, Madjiguène. *Parole de sans-papiers*. Paris: La Dispute, 1999.

Derrida, Jacques. *Adieu à Emmanuel Lévinas*. Paris: Galilée, 1997.

———. "Quand j'ai entendu l'expression 'délit d'hospitalité.' " *Plein droit* 34 (April 1997): 3-8.

———. *Adieu to Emmanuel Levinas*. Trans. Pascale-Anne Brault and Michael Naas. Stanford: Stanford University Press, 1999.

Diop, Ababacar. *Dans la peau d'un sans-papiers*. Paris: Seuil, 1997.

Hargreaves, Alec G. *Immigration, "Race" and Ethnicity in Contemporary France*. London: Routledge, 1995.

Laronde, Michel. *Autour du roman beur*. Paris: L'Harmattan, 1993.

Noiriel, Gérard. *Réfugiés et sans papiers: la République face au droit d'asile XIXe-XXe siècles*. Paris: Pluriel, 1991.

Plamondon, Luc, and Richard Cocciante. *Notre Dame de Paris*. Pomme Music, 1998.

Sané, Mamady. *Sorti de l'ombre: journal d'un sans-papiers*. Paris: Le Temps des Cerises, 1996.

Van Cauwelaert, Didier. *Un aller simple*. Paris: Albin Michel, 1994.

Wacquant, Loïc. *Les prisons de la misère*. Paris: Raisons d'agir, 1999.

VIETNAMESE FICTION
IN FRENCH

Linda Lê and the Prosthesis of Origin

Martine Delvaux

> To write in a language that is not one's own is to make love with a
> corpse. (Linda Lê, *Tu écriras sur le bonheur* 330)

Born in Dalat in 1963, writer Linda Lë left her homeland to escape
communism, arriving in France by boat with her mother and sisters at the age of
fourteen. This is where she now lives and writes "in French for the French"
(Yeager 258).[1] Since 1984, Lê has published a number of novels,[2] some of
which could be described as fictionalized autobiographical texts, and in which
she reflects on exile, mourning, and origins. In particular, she writes about loss,
portraying the complex interactions that link the exiled subject to the native
land she fled and the mother tongue she betrayed.

Lê gives an image of this link at the end of her essay *Tu écriras sur le
bonheur* (1999). She tells the story of a twenty-year-old Vietnamese peasant in
whose stomach was found a dead fetus. This fetus was that of his twin who, due
to a malformation, had developed inside rather than beside his brother's body.
Using this anecdote as a metaphor, she writes: "I carry my country like this
young peasant carried his twin's fetus. It is a monstrous link. A link in which
the native country, the twin, is protected and suffocated, recognized and denied.
And finally carried just as one carries a dead child" (330).[3] This "monstrous
link" with her homeland motivates Lê's relationship to another country--what
she calls her only *patrie*: literature. Writing, for Lê, is dictated by "the
obsession with a malformation" (*Lettre morte* 330)--that of exile--and is
addressed to a dead double, a silent judge--her absent father. Writing is the
means to explore her displacement as an exiled subject, her link to Vietnam as
an origin, both present and absent. Her homeland is lodged within her, a

spectral presence that causes pain and alienation, as does her Vietnamese father's ghost, which inhabits her like a double. In an interview with Catherine Argand, she observes that: "one does not write without some hatred of oneself, without the wish to question . . . the double that is within us, the one that we would have wanted to be, to become, and that we carry within us like a dead person. This is the feeling that survives the horror of having been born, the feeling of having lost, of having killed the twin brother" (31).

Lê's father, who died in 1995 in Vietnam, away from his family, was his daughter's silent witness, the twin that she carried inside her as the reader for whom she wrote: "As long as my father was alive, all my books were addressed to him. He was my ideal reader, my imaginary reader. When he died, I lost my reader, the sky became empty, the world became Godless" (Argand 30). This father's death, like the situation of exile itself, provoked a psychological crisis, an "earthquake" (Argand 31), the aftermath of which gave rise to a questioning of her origins. In the pages that follow, I propose to show how in her fiction, rather than effecting a return to her roots, Linda Lê deconstructs the idea of origins in general and undertakes a disarticulation of her own.

THE MONOLINGUALISM OF THE OTHER

In his autobiographical essay *Monolingualism of the Other or the Prosthesis of Origin*, Jacques Derrida suggests that we tend to invent our own origins, that we make use of prostheses that help us believe in a single origin, in the genesis of our self, in the inception of our subjectivity. The origin, however, can only ever be a prosthesis attached to the stump of an amputated limb, replacing a phantom-limb that, although absent, remains "palpable, painful, but hardly legible--[composed] of traces, marks, and scars" (61). There are no "true" origins, for Derrida, only spectral ones. The "I" is always formed "at the site of a situation that cannot be found, a site always referring elsewhere, to something other, to another language, to the other in general" (29).

Derrida's essay, at once a work of criticism and autobiography, offers a map with which to read the disarticulation of origins staged in Linda Lê's work. He founds his essay on the following contradictory propositions:

> We only ever speak one language. [*On ne parle jamais qu'une seule langue.*]
> We never only speak one language. [*On ne parle jamais une seule langue.*] (7)

A Jewish Franco-Maghrebian, Derrida never learned Arabic, Berber, or Hebrew as a child, although it was officially "allowed," as if an interdict was working through "more subtle, peaceful, silent, and liberal ways" (32). He describes the French he spoke as both a forbidding and forbidden language, a language he was allowed to speak and write but that he never truly owned: "French was supposed to be maternal, but one whose source, norms, rules, and law were situated elsewhere . . . that means, in the Metropole" (41). French, then, was a *substitute* for the mother tongue, a monolingualism imposed by the colonial other, thereby making France, the Metropole, a spectral origin.

This autobiographical tale gives rise to the following question: is there ever anything other than a substitute for a mother tongue? Are origins ever anything other than spectral? The "demeure" that we rely on, suggests Derrida, the home that we imagine as ours and that we perpetually mourn, whose absence makes us nostalgic, can never be anything other than a fiction, an "inalienable alienation" (25)? This impossible monolingualism, the fact that our own language never truly belongs to us, that we never really own it, underlies an essential alienation, a madness constitutive of language and (cultural) identity. The "I" we conceive of as ours, and for which we identify specific origins, has been formed "at the site of a *situation* that cannot be found, a site always referring elsewhere, to something other, to another language, to the other in general" (29). These questions and hypotheses lead Derrida to ask: "In what language does one write memoirs when there has been no authorized mother tongue?" (31).[4]

Linda Lê's linguistic identity is similar to Derrida's in that, like him, she seems to have had no mother tongue, to have never spoken only one language. In her case, the language of the Other is not only French, her language of exile and of choice, but Vietnamese itself. If French is the language of the colonizer, Vietnamese is the language of the colonized, and the hyphen that links them (as in the expression "Franco-Vietnamese" author) is the space of her infinite translation and migration--for she could never be "purely" French or "purely" Vietnamese. She has always evolved, according to the tale that she tells about herself, within a "hyphenated" space, a space which is the locus of all that is "transplanted and lost . . . belonging neither to the one nor the other: the incommunicable."[5]

In *Lettre morte*, the narrator refers to Vietnamese as "a language that I have almost forgotten already" (16), a language that could survive only through her father's letters, his voice and words. With the father's death, she says, "half of myself has fallen silent" (18). The Vietnamese language and Vietnam itself have become a "lettre morte" (a dead letter), a law which is in effect but is no longer enforced. Choosing French over Vietnamese, using the interdicted colonizer's language instead of the interdicted colonized's tongue, Lê invents herself within the space of exile and alienation. She writes in French, in a language "that has become her only language, her tool, her weapon. The weapon that she points at her family, against the Country," and by choosing this weapon, says the uncle in *Calomnies*, "she will always be alone. She is a foreigner [*métèque*] who writes in French" (12). Therein lies the alienation, the "incommunicable" to which Khatibi refers, that is, the madness of language.

In Lê's world, madness and language are intimately linked: "The French language is for her what madness has been for me," says the uncle of his niece, the female narrator of *Calomnies* (12). Commenting on her learning French while she lived in Vietnam, Lê says: "In Vietnam, I studied in French. As a result, I already very much felt like a stranger in my own country. . . . there is a rootlessness and a sort of loss of identity and a madness that comes with all of that. There is the rejection of the family [*le rejet familial*] which is a form of rootlessness and also madness as rootlessness, rootlessness also being a type of madness" (Chung 157). According to Derrida, the alienation due to a form of rootlessness (an alienation experienced by the colonized and the migrant in particular but that each one of us should recognize) which is characterized by the "absence of a stable model of identification for an *ego*"--a model of identification that would originate in one's mother tongue--can generate impulses "that are always on the brink of collapse" (60). He describes these impulses as three types of amnesia, which he also identifies as three types of madness: first, suffering from "an amnesia without recourse, under the guise of pathological destructuring"; second, forgetting who one was and assimilating "stereotypes that homogenize and conform to the model of the 'average' or dominant French person"; third, "committing oneself . . . to traces of writing, language, experience--which take anamnesis beyond the mere reconstruction of a given heritage, beyond an available past" (60).

In fact, one can find in Lê's narrators examples of these forms of alienation. The pathological destructuring staged in *Voix*, the temptation to conform to a stereotypical image of the migrant woman in *Calomnies*,[6] the realization that the past has been rejected in *Lettre morte,* and the ambivalent desire to both retrieve and escape it by way of the father figure all serve to portray the alienation that Lê herself names in relation to autobiographical narrative. As she asserts:

An autobiography is generally the story of one's own life, a quest for one's origins, a search for one's identity, which is the starting point of the novel, but the idea of the novel . . . is rather that of a deranged, crazy autobiography that tries to give some idea of an itinerary but that also attempts to cloud the issue [*brouiller les pistes*] and give as many false leads and improbable interpretations as possible. . . . In fact, it is an autobiography with the idea that, anyway, truth is a lie. (Chung 155)

As these words indicate, Lê purposefully blurs the boundary between autobiography and fiction, demonstrating that "truth is a lie," that there is no single and originary autobiographical story, no single and originary identity, that in effect the "I" is always born of migration or of a form of exile. The various forms of alienation she stages all serve to show that the "I" is foreign to itself, that it is a site and an effect of *différance*, born of an impossible homogeneity and a fundamental alienation.[7] To borrow Derrida's formulation, "absolute replaceability" comes to replace emplacement itself, that is "the being-with-oneself of the self" (89). One can never speak only one language, nor can one be only oneself; one cannot even rely on the past, or the belief in an origin, in order to construct oneself. Indeed, for Lê, the past is not only irretrievable, but its very retrieval is undesirable. Rather than striving to recreate it, she tries to stage the incommunicable, the traces, marks, and scars that have come to represent it as a phantom-origin. She performs what Derrida deems necessary for those who, like him, have no mother tongue to speak of, no language with which to identify and with which to write their memoirs: "One would have to construct oneself," he suggests, "one would have to be able to invent oneself without a model and without any guarantee of having an addressee" (55).

As Jack Yeager points out, Lê has always refused to be pigeonholed, resisting "writing what one had come to expect from Vietnamese writers in French" (257), that is the traditional *bildungsroman*--the coming of age of a Vietnamese child educated in the French system and her subsequent immigration to the Metropole, for instance--and ethnological descriptions of her native culture. Today, Lê still suppresses almost all references to Vietnam, except on one occasion, in her latest work *Lettre morte*, where she refers to the country via its language. Citing the telegram that announces the death of the narrator's father, she writes: "the expression, in Vietnamese, stated loss rather than death. My father had lost his way, had gotten lost, had been unable to find his way back" (16). And like this father, in the image of this death that she describes as "losing one's way," Lê's narrators are essentially displaced. They never find their way back, symbolically dying in order to be reborn other in the other's language.

MOURNING

"Enter everywhere like a dog on a putting green" says her friend Ricin to the narrator in *Calomnies*. "Stay alone. Stay foreign [*métèque*]. Cultivate margins. Plough borders. Make sure that the undesirable, the unsavory, the irreducible remains within you" (33). At the end of *Monolingualism of the Other*, Derrida writes that "rather than constituting an exposition of myself," the essay "is an account of what has placed an obstacle in the way of this self-exposition for me" (70). This obstacle, what she names the "irreducible" in *Lettre morte,* is also what Lê evokes in her work: an endless process of mourning that reveals the traces, marks, and scars of an impossible origin.

This is what we find in *Voix*, a short novel published in 1998 that Lê describes as a daughter's quest for a mythical father (Argand 32). In this text, Lê stages what could be described as a psychotic episode--a "crise," as it is referred to in the novel's subtitle--brought on by the death of the narrator's father. The narrator is recognizable as a portrait of Lê herself, who has spoken of the "three months of stupor" that followed the writing of *Les trois Parques*. After her Vietnamese father's death in 1995, Lê describes having been "pregnant" with an intense feeling of pain that expressed itself in hallucinations, suicidal thoughts, and paranoid behavior (Argand 30). This period lasted two years and ended when she finished writing *Les trois Parques*: "I wrote *Les trois Parques* in a complete and voluntary state of solitude. And this is why there is in this book a real verbal torrent, because I was cloistered within myself. . . . I did not speak for weeks" (Argand 30). It was then, through a period of hospitalization in a psychiatric ward and cohabitation with "mad" people, that Lê recovered her speech: "Strangely enough, speech, a voice, came back to me through what I heard of the others' mad speech. Madness allowed me to retrieve reason" (Argand 31).

At the beginning of *Voix*, the narrator describes being in a "crisis center . . . or a theatre with actors who play their parts and recruit me by letting me choose my own lines" (7). The "lines" that she chooses, however, the lines that will become her own, are the words of others. They are the voices of the mad who surround her inside the hospital walls, but they are also the voices of those who haunt her: the voices of her present (France) and of her past (Vietnam). These voices represent the Other's voice, what Lê calls the "Organization." They constitute an anonymous group of bodies who speak a secret language that, paradoxically, the narrator understands, and in which she can only hear an injunction to sacrifice herself--"They want me to sacrifice myself, they try to suffocate my voice, muzzle my screams" (59)--that is, from both a French and a Vietnamese perspective, to let go of who she was and of who she is, of who she is now, which is also who she was before. One could interpret the Organization as forces that enjoin the narrator to identify herself as a monolithic subject, that encourage her to sacrifice her multiplicity, the fact that she can never be only herself.

Drowned heads floating in the Seine, an endless series of decapitated bodies, strange faces in the streets of Paris: these images mirror the narrator's diffraction, multiplicity, and fragmentation, as well as her displacement. The crisis that she will succeed in surviving represents a confinement within the hyphenation mentioned earlier, the impossibility of belonging either to the country of exile or to the homeland, or of leaving either one of them. The chorus of voices that haunt the narrator and that constitute the symptom of her madness also signifies the complexity of her identity: the perpetual state of mourning which lies at the core of her existence, the perpetual haunting that determines her: "I am a stranger to the world, to the real, to life," says Lê, "[a stranger] to the country in which I live, to my own country" (Argand 31). In *Voix,* the narrator's psychic disintegration symbolizes the burning of her roots and the mourning of a single, originary identity. Here (as in Lê's own life), the father's death has the effect of crystallizing feelings of loss and displacement, feelings of guilt due not only to exile but to the refusal to go back home. Responding to the voices, the narrator burns her father's letters, turning her roots into ashes, killing him a second time: "I am in the land of my childhood. I am looking for the house with the blue shutters. All that is left is a pile of ashes. Some letters shine at the bottom, mutilated vowels, torn consonants. I plunge my hand in, stir the ashes from which a voice arises, You killed him" (47). But in killing her father, in burning his letters, the narrator must also sacrifice her own writing: "With my free hand, I push away the ink pot, the manuscript whose pages fly across the room. I throw the typewriter on the floor. . . . In front of my eyes, I see gigantic letters dancing, black blood-stained letters that almost reach the ceiling and lean over me, TO DEATH!" (25). The symbolic killing of the father, his second death, brings on a second stage of mourning that corresponds to the introjection of the father's ghost and brings about a form of healing.

For if *Voix* presents itself as a collection of voices that exert pressure on the narrator, enjoining her to sacrifice herself by means of a forced identification (either in the present--you must become French--or in relation to the past--you must remain Vietnamese),[8] it is also a sort of exorcism that allows her to identify herself and to survive thanks to the emergence of her own voice and speech. Through the magma of the voices surrounding her, the narrator succeeds in shaping herself, in saving herself and the memory of her deceased father: "My father gets up, disappears through the trees. I take his place and I wait. I look at the inscription on the stone. I am sitting on his grave" (43). In fact, by incorporating her father's ghost, by "saving" him (68), the narrator succeeds in saving herself and moving towards liberation. She drifts away, inscribing herself within displacement rather than striving to find a fixed definition of herself.

Hence, at the end of *Voix*, the narrator sets out on a new journey, whose destination remains a mystery. "I took the train to the mountain" (68), she writes, a mountain that could be located either in France or in Vietnam, and where she makes a descent into the snow (white being the color of mourning in Asian cultures) which counters the burning of her father's letters: "The Organization has lost my trace. My coat is covered with snow. My naked hands, and my feet, in their boots, are numb. But I go forward, my heart happy. I almost reach my goal, the paradise of sadness where the white grains fall" (68).

Finding herself alone in this paradise of sadness, the narrator lies down in the snow as if it were a coffin, as if it were her father's tomb. This tomb, however, is a womb, and signifies rebirth rather than death, movement rather than confinement, the freedom of identity rather than the imprisonment of definitions. And so the novel ends on the following words: "I hopelessly search in the snow for the traces that the chopped-off heads would have left. I am alone. I wrap myself in my coat. I lie down in the snow. I listen to the wind blow. I watch the low-lying clouds. A feeling of deep peace comes over me" (69).

THE PROSTHESIS OF ORIGIN

In *Voix*, the father's ghost is put to rest, projected and then introjected by his exiled daughter, accepted as the lost origin, the prosthesis of origin. Lê has described her "crise" as an earthquake (Argand 31), an image that eloquently names the way in which she questions not only her own origins but the idea of origins itself. *"You can't go home again,"* she writes in *Calomnies* (31), quoting the line of a song in English in the text and echoing it in a second phrase, also in English: *"Nobody is your daddy"* (158). These two sentences represent the two poles of Lê's search: her travel within mourning and migration, and how, in *Calomnies*, this journey becomes anchored in a questioning of her paternal origins.

Calomnies, published in 1993, is structured around two voices: that of the migrant woman, the *métèque*, and that of her uncle, the "Chinetoqué" (17). She, the writer, and he, the madman, are two sides of the same coin, writing being for her what madness is for him: the way to invent oneself inside as well as outside of alienation. She writes, writing being a way to estrange herself, to split herself off from her family, her country, and her native tongue. Books are her stimulants; they propel her. In his case, books are sedatives, an ersatz of death, the most radical form of alienation. Writing saves her from her family's genealogy of madness, a tradition that he embodies, a state that he has fostered. "We are," he says, "she and I, the aborted children, the runts [*les avortons*] of a family of crazies" (19). Her writing and his madness are ways to escape, strategies used to flee familial, national, cultural, and linguistic classifications: "She does not know her native tongue, anymore. I have not spoken this language for fifteen years. . . . We are from nowhere, she and I. The Country has nothing to give her since the men in black [the Vietnamese communists] have chased away the Foreigner--they are the new fathers of the Country. Those fathers have no need for she who has an international forename" (173). Linda Lê's international forename, like the question of language and that of mourning, is central to her own process of deconstruction, to how she rids herself of the prosthesis of origin. In *Calomnies*, alienation is brought to another level: to the impossibility of monolingualism and to the mourning of a home is added the deconstruction of paternity.

In *Calomnies*, the uncle points out that the narrator's mother is trying to subjugate her daughter, to exert control over her and drive her mad by pushing her to question her father's identity. "In the course of a sentence," the uncle says, "her mother has pulverized her father's corpse, killed the obsession" (34) of the Vietnamese father, the father who has brought her up and who was "the great love affair of her life" (13). But thanks to her mother, "she has had the revelation of her bastardom"; "she can give herself another father" (54). Who, then, is this child's father? Is she legitimate or illegitimate? A full blood or a half blood [*sang-mêlé*] (127)? Is her father the Vietnamese peasant or the mysterious, exciting, high-ranking military man (who we are tempted to identify as an American officer) with whom her mother had a love affair during the war and who she describes as the love of her life? Is her father the native or the foreigner? The faithful husband or the exotic lover and the man of good taste ("l'homme de goût") (158), the loser or the conqueror, poor or rich? Was she conceived out of duty or out of love? Which father, which origin should she identify with? The ghost of the one she has left, or the specter of the one who disappeared? What name should she bear: the Vietnamese surname given to her by her mother's husband ten days after her birth, ten days during which she was not registered and did not exist, or the international forename given to her by the "gentleman" and which differs from his own by only two letters (161)? Reality or fiction? "Her mother gave her the two portraits haphazardly," says the uncle: "she only has to choose" (46).

The narrator of *Calomnies* experiences multiple forms of alienation, endlessly dividing herself up, "hungry for revelations, impatient to disrupt [*bouleverser*] her genealogy, rewrite her history" (65). She transforms herself into the prodigal child, the mythical bastard who appeared out of nowhere, born outside affiliation, free of the bounds of legitimacy. Hence, as the uncle comments, to the pride of being a foreigner writing in a language that is not hers, his niece wants to add the possibility of her bastardom in order to become like him, "the model--the free man, the passionate man, nobody's son, born of his own insanity" (87): "She says she wants to give herself to writing like I gave myself to madness" (176). Indeed, the uncle, who chooses French over Vietnamese, who carries with him an incestuous past and is confined to an asylum, is the antidote to the mother's poison: family romance and the myth of origins. He thus comes to represent deconstructed, impure, chosen origins. He found his own prosthesis in madness; here, he found the way to define himself outside of definitions. And so his niece must choose between her uncle and her mother, between her mother's viscous, suffocating life and her uncle's mad freedom (128-129). She must choose between them as between her two fathers, two styles of fathers who are compared to two types of books:

She will have to choose between these two types of fathers. Between the book written by a fashionable novel-writer, a book that deploys his culture and seduction, a book written with ease, a book which will enchant you, a book which is filled with frivolous phrases and which ends with a pirouette--she will have to choose between that charming book and the other one, an austere book that contains only a bit of dried blood. (176)

Lê's narrator must choose between two versions of a father, two pasts and two futures. She must choose between two versions of a book, two styles of writing, two identities: one predictable, recognizable, and therefore enjoyable; the other surprising, disturbing, and therefore dangerously liberating. While her uncle retreated into insanity, she transforms herself through writing--uncle and niece both uprooting themselves, escaping the determinism of origin: "We are lost souls, she and I," he says, "our roots are above water [*à fleur d'eau*]. . . . We drift, in the hope that the water will take us back towards the origin, but we flounder around in an oxbow, we always stir up the same obsessions, we always carry the same corpses" (173).

These corpses, like the heads floating on the surface of the Seine in *Voix*, are decapitated cadavers that reflect *Calomnies*'s female narrator lost "in this sea which she has unleashed" (176-177) by wreaking havoc in her genealogy, by living an alienation chosen over the certainty of a single origin and identity. The voices she hears, the symptom of her madness, are the voices of her writing, the other voices, the other languages that inhabit her, the alienation and recreation that save her from an illusory monolingualism and an affirmed unique birth. The narrator's last words in *Calomnies* are symbolic of the role given to writing. "I am leaving" she says, leaving behind a package filled with her uncle's letters, the words she had desired until then and that could have dissipated the mystery around her birth. Rather than reading these letters and finding answers to her questions, the narrator hands them to Ricin and walks towards the unknown, undertaking, as she does in *Voix*, an endless voyage. "The exile's secret wish," writes Lê in *Tu écriras sur le bonheur*, "is to create, in the adopted language, another language, one deprived of any heritage and of all authority" (335). Leaving behind the "poison" of family romance, Lê's narrators in *Calomnies*, *Voix,* and *Lettre morte* leave in order to create their own origins: "I have to go," says the narrator of *Lettre morte*, "The day is rising, Sirius. Why don't you open that window? Let the freshness of dawn come in" (105).

Lê's narrators always leave, but they never reach the end of their journey, for writing, like madness, is an eternal migration entailing countless departures without arrivals, travels that never really lead to a destination or bring them back to their point of origin. And mourning, like migration, is also a process that never ends. "The dead never let go of us," says the narrator at the beginning of *Lettre morte* about the ghost she carries inside her like a dead fetus, her father's ghost with which she is pregnant: "he comes into me as into a deserted house" (12). She will forever wait for him to come back and wait for him to leave, eternally haunted by the past and divided against the present. Lê's novels trace an endless uprooting, the perpetual loss and recreation of origins. Hence, rather than reproducing the image of a family tree, Lê represents the past as a network of nerves running through an amputated body, projecting in the mind the image of the missing limb, creating a phantom-limb, a ghosted body which is at once present and absent.

"The writer is the foreign land" (76), writes Marguerite Duras in *La vie matérielle*. Writing, because it is always done in the Other's language, because there is no language that we can simply, naively call our own, is a form of estrangement, of alienation. And this is what Linda Lê's work shows us. From the Vietnamese house with the blue shutters to the Seine, from her father's body to his ghost, from his voice and words to her own ink and letters, "she became a writer" (*Calomnies* 11): one who eternally recreates her story and her self, who is hyphenated, located between here and there, necessarily ghosted. Lê's decision to write in French, like her questioning of paternity, indicates her refusal to believe in monolingualism and the purity of origins, her resistance to monolithic identities. Lê's novels present the migrant author as someone in constant mourning and infinite motion, and migrant literature as a literature of displacement--a "littérature déplacée" (*Tu écriras* 329)--neither from here nor there, breaking away from the authority of the country that was left as well as from the authority of the language and the literary tradition that have been chosen. According to Lê, displaced literature legitimates itself through illegitimacy: "For the exiled, the coming to literature will have happened under the sign of loss rather than heritage. Of dispossession rather than ownership. He comes from nowhere. He has abandoned everything" (332). From this perspective, the migrant author's task, according to Lê, is to invent a form of speech that opens people's eyes, that gives them something to see and grants them clear vision,[9] the ultimate goal being to write against expectations, stereotyping, and rigid classifications in order to create a displaced form of speech "located at the heart of pain without trying to soothe this pain with the panacea of words" (336). Linda Lê writes within the space of hyphenation, within migration and illegitimacy. Her novels suggest that even though we seem to speak only one language, we never really speak only one language; that we never have only one father nor do we have only one autobiography. In fact, we never write only one text.

NOTES

1. Jack Yeager's article "Culture, Citizenship, Nation. The Narrative Texts of Linda Lê" explores the question of language and origin in fiction published by Lê before 1996 and most importantly her desire to escape rigid categorizations, that is, being identified as a Vietnamese francophone writer (257).

2. *Les évangiles du crime, Calomnies, Les dits d'un idiot, Les trois Parques, Voix, Lettre morte.* She has also published a literary essay entitled *Tu écriras sur le bonheur.* Lê describes *Les trois Parques, Voix,* and *Lettre morte* as a trilogy born of her experience of her father's death. In writing these novels, she says, her goal was to present mourning as a universal experience and the father's death as a symbolic one, "so that mourning is not a singular mourning anymore" (Argand 28). In this respect, she describes *Les trois Parques* as belonging to the register of myth, *Voix* to that of dream, and *Lettre morte* to that of fantasy.

3. All translations of Lê's works and interviews are my own.

4. In *L'amour, la fantasia*, Assia Djebar writes that "autobiography practiced in the enemy's language has the texture of fiction [*se tisse comme une fiction*]" (cited in Lionnet 332).

5. The quotation is from Abdelkebir Khatibi and is cited by Derrida (8).

6. As Ricin says to the narrator in *Calomnies*: "The counselor wants you to be taken for his protégée--the writer who comes from the old colonies, the starved little bird, the fragile young woman that he sponsors" (37). In her interview with Lê, Catherine Argand states that she "resists the dominant discourse that wants her to be an appealing novelist, or a token Vietnamese writer" (28).

7. This, of course, has been explored at length by Julia Kristeva in *Etrangers à nous-mêmes*. In *Monolingualism of the Other*, Derrida suggests that "it could be demonstrated that absolute uniqueness renders one as crazy as absolute replaceability" (89).

8. Even in relation to Vietnam, the situation presented in *Voix* is complicated. We know that Lê's mother left Vietnam with her daughters after the rise of communism. The communists are represented in the novel as the "men in black," and they are also present as members of the phantasmatic "Organization." Hence, *Voix*'s narrator is torn not only between her homeland and her country of exile but in relation to Vietnam itself. In fact, Lê says of her female narrator in *Calomnies* that the new leaders of the Country want nothing to do with a girl whose origins are possibly international.

9. Lê uses the expression "dessiller les yeux"--to remove the eyelashes from the eyes (to open one's eyes), an expression borrowed from writer Ingeborg Bachmann.

WORKS CITED

Argand, Catherine. "Linda Lê." *Lire* 274 (April 1999): 28-33.
Chung, Ook. "Linda Lê, 'tueuse en dentelles.' " *Liberté* 212 (April 1994): 155-161.
Derrida, Jacques. *Monolingualism of the Other or the Prosthesis of Origin.* Trans. Patrick Mensah. Stanford: Stanford University Press, 1998.
Duras, Marguerite. *La vie matérielle.* Paris: P.O.L., 1987.
Kristeva, Julia. *Etrangers à nous-mêmes.* Paris: Fayard, 1988.
Lê, Linda. *Les évangiles du crime.* Paris: Julliard, 1992.
---. *Calomnies.* Paris: Christian Bourgois, 1993.
---. *Les dits d'un idiot.* Paris: Christian Bourgois, 1995.
---. *Les trois Parques.* Paris: Christian Bourgois, 1997.
---. *Voix.* Paris: Pocket, 1998.
---. *Lettre morte.* Paris: Christian Bourgois, 1999.
---. *Tu écriras sur le bonheur.* Paris: Presses Universitaires de France, 1999.
Lionnet, Françoise. "*Logiques Métisses.* Cultural Appropriation and Postcolonial Representations." *Postcolonial Subjects: Francophone Women Writers.* Ed. Mary Jean Green et al. Minneapolis: University of Minnesota Press, 1996, 321-343.
Yeager, Jack. "Culture, Citizenship, Nation. The Narrative Texts of Linda Lê." *Post-Colonial Cultures in France.* Ed. Alec G. Hargreaves and Mark McKinney. London: Routledge, 1997, 255-267.

Tainted Blood: On Being Impure in Kim Lefèvre's *Métisse blanche* and *Retour à la saison des pluies*

Ching Selao

Kim Lefèvre, a writer and translator, was born in Hanoi of a Vietnamese mother and an unknown French father. While the reunification of Vietnam in 1975 led to the massive emigration of Vietnamese refugees to France, Lefèvre had chosen to leave her country and abandon her family in 1960, when she was in her early twenties. For this author, who claims that her bicultural heritage had made life in her motherland unbearable, immigration to France was the only way to free herself from the burden of her illegitimate origins. Lefèvre's life as a *métis* woman in a Vietnam torn by political instability and conflicts between the Vietminh and French settlers has left her with wounds that have never completely healed, and with a need to purge herself of her Vietnamese identity in order to pursue a life in France. Both of her two autobiographical novels deal with her hybrid roots and her experience of being Eurasian. Whereas *Métisse blanche* (1989) focuses primarily on Lefèvre's life in Vietnam and on the circumstances that explain her decision to leave for France, *Retour à la saison des pluies* (1990) presents her as an immigrant living in Paris and portrays the events that lead to her being reunited with her family during a trip to Vietnam after a 30-year absence.

In recent years, as issues of cultural diversity, multi-culturalism, and the right to difference have moved to the forefront of debates about immigration and identity, the notion of *métissage* has acquired increasing currency in both cultural and literary theory. While in the nineteenth century the presence of the *métis* was associated with the decline and degeneration of the white race, the same figure now heralds a new era in which *métissage* is coded in a positive sense. Indeed, the "scientific" basis of theories condemning interracial mixing has been largely discredited. Within the field of post-colonial studies, critics such as Françoise Lionnet now define *métissage* as a space of indecidability and indeterminacy that undermines simple dichotomies and that serves as a productive form of opposition against hegemonic practices (326). Like Lionnet, Homi Bhabha highlights the fact that the notion of hybridity allows for the creation of new identities and political positions by subverting traditional binary structures: "I believe that hybridity is the 'third space' that enables other positions to emerge" (in Rutherford, 211). In this sense, the concept of *métissage* makes it possible to articulate forms of resistance that challenge traditional discursive powers.

This positive reappropriation of the notion of *métissage* in contemporary discourse often leads us to lose sight of the theme of impurity that was originally associated with the *métis*. In the nineteenth century, the *métis* symbolized degeneration and was perceived as having tainted what were then seen as "pure races." Indeed, as anthropologist Jean-Loup Amselle reminds us, it is difficult to escape the myth of pure origins when discussing hybridity: "in order to consider the question of *métissage* or of syncretism, which is one of its many incarnations, it is necessary to postulate an initial purity"[1] (iv). Although this initial purity now supposedly belongs to the mythic realm of the distant past, it still resurfaces in everyday speech: "every time a commentator uses the epithet 'full-blooded,' for example, he or she repeats the distinction between those of pure and mixed race" (Young 27).

A preoccupation with the concepts of racial purity and impurity lies at the heart of Kim Lefèvre's texts. The fear of "mixed blood," which is a central theme of *Métisse blanche*, is closely related to the rejection of Eurasians by the Vietnamese. Indeed, this text portrays a society that appears to subscribe to the so-called scientific line of thought that condemns hybridity--the narrator's "mixed blood" results in her exclusion and in a severe identity crisis which eventually causes her to leave her family and her homeland. It is in this novel that Lefèvre first reveals her desire to purify her "tainted blood." Here, in a Vietnam undergoing its own search for identity after eight decades of colonization, it is her French blood that the narrator wishes to flush from her veins: "As a little girl, I dreamt of providential accidents that would empty me of this cursed blood, leaving me a pure Vietnamese and reconciled with those around me and with myself" (18). From the beginning of the text, then, it is clear that her mixed blood symbolizes her impurity and is the cause of her rejection. For the Vietnamese, this foreign blood represents colonial contamination and humiliation, and it is experienced by the narrator as a form of invasion, for she herself has never lived the easy life of the colonists and knows nothing about the behavior of the French, the race with which she is continually identified.

The narrator of *Métisse blanche* embodies the "péché contre le sang" (sin against blood) Pierre-André Taguieff presents as a defining element of the *métis* ("Doctrines" 54). In the eyes of the Vietnamese, her illegitimacy and the fact that her father was French implicate her in a negative way in the "relation between colonizer and colonized--master and slave" (54). In an anti-colonialist atmosphere where the rise of nationalism and the return to traditional values are becoming increasingly widespread, the Eurasian child is made to pay for her mother's betrayal of her own country. At school, for instance, the teacher punishes the narrator with a relentlessness which reflects her political beliefs: "She takes every opportunity to punish me with a near-patriotic ardor, as if in hounding me she were saving the entire country from colonial venom" (36). For the teacher, this venom, which has poisoned the lives of the Vietnamese for many years, has now invaded the body of the young *métisse* and must be eliminated. By severely punishing her pupil, the teacher symbolically purifies her "blood," as if she were also casting out the colonizer.[2]

In the politically volatile context of a Vietnam trying to rid itself of the colonial yoke, it is clear, as Taguieff observes, that "*jus sanguinis* unconditionally and exclusively determines national belonging" ("Doctrines" 83-84). Although the narrator has no desire to be a hybrid, and feels she is Vietnamese, she is never considered such because enemy blood flows in her veins. She is not rejected only by the Vietnamese, however. The French, or those who consider themselves French, clearly see her as a native. In their eyes, as her Aunt Odile points out, she "will never be anything but an Annamite!" (30).[3] One of the most significant examples of the condescending behavior the French display towards her concerns her stay at the *Institut Océanographique de Nha Trang*, where her mother works as a cook. As Emily Roberts observes: "The French employer initially plays language games with the narrator, but stops abruptly when the mother asks him, in a mixture of pidgin French and Vietnamese, to help provide her eldest daughter with a proper education. After this the employer resurrects the boundaries of class and race. . . [the narrator] should have no pretensions to equality with whites" (55). If the narrator seems more intent on denouncing the fear of mixing exhibited by the Vietnamese, it is primarily because she finds herself in a Vietnamese milieu more often than in a French one. The colonial situation produced the *métis*, whom both the French and the Vietnamese subsequently marginalized and refused to consider one of their own, each community thus rejecting the impurity "which disrupts the order of each mother group" (Le 90).

Nevertheless, the *métisse* narrator is perceived by some--her mother, for instance--as belonging to a "superior" race. When the mother sees her daughter coming home, weighed down by their share of the pig slaughtered for Têt (the Vietnamese New Year), the mother bursts into tears, saying: "My poor child!. . . A girl of your race is no peasant!" (86).[4] For this reason, her mother persists in trying to find a way to give the protagonist an education worthy of her French blood: "they [the mother and the aunt] both agreed that I could not be left ignorant like those Vietnamese children. It would dishonor the French blood that flowed in me" (150). From her mother's perspective, the superiority of the French can be genetically acquired; thus, it is the daughter's *blood* that elevates her to this higher level rather than leading to degeneration, as earlier arguments against *métissage* suggest.

Whether inspiring apparent contempt or secret admiration, the narrator's *métissage* causes her to be excluded and leaves her feeling alienated from a very young age: "I have no memory of the first years of my life other than the feeling, which began early on, of being displaced and foreign everywhere" (18).[5] Even as a child, then, the protagonist's sense of displacement reflects Taguieff's description of the impure as "first and foremost that which is not in its place"

(*La force* 343). Because the narrator always feels foreign, she dreams of a "nouveau pays, peuplé de métisses" (new country populated with *métisses*) (37), in which she would be like everybody else. When this imagined site becomes reality, it disappointingly turns out to be an orphanage, and even there, when surrounded only by *métisse* children, she is unable to free herself from her feeling of alienation: "Now, I found myself amongst my own--hybrids--and continued to feel like a foreigner" (49-50).[6]

The protagonist moves symbolically towards the French side of her identity after this transitory period in the hybrid space of the orphanage, when she goes to a new exclusive French school in Dalat, the *Couvent des Oiseaux*. Here, she has the impression that she is changing countries: "I felt disoriented, as if I had left Vietnam for another country (268)."[7] It is in this new territory, which has "un parfum de France" (the smell of France) (267), that she learns to appreciate the other side of her cultural heritage. The convent is presented as an ideal place where she can learn about Paris and dream of going there. Indeed, her Vietnamese classmates appear to consider France itself as their native land, as if colonization had never existed. Furthermore, in order to maintain the friendship of her peers, she is encouraged to minimize her Vietnamese identity: "We continued to be friends as long as I shared their tastes, while mine were definitively put aside" (278).[8] For this reason, Jack Yeager observes that "the narrator feels as disoriented in this isolated location as she did anywhere else, *étrangère*" ("Blurring the Lines" 216).

The *Couvent des Oiseaux* is also the place which encourages the narrator to further detach herself from her mother culture: "I was in the process of losing my roots" (283).[9] This process of detachment inevitably has consequences for her relationship with her mother. When she returns to the family home during the vacation and asks for a room of her own, for example, she displays a growing resentment of her mother who, in her eyes, has chosen to live like a "native": "I was full of rancor, I thought that she was a peasant, a *Nhaquê*, and that she always would be" (287).[10] Such negative thoughts about her mother only reinforce her alienation: "I was ashamed of myself. How could I disown my family? I was not really at ease in the boarding school either. I didn't understand anything anymore, but that's the way it was: when I was in Dalat, it was my family and their lifestyle that mattered to me, and as soon as I was among them, their life no longer interested me. I then had only one wish, to return to the convent" (287). These scenes reveal that the narrator--who at times dreams of being Vietnamese and at other times of being French--experiences her body and her identity as inherently unstable owing to her mixed heritage. Yeager emphasizes the importance of this link between *métissage* and instability: "The narrator is never settled in one place but always on the move, unstable, ephemeral, impossible to pin down and define. Whatever the stated reasons for this instability, everything leads back to the presence of the body that incarnates the mixing of French and Vietnamese blood" (*Retour* 47).

This mixing of blood not only causes her to feel unstable, but also arouses feelings of monstrosity, a recurrent theme in the text: "Je me sentais monstrueuse" (I felt monstrous) (93). Indeed, monstrosity is one of the main stereotypes associated with mixed blood and, in addition to being used to characterize the *métis's* physical and psychological state, is also related to the notion of degeneration. Since she has so often been reminded that she is genetically faulty, the narrator has internalized this negative view of herself, referring to her *métissage* as a "porteur d'immoralité, atavisme auquel je croyais moi-même" (carrier of immorality; an atavism in which I myself believed) (320). She finally realizes that she cannot change the tendency of the Vietnamese to view her identity in essentialist terms and that she will always be excluded: "I had spent my life wanting to prove my innocence by conforming to all of the rules of my society. But it was my very essence which was unacceptable" (343).[11] It is this realization that she will never be accepted in Vietnam, that she will always be seen there as the embodiment of "l'humiliante colonisation et l'arrogance du Blanc" (humiliating colonization and the arrogance of whites) (342) that motivates the narrator's decision to move further towards the French side of her identity by going to France.

Lefèvre's move towards a French identity is underscored in her experience teaching French at a high school in Saigon just before she leaves for France. Here, her pupils, who are used to hearing French spoken with a Vietnamese accent, perceive her as "une étrangère, une véritable Française" (a foreigner, a true French woman) (334). Her feelings about leaving Vietnam are, however, ambivalent. During the period when she is waiting for her departure, she thinks of France with "un mélange de panique et de répulsion" (a mixture of panic and repulsion) (340), admitting that the dream of emigrating had been enough to sustain her; the actual possibility of leaving comes as a shock. Most importantly, her ambivalence derives from her association of France with the father who abandoned her, and she contemplates turning down the scholarship she has been awarded: "France was for me no more than a name, a series of abstract images, a country associated with the father I hated" (339).[12] Her mother, on the other hand, perspicaciously sees her daughter's departure as permanent, despite the fact that the scholarship is renewable for a maximum of only three years. She senses in particular that by emigrating to France, her daughter will be reconciled with the French part of her identity and will finally find her place: "There, you will find your own people, those of your race" (341).[13]

Since the narrator leaves for France as part of "une collaboration culturelle franco-vietnamienne" (a Franco-Vietnamese cultural collaboration) (342), her integration into French society is facilitated by her prestigious doctoral fellowship to study French literature at the Sorbonne. This award places her in the privileged category of intellectual immigrants who arrived in France before the wave of massive immigration which did not begin until 1975. At this time (1960), the number of Vietnamese in France was still relatively small. Lefèvre's experience of immigration was therefore largely positive, and her autobiography says little about her adaptation to French society and daily life in Paris, summarizing her integration very briefly with the words "what Vietnam refused me, France granted me: she received and accepted me" (340).[14] Above all, she did not experience discrimination because of her *métissage*: France welcomed her not as a *métisse*, but as Vietnamese, "comme on reçoit un objet rare" (as one would receive a rare object) (77), thus enabling her to feel in her place for the first time. She compares France very favorably with Vietnam in this regard, realizing, however, that the lack of prejudice shown towards her is not necessarily typical of attitudes towards immigrants in France: "Indeed, I'm not unaware of racist attitudes directed towards the Maghrebi community, and, in the future, perhaps, towards the increasingly large Asian community" (340).[15]

Unlike many immigrants whose new life in France is experienced as exile from a cherished homeland, Lefèvre fled a country which had always rejected her, and immigration allows her to bury the past. Upon arriving in France, therefore, she seeks to erase her Vietnamese heritage, carefully avoiding any places frequented by Asians and refusing to use her mother tongue: "I haven't spoken my language or opened a Vietnamese book for thirty years. I think in French, I dream in French and when I speak Vietnamese, I often use expressions translated from French" (*Retour* 57).[16] Although she had earlier tried to prove she belonged in Vietnam by speaking a very correct form of Vietnamese, she now relinquishes her mother tongue and sounds like a French person trying to speak a foreign language. As a friend reminds her, "Now you search for words as if you were a foreigner" (116).[17] Immigration thus allows Lefèvre to consciously avoid all reminders of her *métis* identity and to view herself as wholly French: "During the long years spent in France, I secreted a sap of forgetfulness. With time, this sap has hardened into a second, more resistant skin" (120).[18] This transformation, which is described in terms of molting and taking on another skin, presents her new life in France as liberating and relatively easy.

Lefèvre's experience of immigration contrasts with that of a series of friends and acquaintances she establishes contact with after the publication of *Métisse blanche*, and who emigrated to France after 1975. These encounters provide a picture of a very different kind of immigration, which serves to highlight Lefèvre's privileged position. Whereas Lefèvre's immigration is presented as largely problem-free, her friends' accounts emphasize hardship, the pain of exile, and the loss of financial and social status. Nam, for example, who used to be a lawyer, now works in a cafeteria, while her husband, once a doctor, is a night watchman in a factory in Lyons. Likewise, another old friend is subjected to eight years of exploitation and racism as a nurse at the Val-de-Grâce military hospital before deciding to leave France. Unlike Lefèvre, many of these immigrants were boat people who did not leave Vietnam of their own volition, and they immediately sought to alleviate their homesickness by recreating a Vietnamese community in Paris. Learning about their experiences forces Lefèvre to envisage a very different type of immigration, and the graphic images of suffering she conjures up in her imagination lead to feelings of anger she finds hard to repress.

Lefèvre's encounter with friends from the past also awakens in her a new interest in Vietnam and arouses feelings of guilt about her own positive experiences. The writing of *Métisse blanche* had already constituted a form of return to the past, and Lefèvre now begins to actively seek out the Vietnamese neighborhoods of Paris, particularly in the thirteenth *arrondissement*. Without knowing exactly what she is searching for, she begins the rediscovery of a world that has become largely unfamiliar to her: "I didn't question the precise goal of my quest, I only wanted to soak up the atmosphere I seemed to have forgotten long ago" (*Retour* 37).[19] This contact with the typical life of a Vietnamese immigrant in Paris comes 30 years after she emigrated and occurs to a large extent because she announced on the television program "Apostrophes" that she intended to return to Vietnam. Little by little, she reimmerses herself in the sights, sounds, and smells of Vietnam, each sensual experience triggering a flood of memories. It is clear, however, that other Vietnamese immigrants do not perceive her as a native Vietnamese. In one of the Asian grocery stores, for example, she is viewed as a foreigner when she asks a young woman the name of a fruit. In the woman's answer--"Nous, on l'appelle 'Gâc' " (We call it "Gâc") (40)--the use of the pronoun "we" implies that Lefèvre is an outsider.

The narrator's preparations for her return reinforce her impression of not really being Vietnamese, and in many respects resemble those of a French person planning a vacation. At the consulate where she goes to obtain her visa, she is immediately aware of two or three Vietnamese women speaking their language loudly, "comme au pays" (as in the home country) (120), so she asks for the visa form in French--a tourist visa--in order to distance herself from these women. Her French identity thus represents a kind of refuge, but it does not spare her from the feelings of guilt that have begun to haunt her--for being French also means having betrayed her people.

Lefèvre's emotions before her trip to Vietnam again contrast strongly with those of her fellow immigrants. Unlike her compatriots, who are happy to return to a country they were forced to leave, Lefèvre confronts another kind of guilt, that of having abandoned her family. In particular, she contemplates the gap between her "wealth" and her family's poverty, which she has learned about recently in letters from her mother and sister, from whom she had been estranged for many years. While she lives a relatively comfortable life, has good accommodations, and money to spend, her family barely has enough to pay for one meal after working hard all day. *Retour à la saison des pluies* thus forcefully brings out the guilt brought on by Lefèvre's immigrant condition.

Lefèvre's return to Vietnam confirms her identity as an immigrant. As she soon realizes, the distance created by her departure 30 years earlier has become an abyss that can no longer be crossed. Her decision to stay in a hotel rather than in the crowded family home is that of a tourist, and it is again her mother who accurately senses what her daughter's identity in Vietnam will be: "Alas, you'll come to see us as a guest and will leave as if you were a stranger" (*Retour* 160).[20] For the same reason, she is reproached by her sister for only "partially coming back" (161). She herself acknowledges that she is visiting rather than returning, that she is a tourist, "quelqu'un d'étranger, une Occidentale égarée dans une famille du tiers monde" (a stranger, a Westerner who has strayed into a Third World family) (156).

As we have seen, the work of Kim Lefèvre raises a number of interesting questions concerning *métissage* and social integration, as the narrator moves from rejection in Vietnam to a new life and identity in France. However, her positive experience of integration and rebirth left her with feelings of guilt that rose to the surface over the years, and it is only through becoming a writer that she has been able to "exorcise the past" (*Retour* 16). Indeed, both *Métisse blanche* and *Retour à la saison des pluies* constitute forms of re-membering, as Lefèvre attempts to reassemble the pieces of her life. But as Homi Bhabha suggests, "remembering is never a quiet act of introspection or retrospection. It is a painful re-membering, a putting together of the dismembered past to make sense of the trauma of the present" (63). For Lefèvre, writing, like immigration, brings liberation from her painful past, and perhaps more importantly, the process of writing provides a release from the pain of the present, the guilt of having abandoned her loved ones in an elsewhere that is no longer her own.

NOTES

I would like to thank Michelle Tracy for translating this chapter.

1. "pour penser la question du métissage, ou du syncrétisme, qui n'en est que l'un de ses avatars, il faut postuler une pureté première."

2. In this regard, Philippe Franchini's observations on the September 1945 massacre at Hérault--a Vietnamese district inhabited by *métis* families--shed light on the schoolmistress's motivations: "The crime [in this case, the punishment inflicted by the teacher] belongs to a type of expiatory immolation capable of exorcising the evil of foreign domination which the victims represented" (61).

3. The aunt's actual words are: "tu ne seras jamais qu'une Annamite!"

4. "Ma pauvre enfant! . . . Une fille de ta race n'est pas une paysanne!"

5. "Je n'ai gardé aucun souvenir des premières années de ma vie, hormis ce sentiment très tôt ressenti d'être partout déplacée, étrangère."

6. "Or voici que me trouvant parmi les miens, des alliages, je continuais à me sentir étrangère."

7. "J'étais dépaysée comme si j'avais quitté le Viêt-nam pour un autre pays."

8. "Nous continuâmes d'être amies dans la mesure où je partageais leurs goûts, tandis que les miens étaient définitivement mis sous le boisseau."

9. "J'étais en train de perdre progressivement mes racines."

10. "J'étais chargée de rancune, je pensais qu'elle était une paysanne, une *Nha-quê*, et qu'elle le demeurerait à jamais."

11. "J'avais passé ma vie à vouloir prouver mon innocence en me conformant à toutes les règles de ma société. Mais c'est mon essence même qui était inacceptable."

12. "La France, c'était pour moi un nom, des images abstraites, un pays associé à un père haï."

13. "Là-bas, tu retrouveras les tiens, les gens de ta race."

14. "ce que le Viêt-nam m'avait refusé, la France me l'a accordé: elle m'a reçue et acceptée."

15. "certes, je n'ignore pas les courants racistes dirigés contre les communautés maghrébines et demain peut-être contre celles des Asiatiques de jour en jour plus nombreuses."

16. "Cela fait trente ans que je n'ai pas pratiqué ma langue, trente ans que je n'ai pas ouvert un livre vietnamien. Je pense en français, je rêve en français et il m'arrive souvent, lorsque je parle vietnamien, d'employer des expressions traduites du français."

17. "Maintenant, tu cherches tes mots comme si tu étais une étrangère."

18. "Durant les longues années passées en France il s'est sécrété en moi une sève d'oubli. Avec le temps, elle s'est durcie, est devenue une seconde peau, plus dure et plus résistante."

19. "Je ne me suis pas interrogée sur le but exact de ma quête, j'ai simplement envie de me replonger dans une atmosphère qu'il me semble avoir oubliée depuis des lustres."

20. "Hélas, tu passeras nous voir en invitée et tu prendras congé comme si tu étais une étrangère."

WORKS CITED

Amselle, Jean-Loup. *Logiques métisses: anthropologie de l'identité en Afrique et ailleurs*. 1990. Paris: Payot, 1999.
Bhabha, Homi K. *The Location of Culture*. London: Routledge, 1994.

Franchini, Philippe. "Saigon blanche, métisse, rouge" and "La cité blanche." *Saigon 1925-1945: de la "Belle Colonie" à l'éclosion révolutionnaire ou la fin des dieux blancs*. Ed. Philippe Franchini. Paris: Autrement, 1992, 26-91.

Le, Huu Khoa. *L'interculturel et l'Eurasien*. Paris: L'Harmattan, 1993.

Lefèvre, Kim. *Métisse blanche*. Paris: Bernard Barrault, 1989.

---. *Retour à la saison des pluies*. 1990. Paris: L'Aube, 1995.

Lionnet, Françoise. "The Politics and Aesthetics of Métissage." *Women, Autobiography, Theory: A Reader*. Ed. Sidonie Smith and Julia Watson. Madison: The University of Wisconsin Press, 1998, 325-336.

Roberts, Emily. "Place and Identity in Two Autobiographical Novels Set in Vietnam: *Métisse blanche* by Kim Lefèvre and *L'amant* by Marguerite Duras." *Fin de siècle?* Ed. Anne Frémiot. Nottingham, UK: University of Nottingham Press, 1998, 53-63.

Rutherford, Jonathan. "The Third Space: Interview with Homi Bhabha." *Identity: Community, Culture, Difference*. Ed. Jonathan Rutherford. London: Lawrence & Wishart, 1990, 207-221.

Taguieff, Pierre-André. *La force du préjugé. Essai sur le racisme et ses doubles*. Paris: La Découverte, 1987.

---. "Doctrines de la race et hantise du métissage. Fragments d'une histoire de la mixophobie savante." *Métissages*. Ed. Tsadok Abdesalam. Paris: La pensée sauvage, 1991, 53-98.

Yeager, Jack. "Blurring the Lines in Vietnamese Fiction in French: Kim Lefèvre's *Métisse blanche*." *Postcolonial Subjects: Francophone Women Writers*. Ed. Mary Jean Green et al. Minneapolis: University of Minnesota Press, 1996, 210-226.

---. "Kim Lefèvre's *Retour à la saison des pluies*: Rediscovering the Landscape of Childhood." *L'Esprit Créateur* 33.2 (Summer 1993): 47-57.

Young, Robert J. C. *Colonial Desire: Hybridity in Theory, Culture and Race*. London: Routledge, 1995.

Selected Bibliography

Anselin, Alain. *L'émigration antillaise en France: la troisième île*. Paris: Karthala, 1990.

Assouline, David, and Mehdi Lallaoui. *Un siècle d'immigrations en France. 3* vols. Paris: Syros/Au nom de la mémoire, 1997.

Begag, Azouz, and Abdellatif Chaouite. *Ecarts d'identité*. Paris: Seuil, 1990.

Ben Jelloun, Tahar. *Hospitalité française: racisme et immigration maghrébine*. 1984. Paris: Seuil, 1997.

Benguigui, Yamina. *Mémoires d'immigrés: l'héritage maghrébin*. Paris: Canal+ Editions, 1997.

Blanchard, Pascal, and Nicolas Bancel. *De l'indigène à l'immigré*. Paris: Gallimard, 1998.

Bonn, Charles, ed. *Littératures des immigrations*. 2 vols. Paris: L'Harmattan, 1995.

Brinker-Gabler, Gisela, and Sidonie Smith, eds. *Writing New Identities: Gender, Nation, and Immigration in Contemporary Europe*. Minneapolis: University of Minnesota Press, 1997.

Castles, Stephen. *Here for Good: Western Europe's New Ethnic Minorities*. London: Pluto Press, 1984.

Déjeux, Jean. "Romanciers de l'immigration maghrébine en France." *Francofonia* 5.8 (1985): 93-111.

Hargreaves, Alec G. *Immigration, "Race" and Ethnicity in Contemporary France*. London: Routledge, 1995.

---. *Immigration and Identity in Beur Fiction: Voices from the North African Immigrant Community in France*. Oxford: Berg, 1997.

Hargreaves, Alec G., and Mark McKinney, eds. *Post-Colonial Cultures in France*. London: Routledge, 1997.

Jules-Rosette, Bennetta. *Black Paris: The African Writer's Landscape*. Urbana: University of Illinois Press, 1998.

Laronde, Michel. *Autour du roman beur*. Paris: L'Harmattan, 1993.

---, ed. *L'écriture décentrée*. Paris: L'Harmattan, 1996.

Le, Huu Khoa. *L'interculturel et l'Eurasien*. Paris: L'Harmattan, 1993.

Rinne, Suzanne, and Joëlle Vitiello, eds. *Elles écrivent des Antilles (Haïti, Guadeloupe, Martinique)*. Paris: L'Harmattan, 1997.

Rosello, Mireille. *Declining the Stereotype: Ethnicity and Representation in French Cultures*. Hanover: University Press of New England, 1998.

Sayad, Abdelmalek. *L'immigration ou les paradoxes de l'altérité*. Brussels: Editions Universitaires De Boeck, 1991.

Silverman, Maxim. *Race, Discourse and Power in France*. Aldershot: Avebury, 1991.

---. *Deconstructing the Nation: Immigration, Racism, and Citizenship in Modern France*. London: Routledge, 1992.

Simeant, Johanna. *La cause des sans-papiers*. Paris: Presses de la Fondation Nationale des Sciences Politiques, 1998.

Temime, Emile. *France, terre d'immigration*. Paris: Gallimard, 1999.

Viet, Vincent. *La France immigrée: construction d'une politique, 1914-1997*. Paris: Fayard, 1998.

Index

About the Contributors

FARIDA ABU-HAIDAR is a Fellow at the Centre for Cross-Cultural Research on Women at the University of Oxford. She is a specialist in the languages and literatures of the Maghreb, and her teaching and research often deal with the language of Maghrebian fiction and poetry. Her recent publications include contributions on Maghrebian literature in *The Encyclopedia of World Literature in the Twentieth Century*, the *Companion to African Literatures*, and a special issue of *Research in African Literatures* entitled *Dissident Algeria*. She has also written a chapter on the Arabic literature of Africa for the forthcoming *Cambridge History of African Literatures*.

ODILE CAZENAVE is visiting Associate Professor at MIT and adjunct Associate Professor at the University of Tennessee, Knoxville. She is the author of *Femmes rebelles: naissance d'un nouveau roman africain au féminin* (1996), which she has translated into English as *Rebellious Women* (2000). She has published several articles on women writers, the writing of the body, interracial relationships, and issues related to identity. Her most recent work deals with the new African diaspora in Paris.

MARTINE DELVAUX is Associate Professor of Literary Studies at the University of Quebec at Montreal. She teaches contemporary French literature, post-colonial women's writing, and gender studies. Her current research focuses on testimonial writing concerning the Holocaust, AIDS, and trauma, and she is currently working on a book on these topics. She is the author of a book on the writing of female mental illness (*Femmes psychiatrisées, femmes rebelles*). She has also published articles on the intersections between creative and testimonial writing and literary criticism.

ANNE DONADEY is Associate Professor of Comparative Literature and Women's Studies at the University of Iowa. Her book on Assia Djebar and Leïla Sebbar, *Recasting Postcolonialism: Women Writing Between Worlds*, is forthcoming. Her articles have appeared in *World Literature Today*, *French Cultural Studies*, *L'Esprit Créateur*, and *The French Review*. She was co-editor of the Winter 1999 special issue of *Studies in Twentieth-Century Literature* dedicated to Occupation and Empire in France and the francophone world.

SYLVIE DURMELAT is Assistant Professor of French and Francophone Studies in the French Department at Georgetown University. Her fields of interest include urban and migrant cultural productions in hexagonal France and post-colonial literature and culture in the Caribbean and North Africa. She has published several articles on the above topics. She is presently working on a book-length study of cultural reproduction and filiation in immigrant diasporic narratives and films.

PATRICIA GEESEY is Associate Professor of French at the University of North Florida. Her articles on North African literature and immigration in France have appeared in *SubStance*, *Dalhousie French Studies*, *The French Review*, *Research in African Literatures*, *World Literature Today*, and *The International Fiction Review*.

ALEC G. HARGREAVES is Professor of French and Francophone Studies in the Department of European Studies at Loughborough University. His publications include *Voices from the North African Immigrant Community in France: Immigration and Identity in Beur Fiction* (1991; second edition 1997), *Immigration, 'Race' and Ethnicity in Contemporary France* (1995) and, co-edited with Mark McKinney, *Post-Colonial Cultures in France* (1997).

NICKI HITCHCOTT is Lecturer in French at the University of Nottingham, United Kingdom. She is the author of *Women Writers in Francophone Africa* (2000) and co-editor of *African Francophone Writing: A Critical Introduction* (1996).

SUSAN IRELAND is Associate Professor of French at Grinnell College. Her research interests include contemporary French fiction, Quebec women writers, the Algerian novel, and the literature of immigration in France and Quebec. She has published articles in these areas and is also an editor of *The Feminist Encyclopedia of French Literature* (Greenwood Press, 1999).

MICHEL LARONDE is Associate Professor of French at the University of Iowa. He is the author of *Autour du roman beur* (1993) and editor of *L'écriture décentrée* (1996), a collection of articles on major *Beur* texts. He is currently working on two books on post-colonial Arabo-French literature, one on the representation of education and the literary canon, the other dealing with images of post-colonial authors. He is also editing a collection of essays on Leïla Sebbar.

MARK MCKINNEY is Associate Professor of French at Miami University (Ohio). He co-edited, with Alec G. Hargreaves, *Post-Colonial Cultures in France* (1997) and has recent and forthcoming publications in *Comics: An International Idiom*, the *Encyclopedia of Contemporary French Culture, The Feminist Encyclopedia of French Literature, Modern and Contemporary France, Sites*, and *Women, Immigration and Identities in France*.

H. ADLAI MURDOCH is Associate Professor of French and Francophone Literature at the University of Illinois at Urbana-Champaign. His areas of scholarly interest are French literature and post-colonial studies, with a special interest in the narratives of the francophone Caribbean and francophone West Africa. His articles have appeared in *Callaloo, Yale French Studies, Research in African Literatures,* and the *Journal of Commonwealth and Postcolonial Studies*. He has recently completed a book entitled *Creole Identity in the French Caribbean Novel.*

PATRICE J. PROULX is Associate Professor of French and a member of the Women's Studies faculty at the University of Nebraska at Omaha. Her research interests include the notion of identity and exile in the works of contemporary French and francophone women writers. Her articles have appeared in such journals as *The French Review* and *L'Esprit Créateur*, and she has essays in several edited collections on contemporary francophone literature. She is an editor of *The Feminist Encyclopedia of French Literature* (Greenwood Press, 1999).

MIREILLE ROSELLO teaches at Northwestern University. Her main research and teaching interests are post-colonial literatures and theories (especially in the Caribbean and the Maghreb). She has written on surrealism (*L'humour noir selon André Breton*), Tournier (*L'in-différence chez Michel Tournier*), and Caribbean literature (*Littérature et identité créole aux Antilles*). Her latest books are *Infiltrating Culture: Power and Identity in Contemporary Women's Writing* and *Declining The Stereotype: Representation and Ethnicity in French Cultures*. She is currently completing a manuscript on hospitality and immigration.

CHING SELAO is a graduate student in French at the University of Quebec at Montreal. Her dissertation, entitled *Les lieux du métissage: contamination raciale et discursive dans Métisse Blanche de Kim Lefèvre et la trilogie indochinoise de Marguerite Duras*, examines questions surrounding the theme of *métissage* in the context of post-colonial Vietnam. She is particularly interested in how Vietnamese identity is constructed within colonial discourse and in the impact of this construction on Vietnamese francophone literature.

DOMINIC THOMAS is an Assistant Professor of French at the University of California at Los Angeles, where he teaches francophone literatures and cultures. A recent recipient of a Mellon Postdoctoral Fellowship at the Cornell Society for the Humanities, he is the author of *Engineering the Nation: Literature, Propaganda and Reconciliation in Francophone Africa* (forthcoming), and of essays on francophone African literature.